LaKOTA
GUIDE TO
NATURAL
PAIN RELIEF

LAKOTA: GUIDE TO NATURAL PAIN RELIEF
is a collaboration between Lakota and the custom publishing division of Reader's Digest Association (Canada) ULC, 1100 René-Lévesque Blvd. West, Montreal, QC H3B 5H5

ISBN: 978-1-55475-102-0

Lakota: Legendary Native American Formulas
For more information about Lakota products, visit us on our website at **www.lakotaherbs.com**

READER'S DIGEST CUSTOM PUBLISHING

VICE-PRESIDENT, EDITORIAL
Robert Goyette

MANAGER, ENGLISH BOOK EDITORIAL & CUSTOM PUBLISHING
Pamela Johnson

PROJECT EDITOR
Matthew Brown

PROOFREADER
Alison Ramsey

SENIOR ART DIRECTOR
Andrée Payette

DESIGNERS
Olena Lytvyn, Ann Devoe, Adam Snellings, Alyssa Howes

PRODUCTION ARTIST
Chris Cant

ACCOUNT MANAGER
Jennifer Woolcombe

ADMINISTRATOR
Lisa Pigeon

THE READER'S DIGEST ASSOCIATION, INC.

PRESIDENT & CHIEF EXECUTIVE OFFICER
Robert E. Guth

EXECUTIVE VICE-PRESIDENT, RDA AND PRESIDENT, NORTH AMERICA
Dan Lagani

EXECUTIVE VICE-PRESIDENT, RDA AND PRESIDENT, ALLRECIPES.COM
Lisa Sharples

EXECUTIVE VICE-PRESIDENT, RDA AND PRESIDENT, EUROPE
Dawn Zier

LaKOTA
GUIDE TO
NATURAL
PAIN RELIEF

TABLE OF CONTENTS

FOREWORD

This book is for all the people out there who are able to move around better than ever. People like Rick Starr, a construction contractor who "suffered for years with back and joint pain" until giving in and trying Lakota. People who wake up one day after a few weeks of using Lakota and find that their pain is gone. People who take control of their health without subjecting themselves to heavy doses of pharmaceuticals. People who are willing to try a natural option.

Making natural pain relief available to all Canadians is Lakota's vision. With this book, we are pushing that vision forward, giving people more tools to manage their pain without resorting to drugs. The *Lakota Guide to Natural Pain Relief* provides a wide range of natural options for managing all types of pain, as well as background information about conditions that cause pain. We all need information so that we can take charge of our own health.

The book covers arthritis, back pain, muscle pain, sleeplessness and diabetes-related pain. It also contains a chapter with helpful home remedies submitted by actual Lakota customers. (We haven't tried them all, so make sure they're right for you before using them.) Also, for the first time, take an inside look at how Lakota became one of the most successful products in Canada.

Information about Lakota products is provided in an appendix. In that chapter we describe how we and many of our customers use our products.

We also include a selection of customers' success stories throughout the book. Our customers often write to tell us how Lakota changed their lives. Hearing success stories from real people motivates us to keep making better pain relievers. Relieving a person's pain is its own reward.

Finally, we want to thank those who made this book possible. Here's to those people: people like Rick Starr, and people like you— Lakota customers. Thank you for helping us share natural pain relief with even more Canadians. We hope you enjoy this book and find it useful.

YOUR LAKOTA TEAM

THE LAKOTA STORY

Over 10 years ago, Don and Kent Pedersen, a father-son team of farmers in Northern British Columbia, learned of some powerful pain remedies rooted in traditional Native American medicine. The remedies represented the collective traditions and knowledge of many different First Nations. Knowing that these pain relievers could help people everywhere, they decided to found the company they called Lakota.

THE LAKOTA
STORY

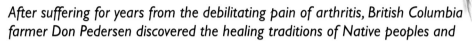

After suffering for years from the debilitating pain of arthritis, British Columbia farmer Don Pedersen discovered the healing traditions of Native peoples and their unique herbal medicines. After seeing first-hand how well these medicines worked, he and his son Kent began developing products based on Native American natural formulations. This is the story of the creation of Lakota, its products and of the two Dawson Creek farmers who, with lots of passion but little conventional business knowledge, built a thriving company that is now a household name all over North America.

Lakota's mission to change the way people treat pain began in Northern British Columbia more than 10 years ago, with father-and-son farmers Don and Kent Pedersen. Don had been the head of the family farm for more than 30 years, but was beginning to slow down—and not by choice. After years of working the farm, arthritis was setting in. The busiest seasons, springtime and harvest, were becoming more and more difficult and the pain more intense.

Springtime on the family farm signaled long days of planting, which requires lifting, bending, twisting, climbing up and down on the tractor, getting in and out to adjust the settings and more. And the Pedersen's didn't operate an ordinary family farm. Standard crops like wheat, barley, oats and canola had given way to specialized grass seed. The margin for error was slim; seed had to be planted at the right depth and the right rate. Mistakes were costly, as the golf courses that bought their specialized seed accepted only the highest quality product.

All farmers require nerves of steel, but growing specialized seed multiplied the risk. Prices for the harvest were much more volatile, seed was much more costly and quality standards were more strict. It was a high-stakes game. But Don thought that he could win, and he was proved right. He and his son Kent plunged into the market.

DON'S ARTHRITIS AND BREAKTHROUGH DISCOVERY

The farm was thriving; Don and Kent's research and careful planning were paying off. But Don's arthritis kept getting worse. Refusing to allow his chronic pain to dominate the life he loved, Don sought a solution. Being a farmer, he preferred something natural to a pharmaceutical drug. He researched and tried several different natural treatments. Not afraid to experiment, he even travelled to Mexico and other clinics to try treatments from around the world.

Work together, play together: A Lakota crew taking in the sun during a team-building exercise.

Time passed, and still nothing was working. Soon, the pain would drive Don to prescription medication. But one day, Don was given a pain remedy by a friend. The friend had developed a treatment that contained herbs used by Native Americans to heal sore joints. Along with these ancient herbs, it was supplemented with modern natural ingredients such as glucosamine and collagen type II.

Don was skeptical at first, especially having tried so many alternatives. But the product worked unlike anything he had tried: He became completely pain-free. After 30 days of use, he regained the kind of mobility he hadn't had for years—maybe decades. The change in him was obvious; his son Kent noticed it, too.

Don knew people needed to hear about this remarkable pain reliever—he was so convinced that he bought the formula.

BURIED ALIVE

It wasn't long before Kent too would learn first-hand how well the product worked. Kent and his Dad were avid snowmobilers. Not content to ride off-the-shelf snow machines, they spent hours and days tinkering and tweaking and adding aftermarket parts. They rode snowmobiles that produced well over 100 horsepower, long before really high-power snowmobiles were available from the dealer. Their snowmobiles took off like rockets.

These hand-modified snowmobiles were not for trail cruising. They were made for racing—specifically, for hill climbing. Kent was a world-class snowmobile racer and had won many hill climbing competitions. Countless winter hours were spent fine-tuning the machines and practicing hill climbs.

But one day, it all came crashing down—literally. An avalanche struck, and Kent was buried alive. You may have heard that snow in an avalanche packs as hard as concrete. Kent can tell you from experience that it's true.

One day, it all came crashing down—literally. An avalanche struck, and Kent was buried alive under four feet of snow.

Tossed and thrown around in the tumbling onslaught, he came to a stop buried under four feet of rock-hard snow. He was badly injured and had multiple fractures. Trapped under the weight of the snow, he was unable to move.

Thankfully, Kent used proper avalanche safety devices. His locater beacon flashed furiously while his friends frantically searched. They quickly located the beacon and began digging. In minutes, they had him out.

Within one week of trying the pain reliever, Kent felt much much better. And by the end of the month he was pain-free.

Kent was seriously injured and had to be medevaced off the mountain. He recovered over the next few months, but he remained in constant pain, especially with back pain. Don suggested he try **Lakota Joint Care Formula**. Kent hesitated; "Isn't that just for old people with arthritis?" he asked. After several more weeks in pain, he finally relented. Within one week of trying the pain reliever, he felt much better. By the end of the month, he was pain-free. He couldn't believe it. There was no denying this product's extraordinary power.

THE FIRST STEP: A US LAUNCH

Don and Kent felt the time was right to bring Lakota to the world. They decided to launch Lakota in the United States; the larger market would make it easier to find partners. Lakota was essentially a health food product, so they figured the best place to launch it was the Health Food Expo in Anaheim, California—the largest health food show in the world. They put together a trade show booth that highlighted Lakota's Native American roots, including an authentic Plains Indian teepee made from buffalo hide. It was a great success. Crowds of people wanted get a closer look at the Lakota booth, and the lineups overflowed into neighboring booths. The excitement around the product was phenomenal. Don and Kent were confident they would soon find the right partner to help them introduce Lakota to the world.

The Lakota teepee, made with real buffalo hide, that made a splash at the Health Food Expo in California.

One well-known over-the-counter (OTC) pharmaceutical manufacturer—a billion-dollar company—saw the potential of the Lakota product, and approached Don and Kent for an exclusive deal for the US. They would introduce Lakota to health food stores, and promised to get the product into large US retailers like Walmart and Walgreens.

Thinking that this would be the best way to get Lakota to the masses, Don and Kent signed the deal. Knowing how Lakota changed his life, Don really was anxious for the product to be widely available as soon as possible. By themselves, they may only have been able to get Lakota into a few health food stores; to get into big US retailers they needed major backing.

Sure Lakota would succeed, Don and Kent turned over the formula to the OTC manufacturer. "It will be in health food stores within a year," they were told. But a year came and went, and Lakota languished. The US partner explained that this was because the plants were running at capacity—but once manufacturing started, Lakota would soon go to Walmart. Don and Kent remained patient—they were farmers, after all. They knew that some things can take time, like the wait before harvest, and getting impatient doesn't speed things up.

Two years went by without any progress. Finally, Don and Kent went to meet with the US partner at the American head office. By this time the company had merged with another OTC manufacturer and was even larger than before. Kent and Don asked if there was anything they could do to speed things up. But after a few meetings with key personnel, they left with a bad feeling. No one seemed to share their eagerness to get Lakota into stores.

The excitement around the product was phenomenal. Don and Kent were confident they would find the right partner to help them introduce Lakota to the world.

On the trip home they started to realize that they had given away the farm, so to speak. Don and Kent hadn't received any money up front—they'd never imagined their US partner would balk at manufacturing the product. They had even invested some of their own money into advertising. Now that the OTC had a new owner, there was little incentive to manufacture Lakota; in fact, there was actually motivation to keep it off the shelves. The new OTC sold products that competed directly with Lakota, and they were cheaper to manufacture.

OBSTACLES OVERCOME, LESSONS LEARNED

Don and Kent were shocked at the way things had happened. It should have been simple, they thought: Lakota was obviously a great product, so everyone should jump at the chance to manufacture it. It was Don and Kent's first lesson in "big pharmaceuticals." Big pharmaceuticals are not always interested in the most effective products; they're interested in the most profitable products, which often means the cheapest ones to manufacture. But the knowledge came too late: Lakota had signed over US rights to the OTC for five years, and there was nothing they could do.

Since the US was locked up for another couple of years, Don and Kent turned their sights to the Canadian market. They would not make the same mistake they made in the US by partnering with a large OTC manufacturer: This time they would go it alone. Don and Kent talked about the fundamental strategy that would come to define the Lakota approach. "No one believes in this product more than we do," they agreed. "And no one can do a better job getting the products into the hands of consumers than we can." So Lakota set up operations in Canada, and started selling directly to health food stores.

A NEW PLAN OF ATTACK

Some health foods stores readily embraced Lakota; others were hesitant. It wasn't surprising; stores are inundated with so many new products that saying "no" is just a reflex.

After a few stores agreed to stock Lakota products, Don and Kent placed an ad in the *Edmonton Journal*. The ad explained what Lakota was and how it was different from other arthritis treatments on the market. Not being professionals in marketing, Don and Kent prepared the ad as if they were describing the product to friends and neighbours. They didn't know marketing spin; but they knew their product and how well it worked.

The ad was a success; the product sold out of health foods stores that stocked it. They didn't make nearly enough to pay for the ad, but the victory convinced Don and Kent to continue investing and getting their message out. They knew that once people tried Lakota, its popularity would grow and grow.

After the ad in the *Edmonton Journal*, they took the next step: national advertising. Unable to afford television advertising or pages in major consumer magazines, they opted for *Alive* magazine. *Alive* is a leading health magazine in Canada, freely distributed at most health food stores.

They knew instinctively that they needed to create a big impact. Too many ads in too many magazines spread over time would thin out the message. So they took a gamble. They took all of their ad money and splurged on a two-page spread.

It was a huge amount to risk on advertising, but they wanted to make a big bang. When advertisers use two-page spreads, they usually want to show off flashy photos or eye-catching graphics. Don and Kent had a different idea: They would simply fill the pages with information. There were details about Lakota's natural ingredients and references to clinical studies. In short, they broke pretty much every established rule of advertising. The ads were a solid grey mass of text. The typeface was actually smaller than the regular magazine font. And they didn't shy away from detailing the technical aspects of the product and its ingredients.

"No one believes in this product more than we do," they agreed.

It's fairly common for advertisers to assume that customers don't understand technical information, or don't want to. But Lakota took a different approach. Don and Kent wanted to explain the product as if they were speaking to people just like them. They created the kind of ad that they themselves would like to see.

The response was overwhelming—the phone at Lakota rang off the hook! The number one question they received was, "Where can I find Lakota?" Over and over, Don and Kent directed people to their local health food store. Some stores, however, were still unwilling to stock this new product, so Don and Kent faced a unique dilemma. "How can we distribute a product that consumers want but stores are reluctant to carry?" they wondered. They came up with their own solution—not one found in any business-school textbook.

SPECIAL DELIVERY

Don and Kent knew that hiring a sales force would be a long, expensive process. It would raise the product's cost, but add nothing of value for the consumer. So instead of hiring a sales force, they came up with a radically different approach—sending their product directly to stores, free of charge. They sent six units of **Lakota Joint Care Formula** to almost every health food store in Canada.

It was a huge gamble; had it failed, it would have spelled the end of Lakota. But Don and Kent were so confident in their product that they were willing to prime the pump by giving it away. They cleared out a shop on the family farm and started boxing product, six bottles at a time. They crammed the back of their pickup with boxes and hauled them to the post office. (Understandably, the post office was less than thrilled to handle loads by the pickup-truckfull!) They paid for each parcel as it was weighed, until the post office set up a commercial account for them. For days, all they did was haul parcels to the post office, and hundreds of stores began to receive free bottles of Lakota along with brochures. Don and Kent also ran more two-page ads in *Alive* magazine.

Care package: A box of Lakota Joint Care Formula, ready to be shipped.

The huge bet on the power of their product paid off. Thanks to the *Alive* magazine ads, the health food stores sold every last bottle and placed orders for more. Word of mouth was spreading rapidly, and Lakota was on its way to becoming a health sensation. Production had to be ramped up to keep pace with increasing demand.

DON AND KENT RISK EVERYTHING

It wasn't long until big retailers came knocking. Shoppers Drug Mart was excited about Lakota. They agreed to put in a large display of Lakota product, shaped like a teepee, with real feathers dangling from the sides. True, they were actually turkey feathers painted to look like eagle feathers, but

They put in a large display of Lakota product, shaped like a teepee, with real feathers dangling from the sides.

each display was handmade on the Pedersen farm. The display was massive, filled with more than $1,000 worth of Lakota products.

Unfamiliar with drug store industry practice, Don and Kent thought it was perfect: It looked great and attracted attention. Unfortunately, the plan was too ambitious. At the end of the promotion the displays came back with lots of product unsold.

Yucca root

Absorbing this much inventory in returns would have sunk many fledgling companies. But one of Lakota's founding principles was "no debt," and this principle served the company well over the years.

Many of the ingredients in the Lakota formulas, such as white willow bark and yucca root, have been used in traditional Native American medicines for centuries, although modern natural ingredients, such as glucosamine and type II collagen, have been added to enhance the effects.

Taking on debt would have been easy for a fast-growing business like Lakota. But it comes at a cost, not limited to interest payments. Borrowing from a bank means the banker has a say in how the business is run. Don and Kent preferred to put up their own money, pouring income from the family farm into Lakota.

Few people would keep sinking money into a business that isn't earning a profit, but Don and Kent were thinking long-term. They cashed in their RRSPs and invested everything they had into the company. Once people tried Lakota, they thought, the product's results would speak for themselves. But Don and Kent knew they needed more advertising to get the message out. It was time for an even bigger national ad campaign.

THE *LAKOTA ARTHRITIS NEWS* IS LAUNCHED

To reach a broader audience, Don and Kent could have advertised in major consumer magazines. Instead, they went directly to the people. They created a four-page newsletter called *Lakota Arthritis News* and paid for it to be inserted it into local newspapers across the country.

Like the *Alive* magazine ads, the newsletter was packed with information. The conventional wisdom is that people don't like to read technical information. But, as you probably know by now, Don and Kent weren't interested in following convention.

Unable to compete with the advertising budgets of major pharmaceutical companies, Lakota needed a way to stand apart. Consumers are used to being bombarded with ads about conventional drug therapies, so persuading them to try a natural-source pain reliever wouldn't be easy. Don and Kent believed that lots of convincing information would help them make their case.

The first *Arthritis News*, distributed in British Columbia in January 2003, convinced thousands of consumers to buy **Lakota Joint Care Formula** at their local health food store. With the money from the first set of orders, the newsletter was sent to Alberta households. The same thing happened there. After several months, Lakota's *Arthritis News* had been distributed across the country. Lakota now had a national presence. Things were getting exciting: Customers from BC to Newfoundland were using Lakota and finding relief for arthritis and joint pain.

Things were getting exciting: Customers from BC to Newfoundland were using Lakota and finding relief for arthritis and joint pain.

The newsletter was working, so Don and Kent decided to broaden their message by creating television ads. And, of course, they did so in their own inimitable style. Relying on the strength of the message rather than flashy high-end techniques, they used their home video recorder to create their own now-famous commercials.

To make the ads, they went to a neighbour's farm, which had a nice, typical red barn. They convinced one of the early developers of Lakota products to be the TV spokesman. He was a real cowboy—not a person who plays a cowboy on TV. His cowboy hat goes with him wherever he goes. Having suffered some hearing loss as a child, he speaks with a slight acoustic irregularity. He was not an actor or professional spokesman: He was simply a regular person who worked with Lakota.

They set up the handy cam on a tripod and started taping. The script was put together with the goal of being as informative as it could be within the confines of television. The cowboy was not the commercial's only star: It co-starred the neighbour's horse. The horse wasn't the most cooperative co-star. It absolutely refused to stand still during shooting. Take after take was recorded and, in the end, one take stood out as the best. But it had a small problem: The horse started nibbling the cowboy's coat. The delivery of the lines, however, was perfect; so they used it for the final commercial, hungry horse and all.

The conventional strategy is to create a carefully researched and well-documented media plan before buying air time. Media plans often stipulate that ads should appear during popular shows—programs with high ratings and a large audience. The obvious downside of this media purchasing strategy, of course, is the extremely high cost of prime-time slots.

Don and Kent couldn't see a lot of value in paying extra for high-profile programming. Instead, they thought, why not advertise in a variety of shows, avoiding the expensive ones and keeping costs down? Also, unlike larger corporations, Lakota didn't need to have a media plan or advertising budget approved far in advance, so they could buy whatever was available at the last minute. TV advertising is perishable, like day-old bread, and unused air time goes on sale at the last minute. So Don and Kent bought up last-minute air time, and they weren't selective about programming. They bought early morning news, late-night movies,

A television commercial featuring the Lakota cowboy—with a horse cameo.

and even shows with lousy ratings. The ads ran nationally on CBC and on The Weather Network. They saved huge amounts of money, buying so much air time that competitors assumed they were spending 10 times more than they actually spent.

The successful TV campaign was followed by a second national newspaper insert in October 2003: *Lakota Arthritis News* volume 2. Television is great for promoting your name and getting one simple message across, but Don and Kent knew that a widely distributed newsletter was still the only effective way to get detailed product information to millions of arthritis sufferers.

They knew they were onto something when *This Hour Has 22 Minutes* began to run spoofs of their ads. The CBC TV comedy show had a field day doing parodies of Lakota commercials in early 2004. Some business owners would probably have been offended, but Don and Kent realized what it really meant: Lakota had become a household name. *This Hour Has 22 Minutes* doesn't make fun of advertising no one has seen. Don and Kent also knew not to take themselves too seriously. Their ads were intentionally low budget; that was the point. They wanted to get the message to Canadians in the most economical way possible—they

Why not advertise in a variety of shows, avoiding the expensive ones and keeping costs down?

didn't set out to win advertising awards. And once the CBC started spoofing them, they were confident that the ads worked.

COSTCO BECOMES A CUSTOMER

After seeing the product rocket to national success, Costco called. Don and Kent were initially hesitant to do business with Costco because people had said the company was difficult to work with. But they eventually made the move, and never regretted it. Costco continues to be a supportive partner today.

After a year of airing the television ads featuring their cowboy friend, Don and Kent wanted something different. They wanted to create a commercial that expressed the Native American heritage of the products. Through a friend, they contacted Floyd "Red Crow" Westermann. They thought that Floyd, a long-time Native American activist, would be the perfect spokesman.

Knowing that they would need a good-quality camera to record the commercial, they bought a used one on eBay and spent time learning how to use it. In July 2004, they packed up their gear and headed to Los Angeles, where Floyd lived. They rented a studio for a day, set up the camera and began shooting. They spent one day taping variations of the script they had written, filming hours of footage.

When they arrived home, they sat down with a film editor friend to edit the final commercial. When it was ready to air, they used the same strategy as before, buying air

They knew they were on to something when **This Hour Has 22 Minutes** *began to run spoofs of the Lakota TV ads.*

time many advertisers don't want. Sure, some of the ads came on at 3 a.m., but they also got last-minute deals for prime-time news and some major programming that hadn't sold out.

Soon afterwards, **Lakota Joint Care Roll-on** and **Joint Care Formula** capsules became the number one products in their respective categories. Don and Kent were thrilled, but they weren't content to stop there; they decided they needed another product. So they developed **Arthritis Roll-on**, a capsaicin-based

The other public face of Lakota: Floyd "Red Crow" Westermann, who appeared in various Lakota television spots.

product. Like **Joint Care Roll-on**, the **Arthritis Roll-on** uses natural capsaicin extract that Don and Kent had succeeded in sourcing—the key to the product's success. Synthetic capsaicin extract is what most products contain, but it doesn't have all four of capsaicin's molecular components that are essential for effective pain relief. Synthetic capsaicin is cheaper; but to make good products, you have to use good ingredients.

KENT TAKES ON IRONMAN

Don and Kent were not afraid of hard work or trying new things. Once Kent had fully recovered from his painful snowmobile injuries, he decided to get into shape. He had never been a runner, and the only biking he had done was as a child. He could barely swim. Nevertheless, he decided to race in a triathlon. He trained

A meeting of minds: Discussion and brainstorming at Lakota's offices.

endlessly, pushing himself further and improving his technique. Eventually, he did it: He completed a triathlon. Then he decided to raise the bar, and set his sights on a bigger challenge: the Half Ironman.

A Half Ironman is 1.9 km of swimming, followed by 90 km of biking, followed by 21 km of running. Anyone who knows the demands of a Half Ironman knows that it takes years of training to reach that level of athletic performance. Kent completed his first Half Ironman before long, and he needed a new challenge. He set his sights on a full Ironman: a 3.8 km swim, a 180 km bike and a 42 km run, one after the other. After completing his first full Ironman competition, Kent began to travel the world to compete in Ironman competitions, even going as far as China. It was this same type of sheer determination that made Lakota successful.

FREE-SAMPLE FIASCO

A few months after the Floyd television ads aired, Lakota published a new issue of the *Lakota Arthritis News*. It was their most successful ad campaign yet. And, for the first time, it featured an offer for free samples—the response was huge. Thousands of free samples were sent out from the post office, packaged in regular envelopes. Each sample came in a small pouch—somewhat like a tea bag packet, but filled with a bit of Lakota rub. But eventually Don and Kent received a phone call from Canada Post. They were given a stern warning: Canada Post regulations did not permit liquid or gel samples to be sent by mail.

Don and Kent hadn't even thought to check. They assumed that as long as the product was not hazardous and the liquid pouch was well sealed, mailing it wouldn't be a problem. Of course, if Don and Kent had known everything they weren't supposed to do all along, Lakota would never have happened. You don't hear about success stories featuring corporate bureaucrats who say, "You can't do that!" Luckily, Don and Kent didn't have that problem—they just figured things out as they went along, doing what they thought was best.

SPECIAL DELIVERY: TROUBLE

Admittedly, not having a big bureaucracy did cause a few snags. It wasn't only Canada Post that got upset about the free samples. According to federal regulations, you can't give Canadians free samples of natural health products. Health Canada was not amused.

Don and Kent had always been careful to ensure that they complied with Health Canada regulations, hiring expert consultants to be certain. And in every area of production—from raw materials to manufacturing to testing—Lakota far exceeded Health Canada requirements. But the free sample prohibition was something they were totally unaware of. Health Canada invited Lakota to a meeting in Vancouver, and two members of the Lakota management team made the trip for a 9 a.m. appointment the next day. Humour and confusion ensued: It was an all-too-perfect example of your typical farmers-in-the-big-city tale.

The Lakota team arrived at the Health Canada building, went to the designated floor and found the door to the regulatory office. They tried turning the door handle, but the door wouldn't budge—it seemed to be locked. Through a large window next to the door, they could see inside the regulatory office: Some people were already in the room. The Lakota managers assumed that the office just wasn't open yet; it was only 10 to nine.

They waited for awhile and tried the door again—still locked. They peeked through the window and saw a closed-circuit television screen on the wall, showing the two of them standing there. At 10 minutes past nine, they tried the door again: Still locked, yet still no one inside the room rose to let them in. After another 10 minutes, they wondered if they had made a mistake about the meeting. They headed back to the car, and double-checked: It was indeed the right place and time.

Don and Kent wanted Lakota to be about the products, not about them.

They went back up, but still couldn't get in. A buzz of activity could now be heard from inside the room. Further down the hall, an unmarked door opened. Someone came out, walked up to the locked door and—to their amazement—walked right in. The Lakota team was flabbergasted. They tried the door again: nothing. In frustration, they gave it a hard yank. And it swung open. When they walked in, every eye in the office was upon them. The office staff had had a great time watching the closed-circuit television, as the two Lakota managers tried, like chimps, to figure out how to open the "locked" door. The Health Canada inspector they were meeting could barely suppress his laughter. It all turned out well, and the jovial start to the meeting helped things go smoothly. The Lakota sample problem was ironed out without difficulty.

LAKOTA BECOMES A HOUSEHOLD NAME

By now, Lakota was a high-profile name. The company was used in business schools as a case study; magazines, newspapers and TV programs called for interviews. Don

A helping hand: Lakota staff in Ontario for a charity event.

Lakota products being prepared and packaged for distribution.

and Kent, being farmers, were not used to the attention. They generally wanted Lakota to be about the products, not about them.

One program they did agree to was CBC Venture, a show featuring Canadian business success stories. Don and Kent had always liked the reporters on the program, and they couldn't believe that Venture was doing a story on Lakota. It meant that a longtime dream of theirs had come true: They had reached national success.

Of course, that meant that Lakota was attracting attention from large pharmaceuticals and investment bankers as well.

DECISION TIME:
WHAT'S THE RIGHT MOVE?

Corporations were putting a high value on Lakota, so Don and Kent agreed to meet with a representative from a well-known pharmaceutical company to discuss opportunities. During the meeting, the rep spoke cryptically about "strategic synergies" and "volumetric studies" and used other business buzzwords. By the end of the meeting, Don and Kent weren't even sure what he was talking about. Over the next few weeks, the pharmaceutical corporation finally said that it was interested in buying the Lakota company.

Don, Kent and some of their team flew to the corporation's Canadian headquarters for a meeting. They walked into a large lobby and called up to let their contact know they had arrived. As they waited, a female security guard with a strong German accent asked if they needed badges. They looked at each other in confusion, not understanding what she was saying. Their silence caused the woman at the reception to ask again in, German-tinged English, "You need badges?" "No," they answered, "I think we're OK." The security guard started making motions as if she were playing a guitar. "You singer?" she asked. Thinking they had misunderstood her, they asked again what she had said. "You country western singer?" she asked, strumming an air guitar again. Finally they understood; one of them was wearing a cowboy hat. Apparently, the only time they see cowboy hats in Toronto is when a country singer comes to town!

After making it past the security guard (who insisted they don badges), they met with the pharmaceutical company's head honchos. During phone calls the rep had promised big numbers. But when things became more serious, the honchos hedged. On top of that, the process required so many layers of bureaucracy that Don and Kent knew it would be a waste of their time. So they turned down the offer and went back to their focus, making the best natural pain relievers anywhere.

Also around this time, Wall Street and Bay Street banker types starting coming around, urging Don and Kent to take Lakota public. They talked about huge stakes. But both Don and Kent found the whole process distasteful. Going public would require a big chunk of money. Ultimately, they couldn't see how Lakota customers would benefit from it being a public company; the big winners would be the investment bankers.

LAKOTA'S FANS MULTIPLY

By this time, Walmart's natural-health products buyer was a big fan of Lakota. He proposed that Lakota would be the Volume Producing Product of the year, which means that the whole Walmart company gets behind the product and pushes to make it successful. Walmart put in fixed end-aisle displays featuring Lakota and supported Lakota with ads and in-store features. Walmart had been another store that people had warned Don and Kent about, but, in the end, they found Walmart both helpful and easy to deal with.

Ever since the start of Lakota, customers has been writing letters to Don and Kent, describing how Lakota products changed their lives. The many letters were a constant source of encouragement. Some customers also requested new product features. One frequent request was for a softer roll-on applicator. Some people with arthritis in their hands found the roller too hard and said it was sometimes painful to use. Don and Kent set out to solve this problem. They exhaustively investigated different styles of soft sponge applicators and finally, in early 2005, they found just what they were looking for. The **Lakota Soft Touch** applicator was born.

LAKOTA' S "FLIP 'N GRIP" LID INNOVATION

Another innovation that came to fruition around this time was the unique Lakota lid, which is now on all Lakota capsule bottles. It came about because some customers had trouble opening the lid on the original bottles. The plastic tear strip had to be pulled all the way around the rim of the lid and the lid flipped off using the tips of the fingers—not exactly an arthritis-friendly feature. Don and Kent knew they had to find a solution. They looked at stock lids from many different suppliers, but no one had what they were looking for. Once again it seemed that they would have to build something from scratch.

They worked with an industrial designer, explaining that they wanted a lid that had two main features. The lid had to be easy to turn, so it could be painlessly removed with arthritic hands; that meant the lid would have to have large knobby grips. They also wanted easy flip-open access, for those who find it easier to flip the lid open using the large tab. The name was catchy and obvious: the "**Flip 'n Grip**" lid. Arthritis sufferers across the country praised it as a wonderful innovation.

COMMERCIAL APPEAL: CONSIDERING THE AD STRATEGY

When you become successful, people from all over come to sell you things. One of the groups that wanted to sell Lakota a "better way" was advertising agencies. A number of big agencies came to Dawson Creek to pitch their advertising prowess. One made a particularly convincing pitch for a new set of ads. It was adamant that expensive television ads would propel Lakota sales through the roof. "If you can sell this much with home-made ads, imagine how much you could sell with professionally produced TV ads," they argued.

Big agencies rely on market research, statistical reports and surveys—studies that treat people as numbers. But Don and Kent knew their customers face to face. They had talked with them on the phone and written them letters. And, most of all, they knew their customers because *they were their own best customers.*

The professional TV campaign was a flop. A lot of money was spent making the slick ad using a standard media plan, but it didn't work. Don and Kent had made the mistake of not following their gut instincts, instead listening to the advertising agencies. "They must know better, since they do this every day," they thought. The mistake became another learning experience, and when young entrepreneurs ask for advice, Don and Kent always tell them to trust their instincts: Be self-reliant, and don't let the experts tell you what can and can't work.

Ever since the start of Lakota, Don and Kent had received many letters from customers describing how Lakota products changed their lives. The letters were a constant source of encouragement.

LAKOTA DECIDES TO TACKLE MORE PAIN PROBLEMS

By early 2007, Lakota was the leading natural pain reliever for arthritis. Don and Kent started working on developing a product specifically for back pain—one of the leading causes of lost work days in Canada. Addressing this problem could have a big impact on Canadians.

They decided on a two-pronged approach: a supplement and a roll-on pain reliever. The roll-on pain reliever would use the natural capsaicin extract used in other Lakota pain relievers, but the back pain roll-on would also have menthol as an extra pain-relieving enhancer. The menthol provides initial cool relief, while the capsaicin provides long-term pain reduction.

They called their pain-relieving tablets the **Triple Action Back Pain Formula**. The formula was based on extensive research into natural-source pain relievers. After tens of thousands of dollars and many months of research, they created a formula based on white willow bark, devil's claw and natural-source muscle relaxants. A huge amount of resources was dedicated to researching this product, and it may be the best Lakota product yet! The two back-pain products, released in 2007, were a hit. By now, Lakota was well known and stores were eager to stock the new products. National distribution was nearly instantaneous.

And Lakota didn't stop with back pain. Another common complaint from customers was that they had trouble getting a good night's sleep when they were in pain. This led to the development of **Lakota PM**: a combination nighttime pain reliever/sleep aid.

Lakota had a huge impact in the arthritis and back pain areas, but there was another big group that needed relief—people with muscle pain. This was definitely an area where Lakota could make products better than the competition's. Tweaking the natural capsaicin formula with some herbal extract, they developed a **Muscle Pain Roll-on**. It became the number-one bestseller in some stores; in fact, it is the *only* natural source muscle pain rub.

In 2011, Lakota tackled another type of pain. Diabetic nerve pain, one of the most debilitating types of pain, had a complete lack of natural-source options. The resulting product was a **Diabetic Foot Pain Cream**, which moisturizes while providing pain relief.

THE LAKOTA STORY CONTINUES

Lakota is a success story in the best possible way: It has succeeded in helping countless people to deal with pain, improve the quality of their lives, and get back to the important things. And the team at Lakota didn't succeed by changing who they are or what they stood for: They did things their own way, and showed everyone that with a good product, commitment, and a lot of hard work, anything is possible.

What will the future hold for Lakota and its line of products? No secrets will be revealed here. But there is no doubt that Lakota will continue to be the natural remedy that people reach for, the one they tell their friends about—"You have to try it, it really works!"—and the one they trust. The Lakota story continues.

TAKE CHARGE
OF YOUR ARTHRITIS

Knowing how a healthy body works and understanding what goes wrong when arthritis strikes can help you get the upper hand on treatment and pain relief. Knowledge and a good attitude will also transform you into a motivated, full-time partner in your own health care. The result? Increased mobility and independence, and a better quality of life.

UNDERSTANDING
ARTHRITIS

Many people suffering from arthritis are caught up in a terrible cycle of pain, stress and depression. But taking on an active role in managing your pain can help break that vicious cycle. Understanding your condition is an excellent way to help take the fear out of the arthritis equation; knowing what's going on with your body can bring a much-needed sense of calm, enabling you to make clear-headed decisions.

An Equal-Opportunity Condition

The word "arthritis" does not refer to one simple condition; it encompasses some 127 different diseases. So when someone says that they have arthritis, the logical response is, "What kind?" Arthritis can strike both sexes at any age. Some forms—rheumatoid arthritis, fibromyalgia and lupus—are more prevalent among women; gout and ankylosing spondylitis are more common in men.

Arthritis may affect only one joint or it may involve an immune attack against many of them. One person may experience excruciating pain and fatigue while another experiences only mild aches. Your symptoms may fluctuate between great pain and periods of relief; a friend's symptoms may remain stable for years. Some forms of the disease are caused by metabolic disorders, others are genetic and still others may result from environmental factors.

But you can take action to fight arthritis. A generation ago, the words "arthritis" and "action" were rarely spoken in the same sentence. Arthritis was thought of as a chronic, debilitating disease that slowed you down and ultimately left you hobbled. Arthritis prevented action.

That was the common belief—but we live in a more enlightened time. Make no mistake: Arthritis remains a leading cause of disability. If you have it, at least 4.5 million other Canadians share some form of your pain. No one has yet found a way to cure arthritis. But passively watching as your function and mobility drain away is no longer an acceptable course of action. Action is actually the key to reducing pain and maintaining a productive, active life.

Action against arthritis takes two forms. The first is fighting the disease itself with all the medical, physical and psychological weapons at your disposal.

The second is simply living life to the fullest—staying active, moving your body, working your joints and stretching your muscles. Living fully also means enjoying a tasty and nutritious diet while controlling your weight. Taking action by living well promises to let you be even more active—and enjoy a better quality of life.

Research shows that by taking charge of arthritis, you can tame arthritis pain, maintain function and even make remarkable improvements. We call it "arthritis self-management;" it centres on exercise and good nutrition. Don't just rely on what your doctor tells you to do. The self-manage-

■ ■ ■ THE MANY FACES OF ARTHRITIS

Many of the 127 separate arthritis disorders have very different causes and symptoms. But they do share a common feature; all of them involve inflammation of the joints. In fact, the term "arthritis" comes from the Greek words *arthron* (which means joint) and *itis* (which means inflammation).

■ ■ ■ **THE FEMININE SIDE OF ARTHRITIS**

According to The Arthritis Society, some 2.9 million Canadian women are believed to suffer from some type of arthritis, and the number is expected to reach 3.9 million by 2026—nearly twice the number of men. Theories abound, ranging from the belief that women's weaker cartilage and tendons are the cause, right up to a link with estrogen. All are unproven, but the statistics are undeniable. For example:

Osteoarthritis affects 3 million (or one in 10) Canadians, with twice as many women suffering from the disease as men, according to the Arthritis Community Research & Evaluation Unit. Most OA sufferers develop the condition after 45, but it can strike at any age.

Rheumatoid arthritis affects 300,000 (or one in 100) Canadians and affects three times as many women as men. Most RA sufferers develop the condition between the ages of 25 and 30, but it can strike anyone, from babies to the elderly.

Lupus (systemic lupus erythematosus, or SLE) affects 15,000 (or one in 2,000) Canadians. Women develop lupus eight to 10 times as often as men, usually between the ages of 15 and 45. But the disease can strike any time from babyhood to old age.

ment view puts you squarely in charge; the role of doctors and other caregivers is to support you with treatment and advice.

Studies show that nonmedical habits, attitudes and activities that you alone control often make the biggest difference in easing pain and letting you enjoy life. Consider the following: Research has found that even 20 months after learning more about exercise, diet and other self-help information, arthritis sufferers on average:

- Reduced pain by 20 percent
- Eased depression by 14 percent
- Cut doctor visits by 35 percent

What's more, patients largely continued reaping these benefits as long as four years after first learning to take charge of their condition.

This chapter offers detailed information and advice aimed at helping you to beat back arthritis. Because you can control your arthritis—to a greater degree than you have ever imagined.

We begin with a primer on the anatomy of a joint—ground zero for virtually every type of arthritis.

OSTEOARTHRITIS: CARTILAGE GONE BAD

Osteoarthritis (OA) is by far the most common type of arthritis, affecting some 3 million Canadians, or about half of arthritis sufferers. Some call it "old folks' arthritis," but it can happen to younger folks, too. Whatever your age, OA needs to be approached with an informed strategy so that you can take charge of your own health care.

Did you know?

Spicy foods can make a difference for arthritis pain. Spices such as cayenne pepper, ginger and turmeric contain compounds that reduce swelling and block pain signals. So spice it up!

What Is OA?

"Osteo" is the Greek word for bone, and many people do think that OA is a bone disorder. In fact, the condition mainly involves the cartilage that covers and cushions the ends of the bones within the joint.

 **CAUTION**

Early diagnosis and treatment is the best approach for any type of OA, but is especially important for OA of the knee. Treatment, including drugs, weight loss, exercise, hyaluronic acid injections and walking aids can all help prevent further joint damage. If left untreated, OA of the knee can become disabling, leaving joint replacement surgery as a patient's only recourse.

■ ■ ■ BURSITIS: CUSHIONS IN CRISIS

Small sacs called bursae are found near certain joints, including the elbow and knee. These sacs are filled with synovial fluid. They act as cushions, taking the pressure off the surface of a bone or easing the friction created on tendons or muscles when a joint is in motion.

Bursitis is inflammation of one or more bursae. It usually occurs when people repeatedly put pressure on a joint. Labourers who must kneel for long periods of time may develop bursitis of the knee. Students who prop their heads on their elbows when studying may develop "student's elbow."

Bursitis or arthritis? Bursitis is a "local" problem—only the bursae are affected—but is often mistaken for arthritis. The inflammation causes pain, tenderness and, sometimes, swelling; moving the joint often makes the problem worse. Talk to your doctor about treatment options. But often the best treatment for bursitis is simply to rest the affected joint. This allows the excess fluid inside the bursae to become reabsorbed into the bloodstream.

➤ **FACT:**

Osteoarthritis can occur in any joint in the body, but most commonly affects the hips, knees, lower back, neck and fingers. OA in the wrists, elbows and ankles can often be traced to an injury or to a job that subjects those joints to repeated stress.

DYSFUNCTIONAL CARTILAGE In OA, the cartilage does not function as it was intended to and slowly breaks down. There may be a number of causes for this breakdown. The result? The cartilage wears away—which is why osteoarthritis is sometimes referred to as "wear-and-tear" or "degenerative" arthritis. As the cartilage erodes, joints no longer move smoothly; instead, they feel—and sometimes sound—creaky.

Most OA sufferers have what is called primary OA, meaning the cause of their cartilage breakdown isn't known. In cases of secondary OA, cartilage damage can be traced to a specific cause, such as a physical injury to the joint, misaligned bones or inflammation due to rheumatoid arthritis.

Unlike some other types of arthritis—rheumatoid arthritis, for instance—OA affects only the joints and not any other parts of the body. OA is most likely to develop in those joints that are subject to the greatest amount of stress: the body's weight-bearing joints, especially the knees and hips.

➤ **FACT:**

If you have arthritis, there is a scientific name—crepitus —for the creaky feeling (and creaky noises) that you may notice when you move affected joints. Doctors feel and listen for signs of crepitus when diagnosing arthritis in patients.

The Road to Osteoarthritis

As cartilage breaks down, it can no longer cushion bones or prevent them from rubbing against each other. In addi-

66 *Lakota Arthritis pills really help my longstanding chronic painful knees. Now I have less pain and more mobility and can now climb stairs more easily.* 99

Marjorie Lyn, Toronto, ON

tion, bony growths, or spurs (known as osteophytes), may develop around the edge of bones in response to pressure on them. These changes lead to the most common symptoms of OA: pain, stiffness and restricted range of motion.

What Causes OA?

Again, the cause of primary osteoarthritis—what triggers joint cartilage erosion—is not yet known. Researchers have identified several risk factors, however, that can significantly increase a person's odds of developing the disease:

AGE Age is the most powerful predictor of whether a person develops osteoarthritis. The condition is rare in young people, but becomes increasingly common in older age groups. But although OA correlates with age, it isn't caused by it.

TOO MANY POUNDS Wisdom isn't the only thing that increases with age. So does the waistline. Carrying around extra weight puts constant stress on the joints, eventually damaging the cartilage. This is particularly true for the weight-bearing joints: the knees and hips.

If you're overweight, losing those extra pounds is one of the most effective of all osteoarthritis treatments available. A study that followed women for 36 years found that the heaviest women (those in the upper 20 percent by weight) were more than *three times* likelier than women in the bottom 20 percent to develop severe osteoarthritis of the knee.

LOOSE JOINTS When the bones of a joint aren't bound tightly to each other, they can bang together and damage their protective cartilage. This "joint instability" is now recognized as a major cause of the pain and early-morning stiffness that may start before cartilage damage has begun. (These symptoms are often felt by young, "double-jointed" women, such as many ballet dancers.) As a preventive measure, people with loose joints may be advised to avoid activities that could increase their risk of developing osteoarthritis prematurely.

■ ■ ■ DO YOU HAVE OSTEOARTHRITIS?

✔ One or more joints has a deep and aching pain that is steady or intermittent.
✔ Pain is worsened by exercise or other activities and eased by rest.
✔ Joint pain won't go away, even after resting the joint for several days.
✔ One or more joints feels stiff for 30 minutes or less after you get out of bed.
✔ One or more joints swells or feels tender.
✔ The affected joint has a grinding feeling or makes a grinding sound.
✔ When you start moving after sitting during the day—after driving a fairly long distance or seeing a movie, for example—you feel stiff for the next 20 or 30 minutes.

ON-THE-JOB EXERTION Certain jobs increase a person's risk of developing osteoarthritis. For example, OA of the knee is common among miners, dockworkers, people that sit in a squatting position over many years as well as others who must constantly bend their knees or do heavy lifting.

LOOK TO YOUR GENES OA has been traced to a gene responsible for making the collagen in cartilage. A mutation in this gene causes the production of defective collagen; this probably weakens cartilage and causes it to break down prematurely.

Genes seem to influence osteoarthritis in particular joints as well. OA involving the end joints of the fingers appears to be an inherited trait. This condition is known as Heberden's nodes [see facing page]. Genes may also influence OA in other joints. Researchers studying identical and fraternal female twins found that genetic factors may be responsible for half of all cases of OA of the hip.

Did you know?

Experts now believe that morning stiffness (also known as gelling) results from the accumulation of synovial fluid inside the joint while the person with arthritis is asleep. Once the person wakes up and starts moving, the excess fluid is pumped out and the stiffness subsides.

STOP

CAUTION

Joint pain that does not abate after a few days of rest is a clear signal that you should see a doctor.

THE ESTROGEN FACTOR Women stand a much greater chance of developing osteoarthritis than men, especially as they get older. This gender difference is most extreme for OA of the knee in older people: Women over 65 are more than twice as likely to develop it as men the same age.

COUCH POTATOING People tend to exercise less as they age—especially if they have arthritis. Unfortunately, inactivity itself increases your risk for osteoarthritis in several ways:

- Inactivity leads to weight gain, which puts extra strain on the joints.
- Tissues vital to joint movement—especially the muscles—can atrophy due to inactivity. Studies have shown that people with weak thigh muscles are more likely to develop OA of the knee.
- Inactivity can kill off chondrocytes, the cells that make and repair cartilage.

Cartilage has no blood vessels, so chondrocytes must obtain nutrients from the synovial fluid. Walking and other weight-bearing activities contract and expand cartilage with each repetition, and this creates the pumping action of fluid vital for chondrocytes. Long story short: Exercise equals nutrients for cartilage.

TAKING A BLOW The sports pages regularly report on athletes who've sustained serious injury to a joint—most often the knee. Unfortunately, an athlete or anyone else who suffers an injury to some part of a joint—cartilage, bone, ligament, or tendon—may eventually develop OA in that joint. With some injuries, such as a compound fracture of the ankle, osteoarthritis is almost a certainty. Professional athletes who incur frequent knee injuries will most likely develop OA of the knee when their playing days are over.

Joint by Joint: The Prime Targets of OA

Osteoarthritis can affect any of the body's joints, but it most often occurs in the hands, knees, hips or spine—or in joints that have been injured or stressed.

HANDS Osteoarthritis of the fingers is usually hereditary. Heberden's nodes, the small bony knobs that form on the ends of finger joints, occur most often in middle-aged and older women. The nodes are usually painless and tend to develop so slowly that a woman may not notice them until, for example, she has trouble slipping a ring over the joint.

Heberden's nodes are twice as likely to develop in women whose mothers also have them. Similar enlargements on the middle finger joints are known as Bouchard's nodes. Both Heberden's and Bouchard's nodes may first develop in one or a few fingers and later affect others. The problem with these nodes is mainly cosmetic.

> 66 *I have played competitive tennis for years, and when the joints started hurting more and more I thought I was done for good. Fortunately, after a few weeks of using Lakota I could get back on the court and run around! Thank you.* 99
>
> Kent Marley, Victoria, BC

CAUTION

If your doctor skimps on either the conversation or the physical exam and tries to diagnose or rule out osteoarthritis on X-rays alone, find yourself another doctor.

A more painful form of OA affecting the end joints of fingers is called nodal osteoarthritis. A single joint suddenly becomes painful, tender and swollen for three or four weeks—and then the problem subsides. Nodal OA is also hereditary and mainly affects women 45 and older, who are 10 times more likely to develop it than men in the same age group.

The joint at the base of the thumb also commonly develops osteoarthritis. By contrast, OA rarely affects the knuckles where the fingers attach to the hand.

KNEES The knees bear more weight than any other joint in the body—which makes them very susceptible to OA. When that happens, the knees may become swollen and feel stiff when you try to move them. You may notice that you have trouble walking short distances, climbing stairs and getting in and out of the car.

According to studies, strengthening the muscles surrounding the knee can often dramatically improve the symptoms of osteoarthritis of the knee.

HIPS Like the knees, hips are susceptible to OA. People with osteoarthritis of the hip may have trouble bending, and the pain and stiffness may cause them to limp when they walk. The pain may also radiate to other parts of the body, especially the groin or down the inside of the thigh. As we've already said, some cases of osteoarthritis of the hip seem to be hereditary. People who are bowlegged or who have other congenital abnormalities that cause the bones of the hip to be misaligned are also at increased risk for hip osteoarthritis.

Losing weight can help—but is not as helpful for relieving hip osteoarthritis as it is for the knee. Exercise can also help relieve pain and improve movement. Hip-replacement surgery is very effective when other treatments fall short of relieving the pain or disability.

SPINE Osteoarthritis of the spine mainly causes stiffness and pain in the neck or lower back. Measures that can help relieve the symptoms include exercises that strengthen the muscles of the back and abdomen, heat treatments, and the use of support pillows when sitting. In some people, bone spurs growing from the edges of the vertebrae may squeeze the spinal nerves, causing pain, weakness or numbness in the arms or legs. When this happens, surgery may be necessary to relieve the pressure on the nerves.

Did you know?

The aerobic exercises that pose the least risk of damaging joints are swimming, road cycling and walking.

> 66 *Thank you Lakota for helping me with my joint pain. I have been quietly suffering joint pain and swelling for the past 10 years, on one joint at a time. I am not the type to just pop a pill and feel better. When I first heard of Lakota, I was skeptical. Then I suffered joint pain and swelling on five different areas on my body and felt totally disabled. I was scared. I got my husband to pick up some Lakota from the health food store. I was ready to try it—the best decision ever. I was able to function the very next day! Thank you Lakota for giving me my life back!* 99

Kitsa Tsivoulas, Scarborough, ON

How Does OA Progress?

The breakdown of cartilage that leads to OA does not occur overnight, even though that first sharp pain in your knee might happen suddenly. The erosion almost always happens slowly, over many months or years, as the once-smooth cartilage becomes thinner, develops a roughened surface and loses its cushioning ability.

Sometimes, the pain and stiffness that accompany the disintegrating cartilage appears so gradually that people ignore it or chalk it up to "getting older." And for many lucky people, this is as far as their osteoarthritis ever progresses. In those cases it remains only a mild problem, causing symptoms they're barely aware of.

When cartilage continues to erode, however, the increasingly bothersome symptoms send many people to the doctor's office. After exercise, knees and other joints may ache or feel stiff for a brief time. You may also feel stiff after you've been sitting for an extended period of time.

BONE MEETS BONE Eventually, cartilage wears away to the point that, in some areas, the bones rub up against one another. People may feel their knees lock briefly as they climb the stairs or they might experience a grinding sensation—or even hear a grinding sound—when they bend affected knees or hips. People may also find themselves avoiding once-routine activities because of the pain—the daily walk to the newsstand, for example, or working in the garden on weekends. If the affected joint is a hip or knee, people may begin to limp as they try to minimize the pain.

Furthermore, small chunks of fragmented cartilage floating in the synovial fluid may begin to irritate the synovial membrane and add to the discomfort. In response, the membrane becomes inflamed and produces excess fluid, which makes the joint swell. In addition to pain, a person may now notice that the joint's range of motion is becoming restricted.

Did you know?

Osteoarthritis pain tends to worsen towards the end of the day. In many other types or arthritis, the pain remains constant during the day or is worse in the morning.

BONE SPURS AND OTHER PAINFUL GROWTHS OA becomes more severe as changes extend beyond cartilage to the underlying bones, which may sprout small growths (bone spurs, or osteophytes) around their outer edges. Bone spurs increase the joint's surface area and may be the bones' defensive reaction to the extra pressure created when their protective covering has worn away.

Unfortunately, bone spurs often make things worse. Spurs on the spine may cause severe pain by pinching the nerves connecting the spinal cord to the muscles; sharp spurs around the rim of the knee joint may worsen the pain and tenderness. By this time, people may find that arthritis pain is keeping them awake at night.

When the cartilage is completely eroded, the bones rub against each other within the joint. At this point, the pain can be excruciating and nearly unrelenting even after the slightest movement. When such severe osteoarthritis affects weight-bearing joints, it can be crippling, especially if:

- Uneven cartilage loss has created uneven joint surfaces, causing bones to become misaligned, leading to instability in the joint itself.
- Extensive bone-spur formation limits the affected joint's mobility.
- The muscles and tendons that support the joint have shortened and weakened due to disuse, which can lead to muscle spasms and even more disability.

Today's joint-replacement operations can be a godsend for people with such severe osteoarthritis.

RHEUMATOID ARTHRITIS

Rheumatoid arthritis (RA) is the most common type of inflammatory arthritis, and it usually affects many joints in the body. RA is much less common than osteoarthritis, affecting only about one percent of Canadians (some 300,000 people), with women accounting for three of every four people with the disease. RA can be-

---

■■■ RA VERSUS OA: COMPARISONS AND CONTRASTS

Age of occurrence Rheumatoid arthritis (RA) usually develops between the ages of 20 and 50, but can occur at any age. Osteoarthritis (OA) is a disease of middle and old age and rarely occurs before age 45.

Pattern of disease. RA often strikes symmetrically, meaning it affects both wrists, the knuckles on both hands, etc. OA rarely affects both joints (e.g., both wrists) at once.

Speed of onset About 20 percent of RA cases develop suddenly, within weeks or months. OA develops slowly, with cartilage breakdown usually occurring over several years.

Extent of illness In addition to causing joint damage, RA can cause fatigue, fever, anemia, weight loss and damage the heart and other organs. OA is limited to the joints.

Joints affected RA usually affects many joints, including the wrists (which are affected in almost all RA cases), knuckles, elbows, shoulders, ankles, feet and neck (but usually spares the rest of the spine). OA most commonly affects the knees, hips, feet, hands and spine; sometimes affects the knuckles and wrists; and rarely affects the elbows and shoulders.

Hand involvement RA affects many of the hand joints, but usually not the knuckles closest to the fingernails. OA affects the knuckles closest to the fingernails more often than other joints of the hand.

Morning stiffness People with RA have prolonged morning stiffness, usually lasting for at least 30 minutes after they get up. With OA, morning stiffness lasts less than 30 minutes.

gin at any age, but most often develops in young and middle-aged adults.

What Is RA?

RA is a systemic disease. What this means is that RA can affect not only the joints but also the blood vessels, heart, skin, muscles and other parts of the body. Most people with RA must contend with daily pain and stiffness, which may wax and wane. They often speak of having good days and bad days, weeks or months and of enduring periods of depression, anxiety and help-lessness. In these cases, a self-empower-ment approach can play a central role in helping people with RA gain control over their disease and their lives.

DO YOU REALLY HAVE IT? RA and osteoarthritis are often mistaken for each other—which can cause serious prob-lems, since the two types of arthritis are treated quite differently. Although symp-toms may be similar, RA and OA are very different diseases.

Osteoarthritis can affect any joint that has cartilage: freely movable joints, such as the knee, or slightly movable joints like the vertebrae. In contrast, RA focuses on the body's freely movable joints and on one area in particular—the synovial membrane, the inner lining of the capsule surrounding freely movable joints. Once this joint becomes inflamed, the characteristic symptoms of rheumatoid arthritis begin to appear: heat, swelling, stiffness and pain.

➤ **FACT:**

Many arthritis sufferers believe their stiffness and pain get worse when the weather changes. They're probably correct. Studies using climate chambers have found that people with arthritis really do experience increased stiff-ness and pain when the barometric pressure drops quickly or when the humidity suddenly rises.

While osteoarthritis confines its damage to the joints, RA is a systemic disease: It can damage not only the joints but also other parts of the body, such as blood ves-sels, the eyes and the heart. This tissue damage is caused by chronic inflammation—the hallmark of RA. Although inflammation can also occur in osteoarthritis, it is con-fined to the affected joints.

What Causes RA?

The causes of RA's key feature—chronic inflammation—are not known. However, scientists do know that a glitch in the immune system is involved. RA is an auto-immune disease, meaning that the body's immune

Did you know?

Bones and bone spurs can be seen on X-rays, but cartilage is invisible because it doesn't contain calcium salts. So cartilage is essential-ly visualized by its absence: In a normal joint, the black and apparently blank space separating two bones is the cartilage at the ends of the bones.

As osteoarthritis pro-gresses, X-rays show this blank space increasingly narrowing as more cartilage is lost and the bones move closer together.

> 66 *I have used Lakota Roll-on for may years and have told many people about it. It is the best remedy for my arthritic fingers. My brother is a painter and his fingers were getting so stiff and I suggested trying the Lakota Roll-on. He says it's almost like a miracle: He is back painting these days and his fingers are much more limber than before. When we travel there is always a Roll-on in my bag. There is not much else I can say except it is the BEST remedy for me. Thank you.* 99

Edie Despas, Camrose, AB

system mistakenly attacks healthy tissue as if it were a foreign invader.

RA'S TARGET This autoimmune attack is directed against the joint's synovial membrane. The joint becomes inflamed and causes pain, warmth, stiffness and swelling—symptoms common to many types of arthritis. But what makes RA different is the potential for the inflamed synovial membrane to severely damage the joints.

Genetic makeup is among the chief risk factors that researchers have identified for RA. Drugs can block RA's spread by deactivating the immune system components that attack the body's own tissues.

What Studies Show

Doctors once believed that damage to a joint's bones did not occur until many years after RA began affecting that joint. But more recent studies show that bone damage starts during the first year or two after RA's onset—pointing to the need for early diagnosis of RA and treatment to halt the inflammation that causes the damage.

■ ■ ■ SURVIVING FLARE-UPS

What is a flare-up? The word "flare-up" is an important part of the vocabulary for many arthritis sufferers. Things may be going along smoothly—so smoothly you've almost forgotten you have arthritis—and then, suddenly, a flare-up.

✔ Arthritis flare-ups are times when things go bad: Inflammation, pain and stiffness resurface with a vengeance. Flare-ups can be set off by many different things—overdoing it at the gym, lack of sleep or even emotional stress.

✔ Flare-ups can severely challenge the patience—sometimes even the sanity—of people with arthritis. Successfully taking charge of arthritis means riding out a flare-up in a way that causes the least amount of aggravation.

Minimizing pain The key is learning how to adjust to a flare-up without giving in to it. When a flare-up comes on, you'll want to give yourself more rest and protect the inflamed joints from further exertion. However, overprotecting a joint can be counterproductive, since long periods of inactivity can cause the muscles and tendons around a joint to weaken.

Unfortunately, flare-ups are an unavoidable part of arthritis. But knowing that you can manage these periodic crises means that you don't have to live in dread of them.

For questions about drugs to deal with flare-ups, consult your doctor.

■ ■ ■ THE FOUR DEGREES OF RA

No two cases of RA proceed in exactly the same way. In fact, experts stress that RA's course in any patient is quite unpredictable. But they have identified four basic ways in which the disease progresses—or, in some cases, doesn't.

1. In a few people—perhaps around 10 percent of those who develop it—RA is a temporary problem; these people experience a spontaneous and lasting remission that can't be attributed to any treatment they might be undergoing. When they happen, these spontaneous remissions usually occur within the first two years that people have RA. Another 10 percent of RA patients experience remissions, but the disease recurs later.

2. In the second type of RA, patients experience periodic flare-ups—weeks or months of painful, stiff and swollen joints—that alternate with intervals of normal health. Their treatment will depend on whether their joints are damaged during the flare-ups and how well their joints function between flare-ups.

3. In the third type of RA, known as remitting-progressive, patients experience periodic flare-ups without returning to normal health between the attacks. Instead, during the periods between attacks, they have lingering joint inflammation that becomes increasingly severe with each attack. If it isn't treated properly, remitting-progressive RA can eventually lead to significant joint damage.

4. The fourth type is called progressive RA, which is self-explanatory: The inflammation becomes more severe over time and causes gradually increasing pain, swelling and—if severe inflammation lasts long enough—joint damage and disability.

ANKYLOSING SPONDYLITIS: BACK PAIN WITH A TWIST

Anywhere from 150,000 to 300,000 Canadians (up to one percent) are believed to suffer from ankylosing spondylitis (AS), a chronic inflammation of the spine. It is three times more common in men than in women, but research suggests that the ratio may be much more equal: Women often have much milder cases that usually escape detection.

AS is mainly a disease of young people, often beginning before age 20 and rarely affecting people over 40. Once thought to be part of rheumatoid arthritis, we now know that it is related but separate.

What Is AS?

AS is a type of chronic arthritis that mainly affects the spine. (Ankylosing means "stiff," spondyl refers to the spine and itis means "inflammation.") In AS, the inflammation occurs in joints and areas where tendons and ligaments attach to bones. In severe cases, inflammation of the spine can actually cause the spinal vertebrae to fuse.

Older people who walk hunched over, looking down at the ground are usually in the late stages of AS. The good news is that today's treatments can almost always prevent AS from becoming such a disabling or crippling condition.

How Does AS Progress?

AS sneaks up on sufferers gradually. The first symptoms are usually aches and pains in the lower back caused by inflammation of the sacroiliac joints, located in the lower back on both sides of the spine, just above the buttocks. Low-back pain that begins gradually and persists for months is often a tip-off for the disease. The backache can be quite severe, interfering with sleep and causing a person to roll sideways to avoid bending the back when getting out of bed.

> ➤ FACT:

One way to distinguish between a ruptured disc and early ankylosing spondylitis is that while disc pain improves with rest, the pain of AS usually gets worse with rest and improves with movement.

ASCENDING PAIN As it progresses, AS and its inflammation may move to the upper back or spread to other joints, especially the neck, hips and shoulders. The spine becomes stiff due to pain and muscle spasms. In the final stages of AS, chronic inflammation can cause bony bridges to form between the vertebrae, resulting in the spine fusing permanently into a bent and inflexible position.

AS is a systemic disease, so it sometimes affects areas of the body beyond the joints. People with AS may experience fatigue, weight loss, poor appetite and—in about 25 percent of patients—an inflammatory eye condition known as iritis, which causes redness and tearing. People with severe and long-standing AS may experience damage to heart tissue that requires implanting a pacemaker.

> ➤ FACT:

Tenderness where a tendon attaches to a bone—a sharp pain in the shoulders, buttocks, back of the knees or the heel—can be a sign of early-stage ankylosing spondylitis.

What Now?

Someone recently diagnosed with AS should feel reasonably upbeat. Chances are you've been diagnosed early in the course of the disease. Today's treatments can almost always prevent AS from progressing to the point of irreversible spinal rigidity. These treatments also do a good job of alleviating pain and stiffness and enabling most people with ankylosing spondylitis to remain active and lead normal, fulfilling lives. Talk to your doctor before making any treatment decisions.

Though most people with AS lead normal lives, a take-charge approach emphasizing exercise is absolutely essential for success.

THE HEALING POWER OF EXERCISE

Regular activity enables AS patients to maintain a limber spine and prevent spinal deformity. Daily stretching exercises for extension of the back, neck and spine, and for improving chest and upper trunk mobility, are especially recommended. Swimming may be the best overall exercise for AS patients, since it stretches the back but doesn't stress it the way running or other weight-bearing exercises do.

Patients suffering from AS must also maintain as straight a spine as possible, by practicing good posture when sitting or standing and by sleeping on a firm mattress. Talk to your doctor for information on treatment.

■ ■ ■ RHEUMATIC RUNDOWN

Painful, swollen joints occur in a large number of joint ailments. Here is a rundown of rheumatic diseases with similar symptoms:

✔ Rheumatoid arthritis
✔ Ankylosing spondylitis
✔ Systemic lupus erythematosus
✔ Arthritis associated with psoriasis
✔ Reactive arthritis
✔ Gout
✔ Pseudogout
✔ Bursitis

TAKING CHARGE

*When you have arthritis, it's easy to let scary words like "degenerative"
and "progressive" become stumbling blocks—as if there's nothing you
can do to ease your pain and stay functional. In fact, this is far from
the truth. Arthritis is degenerative by nature, but there is plenty you
can do to slow its progress—or even halt it altogether. Exercise and
a healthy diet top the list of steps you can take; combine them with
a general self-care approach and you'll be in control of your arthritis.*

The Confidence to Overcome

Thousands of people who suffer from arthritis have discovered a
simple yet powerful truth that can provide hope and strength to
just about anyone who develops the condition: The most successful patients, the ones who go on to live richer, fuller lives,
are the ones who are most confident that they can overcome
the limitations of their disease.

Researchers have studied many patients enrolled in arthritis
self-help programs to find out what behavioural changes are
most important. Much to their surprise, the researchers found
that successfully overcoming symptoms depended above all
on patients' confidence that they could do it.

What's more, a positive attitude was even more important to
a patient's success than following a doctor's advice on
treatment, nutrition or exercise. It's called self-empowerment. A take-charge attitude, it turns
out, can be learned. And this is the key
ingredient for overcoming arthritis.

What Does Taking Charge Mean?

One unfortunate but all-
too-common reaction
to a chronic disease
like arthritis is simply
resigning oneself to
it. This is a condition
psychologists refer to
as "learned helplessness."
A little better is an approach of
simply doing whatever your doctor
tells you to do. But the best approach of
all—the one most likely to ease your pain, improve
your mobility and allow you to live life to the fullest—is to manage your arthritis in a positive way: Choose the life you want to
live, rather than the one you think arthritis will force you to have.

❝ *My husband and I have arthritis and osteoarthritis that cause us a lot of pain and swelling. Since using Lakota, we find our pain is less, the swelling in our joints has gone down and we have better mobility because of this. Our fingers, knees and other joints are more flexible and easier to use. It has made our life so much easier, being able to keep moving without pain. Thank you Lakota for helping us have a better quality of life due to your wonderful product.* ❞

K. Grimster, Brampton, ON

THE TEN STEPS FOR OVERCOMING ARTHRITIS

The self-help approach is based on an indisputable fact: No one cares about your welfare as much as you do. Thoroughly educating yourself about your condition and the treatments that are available to you is a giant step towards that liberation. Just because you have a chronic disease doesn't mean that it has to rule your life. There are ways to alleviate the effects of your condition, and most of them are based on common sense.

Digesting the information and then incorporating these steps into your daily life will give you the upper hand over your arthritis. One warning: Although arthritis self-help programs are often useful, they're not for everyone. You may not want to follow the 10-step program we describe here. But you may find that pursuing just a few of the steps—getting to know your problem, for example, or thinking about your long-term goals—can make an important difference to the way you feel.

CAUTION

Always use the strongest and largest joints and muscles for the job. Getting up from a chair can place a great deal of strain on your hands if you push yourself with your fingertips. Instead of using your fingers or knuckles, use your palms to help you to achieve liftoff.

Did you know?

Mid-course corrections not only help you move towards your goal but they also sharpen your coping skills. People with arthritis are constantly confronting uncertainty; a large part of taking charge of arthritis is becoming skilled at recognizing problems and then working around them.

1. GET TO KNOW THE PROBLEM

The more you know about a problem, the better you will be able to deal with it. And the better acquainted you are with arthritis, the better equipped you will be to overcome it. This isn't a radical new insight, but it is a very powerful one.

Knowledge is power, so take the time to evaluate your condition. Is pain the most troublesome symptom you experience? If so, how bad is it? Is it worse in the morning, or later in the day? By answering these and other questions, you'll be able to develop an effective arthritis program tailored to your needs.

66 *I have arthritis in my spine and without Lakota at times moving my neck and shoulders is a chore. The relief I get from Lakota is amazing, I have recommended it to a lot of friends who are now firm believers in the product.* 99

Judy Greenough, Bentley, AB

2. CHOOSE YOUR LONG-TERM GOAL

Chances are you want to resume a much-loved activity—going for a walk on the beach or playing with the children or grandchildren, for example—that arthritis has taken away from you. The best goals are specific, well-defined ones, such as: "I want to be able to walk a mile without knee pain." It's easier to motivate yourself to achieve a specific goal than a vague one, and it's also easier to tell whether you have attained it. Whatever it is, carving out a clear-cut goal can provide the motivation you need to jump-start your arthritis self-management plan.

3. DECIDE ON A STRATEGY

Once you have your goal, you need a treatment strategy to help you to reach it. Certainly, there is no shortage of treatment approaches available. Books, websites, news segments on the latest arthritis treatments—there is a confusing glut of information to contend with. Do you want to eliminate the pain in your arthritic knee? If so, you could try a number of approaches including weight loss, an exercise program or using anti-inflammatory drugs. Do you want to take the load off your knees by losing 20 pounds? You could avoid high-calorie foods, begin an exercise program, decrease the size of your portions at mealtimes or take a calorie-controlled lunch to work instead of eating out. Or you could combine several of these approaches into your overall strategy.

No goal worth achieving can be reached overnight or without effort. An effective anti-arthritis strategy will require some work or even some sacrifices (forgoing those tempting desserts, for example), but reaching your goal will ultimately make it all worthwhile.

4. DRAW UP YOUR WEEKLY TAKE-CHARGE PLAN

For someone with arthritis, that old Chinese saying, "A journey of a thousand miles must begin with a single step," is literally and figuratively true. In creating your weekly take-charge plan you need to decide on a short-term goal, then assign yourself specific actions to achieve that goal.

For example, if you decide that you want to lose 20 pounds, your take-charge plan might call for a short-term goal of losing a pound a week. Then you identify specific weight-loss actions—eliminating fattening desserts or walking to burn up calories, for example. If you manage to complete those actions with relatively little effort, you can consider writing in slightly more ambitious actions for next week's plan.

What Studies Show

Research shows that the longer pain goes on, the harder it is to treat. Although acute, or short-term, pain can be a good thing (it's your body telling you that something is wrong), ignoring or putting up with chronic pain allows the nerve fibres that carry pain signals to the brain to become oversensitized, to the point at which even a mild irritation can become torture.

5. BUILD A TEAM

It's wise to be inclusive when drawing up your take-charge plan. Ask for your doctor's advice, especially if you haven't yet been diagnosed with arthritis or don't know what kind you have. Many people assume that their aches and pains stem from arthritis, but sometimes their problems are being caused by something else entirely, such as an adverse reaction to a drug or a different health problem.

If you have been diagnosed with arthritis, work closely with your doctor to draw up a management plan that will suit your circumstances before putting it into action. Try to see your doctor and yourself as a team; a good partnership with your doctor can greatly assist you in achieving your goals.

6. PUT YOUR TAKE-CHARGE PLAN INTO ACTION

Now comes the hard part—following through on the strategy you've devised. If your goal of losing a pound over the next week calls for cutting out 500 calories per day, you may have to deny yourself that morning pastry and afternoon cappuccino.

7. MONITOR YOUR PROGRESS.

As the weeks pass, note how well you've done in completing the actions you've assigned yourself in your take-charge plan. Congratulate yourself if you've been able to stick to your plan, but try not to berate yourself if you did some backsliding. Nobody ever said that changing a habit was easy.

Did you know?

Changing behaviour is a process, not a one-off event. It takes most people about 10 weeks to make significant changes in the way they handle pain, for example, and another six months until they are past the point where they risk backsliding.

8. ADJUST YOUR ACTION PLAN

If you don't attain the short-term goal called for in your weekly take-charge plan, work out what went wrong and identify a way to correct it. If you lost only half a pound, maybe losing a pound a week was too ambitious. Or it may have turned out that losing a pound was easy and you could safely lose a little more. Either way, you will probably need to fine tune your action plan.

9. BUILD ON YOUR SUCCESS

Success, as we know, is one of the best of all motivators. If you've achieved your short-term goal for one week, the momentum from that success will carry over into the following week—and inspire you to set a more ambitious goal. As you target and attain new goals, you'll find yourself actually overcoming your arthritis in the process.

10. TRY THE LAKOTA WAY

When you need to manage pain, try the Lakota products best suited for your condition. Use a natural supplement such as Lakota Joint Care Formula or Lakota Rheumatoid to protect cartilage and reduce inflammation. Try a natural roll-on pain reliever such as Lakota Arthritis Roll-on for days when the pain is more intense.

■ ■ ■ THE LITTLE THINGS

A study of women with spine and hip joint pain found that small lifestyle changes—such as stretching before doing any physical activity, rolling out of bed instead of sitting up and carrying a seat cushion to soften hard seating—helped in managing pain.
You might feel like you're too busy, but take the time to consider small changes that can make a difference. When it comes to arthritis, the little things really add up.

GET MOVING

The human body is built to move. Inactivity leads to the wasting away of muscle, and that can increase the strain on joints—which causes even more pain. It might seem painfully contradictory to an arthritis patient, but exercise is indeed medicine in motion: It can help to prevent osteoarthritis, and it can certainly help those already living with the condition.

It wasn't so long ago that doctors endorsed their patients' tendency towards inactivity by advising them to stay off their feet. They assumed that osteoarthritis was an inevitable part of aging and that exercise just made things worse by speeding up cartilage destruction. As for patients with rheumatoid arthritis, doctors believed that exercise would do nothing but trigger inflammation and flare-ups.

THE HEALING POWER OF MOVEMENT

They were so wrong. Science, fortunately, has had the last word on the subject, proving that exercise is good medicine for arthritis sufferers. Study after study has shown that moderate activity does not damage joints or worsen arthritis pain. In fact, regular exercise is one of the best therapies for relieving joint pain; it also improves many other health problems common to arthritis patients.

Activity's Wide Range of Benefits

Arthritis can have a physically damaging effect—and not just on the joints. Studies show that many people with arthritis are in poor general health, particularly when it comes to risk factors for heart disease.

People who have arthritis tend to be much heavier and have higher blood pressure, lower levels of HDL cholesterol (the "good" form that prevents heart disease) and higher blood sugar levels (indicating possible diabetes). And the reason for most of this is inactivity—which was recently declared a major heart-disease risk factor.

➤ **FACT:**
Strong, well-toned muscles, tendons and ligaments can bear the brunt of the force on our joints as we move. Most of the load that the joints bear can be transferred to these supporting structures, taking some of the pressure off the cartilage.

Exercise offers numerous health benefits to people no matter their age or physical condition, but it can be especially valuable for people with arthritis. Regular activity can relieve pain and stiffness as effectively as NSAIDs (non-steroidal anti-inflammatory drugs) and other drugs—while offering two crucial additional advantages:

Everyday Strategies

There are many ways to work on flexibility and lose some pounds in your daily life.

✔ Make vacuuming a total body exercise by stepping forward in a slightly longer-than-usual stride as you move the machine forwards. Keep your back straight.

✔ Stay in motion; fidgeting burns hundreds of calories a day. Stand up and walk around while talking on the phone. Do the same during television commercials.

✔ In the car, roll your shoulders and stretch your arms at red lights.

47

- Exercise, when done properly, rarely causes significant problems. Drugs, however—especially pain-relieving NSAIDs—can cause serious side effects.
- Exercise does something that no drug can do: It modifies the course of arthritis by making joints healthier—stopping osteoarthritis from worsening and possibly even preventing the disease from occurring.

Besides relieving pain and stiffness, the right combination of exercises can help to strengthen and stabilize arthritic joints and prevent them from becoming deformed. Equally important, exercise can go a long way in reducing the mental stress that can worsen physical pain. And, if you need further motivation to get moving, staying active can lower your risk of diabetes, hypertension, heart disease and several types of cancer; provide relief from insomnia and depression; and improve immunity and a sense of well-being.

Exercise and Joints: Working Together

The well-known saying "Use it or lose it" certainly applies to your joints. Unless you put them through their paces with regular activity, they lose their strength and resilience and become weaker, stiffer, more painful and constricted. That's because exercise (or the lack of it) affects the health of all parts of a joint, including the bones and the all-important cartilage that buffers them.

> ➤ FACT:
> Bones are dynamic, not static, constantly changing in response to the demands placed upon them. Bones are like muscles, growing thicker and stronger in response to a heavier workload.

66 *I'm a fairly young man still, but arthritis runs in my family. When I started a summer job some years ago making car rims, I started experiencing joint pain in both my wrists almost immediately. I wasn't sure if I could do the work for the entire summer as the pain got worse. Luckily I gave in to suggestions and started taking Lakota. By the next day I could really notice the difference. Lakota really was a lifesaver. It's a great product and I still use it. Keep up the good work and please don't change the Lakota formula!* 99

Robert Pietrzak, Sarnia, ON

Experts recommend three types of exercise for arthritis sufferers: stretching to increase range of motion; aerobic or weight-bearing activities, like walking and strength training. Each works in a different but important way to strengthen and improve joints.

BE FLEXIBLE. The joint's range of motion—how fully and easily you can bend your knees to pick up a pencil or your grandchild, for example—depends on the flexibility of the muscles, tendons and ligaments that surround and protect it.

When pain and stiffness discourage people from moving their joints, the inactivity causes these surrounding tissues to contract, which further limits the joint's movement. Stretching exercises are vital for flexible muscles, tendons and ligaments, so that the range of movement can be maintained and even enhanced.

STRENGTHEN THE JOINT'S SUPPORT. The bones of a joint do not operate in isolation. Their ability to move depends on the muscles and tendons that pull on them. Exercises aimed at strengthening muscles and tendons can ease movement and help the joints to move with less pain. Bulking up the muscle mass around a joint also helps to protect the joint in the event of a fall or any other physical assault on the area.

We all tend to lose muscle mass as we get older, a reality that unfortunately exacts a double penalty on older arthritis sufferers; not only do they lose muscle mass quite naturally as they age, but they also lose it because of the inactivity that is so often a consequence of their painful condition.

This is why muscle-strengthening exercises are valuable for all older people, but especially for those with arthritis.

CARE FOR YOUR CARTILAGE. Smooth movement within a joint depends on the health of its cartilage. To maximize the health of a joint and its cartilage, the joint must not only move regularly but must actually undergo "repetitive joint loading"—the stress exerted by aerobic, weight-bearing exercises such as walking or jogging.

Did you know?

As recently as 20 years ago, doctors advised arthritis patients against exercising for fear that it would worsen joint damage and inflammation. But it's now recognized that moderate physical activity can be one of the most effective of all arthritis treatments.

■ ■ ■ EXCISE PAIN BEFORE EXERCISE

There are known methods of stopping arthritis pain for short periods of time. Here are some methods you can use before exercising or just going out for the groceries:

Heat Applying warm towels, hot packs or taking a bath or shower for 15 minutes three times a day can relieve pain.

Cold A bag of ice wrapped in a towel helps to stop pain and reduce swelling when used for 10 to 15 minutes at a time. This is especially effective for inflamed joints.

Relaxation therapy Patients can learn to release the tension in their muscles to relieve pain.

Mobilization therapies Traction (gentle, steady pulling), massage and manipulation (using the hands to restore normal movement to stiff joints) can all help to control pain and increase joint motion and muscle and tendon flexibility.

➤ FACT:

For every year that you have been out of shape, you need a month or more of exercise to get back into shape.

Small steps make a big difference

Many people tend to do less and less exercise as they age. In a way, this exercise anxiety is understandable; intense exercise and macho slogans such as "No pain, no gain" are enough to discourage anyone from putting on a pair of running shoes and going out. Fortunately, the best exercise slogan today is actually a very old one: "All things in moderation."

Fitness as Part of Your Lifestyle

The value of moderate exercise is well known. Moderate exercise is an important contributor to overall health and well-being—and you don't have to go to the gym to achieve it. Doing 30 minutes of moderate activity, at least five days a week, is enough. This could include walking, cycling, gardening or even cleaning the house.

Did you know?

Pain and stiffness in one joint often leads to problems in another. The ankle, for example, is rarely affected by osteoarthritis, but people with OA of the knee often develop ankles that are weak and have limited motion. The pain in their knee has caused them to walk more gingerly, and with less weight placed on the foot; the calf muscle grows weak and the ankle becomes stiff. For similar reasons, OA of the knee quite often leads to impaired hip motion, and vice versa.

➤ FACT:

On days when you really don't feel motivated, plan to exercise for just five minutes. If you still don't feel like exercising after the five minutes are over, stop. Most of the time, however, you'll start feeling invigorated and will want to continue.

A simple change in your lifestyle, such as walking up stairs rather than taking the elevator or escalator, is just one example of how to increase your daily activity. Try to set aside some time to do things that you enjoy or have enjoyed in the past—such as dancing, going for walks, cycling or swimming.

If you enjoy doing the activity you are more likely to stick to it and do it more often. You could get off the bus one stop earlier and walk the extra distance, or go for a walk at lunchtime. Cutting down on the time you spend in front of the television or computer will also help.

❝ *My father has terrible arthritis, and will often get shooting pain through his hands. He's tried a few treatments but nothing seemed to give him much relief. One day I was in the pharmacy and spotted Lakota. I decided to give it a try and he loves it!* ❞

David Williams, Langley, BC

This "exercise prescription" is amply supported by research showing that moderate activity offers many of the same health benefits previously associated with full-throttle exercise.

The good news about moderate exercise couldn't come at a better time for people with arthritis. Studies have shown that it is safe for virtually all arthritis patients to engage in moderate exercise—and is extremely useful as well: Low-impact aerobics, swimming, dancing, walking and cycling are all examples of moderate exercise that can ease joint pain and stiffness, while also improving your overall health.

The Essence of Taking Charge

The best way to incorporate exercise into your daily routine is to make it a key aspect of your take-charge plan. Most arthritis patients can find some form of exercise that is appropriate—and even fun—for them. And of all possible treatment approaches, exercise may be the one most likely to lead to self-empowerment.

By now, you know how important it is for arthritis patients to feel confident that they can control their own destiny. In study after study, self-empowered patients have proved most successful in overcoming their symptoms and leading richer, fuller lives. Choose a long-term goal and then reach it through a succession of short-term goals. Exercise fits this approach perfectly.

EXERCISE BUILDS CONFIDENCE. Studies have already shown that exercise gives people confidence that they can meet the physical challenges of life—an essential component of self-empowerment.

ACTIONS CAN BE SPECIFIED. Write up a take-charge plan, in which you list the actions you hope to achieve each week. Exercise is ideal for your take-charge plan, as you can express it as a number of repetitions (12 leg lifts, for example), a distance ("walk one mile"), a length of time ("do stretching exercises for 10 minutes") or perhaps even specify its intensity ("walk 10 minutes on a treadmill set at 3.5 miles an hour").

KEEPING TRACK IS EASY. You know whether you've met your target goal of "two sets of 12 leg lifts on Monday, Wednesday and Friday." Meeting your goal each day will encourage you.

Everyday Strategies

Use the stairs. It's a great way to build exercise into your day—but don't think "all or nothing." You can walk up to the second floor, catch the elevator there and ride the rest of the way. As you get stronger, walk more flights and ride less.

Try two for one. Taking stairs two at a time doubles the exercise—you get the benefits of stair-climbing plus lunging. (And you may even beat the elevator.)

Walk, don't slouch. You can enhance the benefits of walking by practising good posture as you stride. Hold your body so that shoulders and hips are aligned without arching your back. Keep your elbows close to your body. Let arms swing freely forward and back in a straight line.

YOU CAN MAKE ADJUSTMENTS. If doing 12 leg lifts proves too difficult, reduce your repetitions to 10. Straining yourself will not benefit you in the long term. And don't expect immediate results; it may take some time to get into the swing of regular exercise. Getting in shape is all about the process, so make sure to enjoy it.

It is easy to build on your success. The take-charge plan is based on gradual progress—achieving small successes each week until you finally achieve a goal that may once have seemed out of your reach. A well-planned exercise program will follow the same pattern, with requirements becoming slightly more strenuous from week to week.

ASK THE EXPERTS. For most people, exercise is a simple proposition; put on a pair of sweat pants or a swimsuit, start exercising and perspire. But for arthritis patients who may have damaged a joint, strained the supporting ligaments or tendons or have muscle imbalances, consulting your doctor and possibly a physiotherapist may be a better first move.

Physiotherapists are exercise specialists who can work with you to create a program of stretching, strengthening and aerobic exercises that is tailored to your needs and abilities. You may be in particular need of that kind of advice if your arthritis is severe or if you stopped exercising a long time ago.

GET PHYSICAL. A physiotherapist assesses your aerobic capacity, your sense of balance, the flexibility of all your joints and your muscular strength. Then they will develop a program targeting areas where you need help—quadriceps-strengthening exercises for knee pain, for example, or swimming to improve aerobic capacity and overall flexibility.

Don't waste the opportunity to make it fun. The choices should include activities you enjoy, so you'll be motivated to stick with the program for years to come.

A course of physiotherapy generally lasts just a few weeks, although some people may benefit from longer-term care. Therapy sessions usually last less than an hour and may range in frequency from once a week to every day.

The best way to find a physiotherapist is to ask your doctor for a referral to a licensed or registered physiotherapist. Physiotherapists work in hospitals, clinics, health clubs, sport injury clinics and nursing homes. Some even make house calls.

Make sure thar your physiotherapist is fully aware of your medical condition—this will ensure that your program is absolutely right for you.

Stretching It: Unlocking the Joints

Of the three types of exercise recommended for arthritis, stretching is the one you should strive to do every day. It is the least likely of the three types to cause injury or aggravate your condition—this is one of the reasons that some stretching exercises may be recommended even during arthritis flare-ups.

DON'T LET STIFFNESS TAKE OVER. Stretching addresses a problem that affects everyone, whether they have arthritis or not—the tendency for muscles, ligaments, tendons and joints to stiffen with age. Without regular stretching exercises, the average adult's flexibility declines by roughly five percent each decade.

Adding arthritis to the mix makes things considerably worse, since people with the condition are even less likely than others to maintain supple joints. The good news is that inflexible joints can be unlocked—and a conscientious stretching program can help to erase decades'-worth of accumulated joint tightness.

> ➤ FACT:
>
> Stretching exercises to reduce pain are considered a mainstay of treatment for fibromyalgia, a disease that mainly affects women and is characterized by chronic, generalized musculoskeletal pain.

Why It Works

The concept behind stretching (also known as range-of-motion exercises) is simple: When a muscle is pulled slightly beyond its normal length, it gradually adapts to its longer length and increases a joint's range of motion. This improved range accounts for most of the benefits of stretching—being able to tie your shoes,

---

■ ■ ■ **EVERYDAY EXERCISE**

Walking If walking seems too tame, but running is too hard on your joints, try a technique called interval training, in which you crank up the pace periodically—but only for short spurts. Example: Walk at your normal pace for five minutes, then walk much faster for 30 seconds—then slow back down to your usual stride for another five minutes and repeat. This sequence boosts intensity, but poses minimal risk of injury.

Biking Grip the bike properly. Hold the handlebars firmly enough to control the bike, but loosely enough to keep hand and arm muscles from being unnecessarily tense. Keep your elbows slightly bent.

❝ I have suffered with pain in my joints for a long time. My grandchildren wanted to play with me but I could not. I tried the roll-on pain relief and both myself and my grandbabies are thrilled with how pain-free I am. I can now play with them, not just watch. Life is so wonderful and Lakota products have helped my life be one of participation. Lakota products are nature's way of helping us who need and want relief from pain! Thank you Lakota! ❞

Diane Harzan, Beaconsfield, QC

❝ For years, I have suffered from arthritis pain. A friend told me to try the Lakota Arthritis capsules, and I'm sss-soooo glad I did! What a relief! I can now open my hands that were so sore to move before. And my knees don't hurt as much either. I was able to go for a short walk, something I hadn't been able to do in months. And now I can walk almost a city block, Lakota Arthritis capsules have changed my life, and in a good way. Thank you Lakota. ❞

Sherry Harlton, London, ON

■ ■ ■ STRETCHING SECRETS

Breathe deep. Make your stretching more relaxing and pain relieving by using simple breathing techniques. Breathe through your nose when inhaling and exhaling; take at least three seconds to fill your lungs and another three to let the air out.

Relax. Don't let other parts of your body tense up while you're stretching.

Stretching do's and don'ts. The rule of thumb is to stretch until you feel a gentle tug in the muscle. When that feeling subsides, you don't have to stretch further; just hold the position for 15 seconds or as long as it takes your muscles to relax with the stretch. Then, if you want to push it further, stretch another centimetre or so and hold for another 15 seconds. Sometimes called the developmental stretch, this promotes flexibility.

Keep it up. Stretch every day, even if you're not doing any other exercise; muscles only keep their newfound flexibility for a day or less. Keep working them every day and you'll get progressively more pliable. Daily stretching also helps with stress relief—when you need to unwind, stretch it out and lift your mood.

work in the garden or turn your head while reversing your car to watch the space behind you.

THE BASICS OF STRETCHING Stretching can be done in several different ways, but there is one technique that is probably safest and is also simple and effective—static stretching. Static stretching involves easing into a stretch to the point where you begin to feel mild discomfort—never further—and then holding that maximum position for 10 to 30 seconds. Research has shown that holding a stretch longer than that provides no extra benefits—and that briefer stretches probably won't do you any good.

Stretching in water is ideal, since it supports your limbs and helps to minimize the stress on them as you put them through their range of motion. Exercising in warm water—between 28°C and 34°C is especially useful, as warmth helps to relax muscles and decrease joint pain.

Strength Training: Getting Muscle from Metal

You may be surprised to learn that older people are the ones who should be going to the gym. The reason? The older people get, the faster they lose muscle strength.

Believe it or not, between the ages of 20 and 50, muscle strength in the average adult dips by only about 10 to 20 percent. But over the next two decades, remaining strength falls by an extra 25 to 30 percent—and drops even faster after that. Inactivity accounts for much of this muscle loss, so it stands to reason that older people with arthritis become even weaker than other people their age.

Losing More than Muscle

As your muscles slowly fade, it can have serious consequences for your daily life. Many older people have some difficulty performing everyday tasks, such as carrying the laundry upstairs, opening windows or simply getting out of a chair. Muscle loss also weakens bones, which need stimulation from the muscles to stay strong. And, of course, the inactivity brought on by arthritis weakens the muscles around joints, limiting a person's ability to move and eventually impairing balance.

However, there is a silver lining: Strength training can almost entirely reverse the muscle loss that has occurred over decades. One study, for example, found that 70-year-old men who had engaged in strength training since middle age were just as strong, on average, as 28-year-olds who did no strength training. Furthermore, it appears that the older people become, the greater is the proportional gain from a strength training program.

One study found that frail individuals in their 80s and 90s were able to double or even triple their leg strength after strength training for just two months, enabling some of them to return to walking without assistance.

More Muscle, Less Pain

Strength training has also produced impressive results in studies involving arthritis patients, particularly those with OA of the knee. Almost invariably, the inactivity brought on by OA of the knee causes weakening of the quadriceps muscle, the large muscle at the front of the thigh that runs from knee to hip. Exercises that strengthen the quadriceps muscle can produce striking improvements, greatly easing pain and allowing much more movement of the knee joint.

What's more, strength training helps you to stay slim; muscle burns calories faster than fat, even while you're resting. In general, a strength-training session will use up calories as fast as walking does.

BUILDING MUSCLE POWER Engaging in at least two muscle-strengthening sessions a week will build muscle—and even just one weekly session will slow muscle loss, possibly stopping it entirely. The sessions don't have to be time-consuming; you can obtain substantial benefits from as few as four to six exercises that work major muscles in the arms, shoulders, chest, back and legs.

■ ■ ■ BETTER BIOMECHANICS

Although exercise can help your joints and arthritis, poor posture and poor biomechanics can cancel that good medicine. Here are some suggestions that can take the strain out of daily tasks:

✔ If you have arthritis of the hands, use an electric can opener rather than a manual model, and don't hold objects in a tight grip for extended periods. When holding anything, flex your fingers frequently.

✔ If reaching up hurts your shoulder, place frequently used items on lower shelves.

✔ Maintain good posture. It places the least stress on your joints.

✔ Use the largest joint possible to accomplish any task. Carry a shoulderbag rather than a clutch bag, because your shoulder joint is larger than your finger joints.

✔ Try to keep your joints extended rather than bent.

✔ Try not to stay in one position for a long period of time.

✔ If you have rheumatoid arthritis, avoid bending; arrange your rooms so that you reach up for items and use extended shoehorns that are easier on inflamed joints.

Did you know?

Holding your breath when strength training can elevate blood pressure to dangerous levels. Olympic weightlifters can drive their blood pressure to as high as 480/320mmHg. Instead, breathe out while lifting the weight and breathe in while lowering it.

Performing one set of eight to 12 repetitions of any
particular strength-training exercise should improve both
muscle strength and endurance.

For some arthritis patients, lifting weights causes pain
if the weight is moved through the entire range of motion.
Rather than trying to work through the pain, try lifting the
weight through a limited range of motion. You will still
experience significant benefit, and gradually be able to
push it further.

Aerobic Exercise

Exercises that increase your heart rate are called aerobic. More specifically, aerobic exercise is any activity that uses your large muscles in a repetitive fashion long
enough to get your heart beating at 60 to 80 percent of its maximum rate for at
least 20, but preferably 30, minutes.

Aerobic exercise—which includes skipping, rowing, roller-blading, skating or
even cross-country skiing—increases your overall fitness by training your heart and
lungs to deliver oxygen more efficiently to the working muscles of your body. Since
people with arthritis tend to be less active and therefore less fit, they usually have
a lot to gain from aerobic exercise. Additionally, aerobic exercises that also involve
weight bearing, such as walking or jogging, can help to lubricate and nourish the
crucially important joint cartilage.

> ➤ FACT:
> During the first six months of an exercise program, it is best to lengthen your
> workouts gradually. Increase your sessions by no more than five minutes a month.

Some aerobic exercises do double duty for arthritis patients by stretching and
strengthening the joints. Swimming, for example, is both a good aerobic exercise
and ideal for stretching. Walking and dancing are aerobic and also help to build
strength in both the leg and thigh muscles.

The aerobic exercises generally recommended for arthritis patients offer a good
workout without putting a lot of pressure on your joints. They include walking,
cycling, swimming, aerobic
dancing, and aerobic pool
exercises—all of which have
been shown to produce defi-
nite benefits.

To improve your aerobic
capacity, try to exercise at between 60 and 80 percent of
the maximum heart rate for
your age. This range is called
the target heart rate.

In one study, patients with
painful hip or knee OA were
randomly assigned to three
treatment programs—aerobic
walking, aerobic pool exercises, or non-aerobic stretching exercises—for 12 weeks.

❝ *I play soccer in a master's men's league, which is very competitive. As I get older the wear and tear on my joints increases each year, especially since I badly sprained my ankles several years ago. I don't want to give up playing as I love the game too much. Using Lakota Joint Pills and Roll-on Pain Relievers allows me to enjoy playing soccer without pain. They are the one product that I have stocked up on and use when joint and muscle injuries occur. I highly recommend Lakota to family and friends.* ❞

Ron Ypma, Woodstock, ON

Both of the aerobic groups showed significant gains in aerobic capacity compared with the stretching group, while all three groups showed similar lessening of joint pain and tenderness. In case you fear that exercise will send you to the medicine cabinet for pain relief: None of the three groups increased its use of pain medication throughout the study period.

Exercise Dropout? How to Keep in Motion

Many people are eager to begin working out, but more than half give up within three months. All too often, "exercise dropouts" injure themselves by plunging in too aggressively rather than starting off slowly. But by taking basic precautions, you can minimize the risk that an exercise injury will derail your efforts to strengthen your joints.

GET A CHECKUP. If you are over 50, or haven't been physically active for many years, you should see your doctor to find out if your heart is up to the rigours of moderate exercise. A doctor's visit is also advisable if you know that you have heart disease or one or more risk factors for heart disease, such as hypertension, diabetes or a high cholesterol level.

Even if vigorous exercise is out, you should work with your doctor in choosing stretching or another less strenuous activity that can still be quite helpful.

CHOOSE YOUR EXERCISES WISELY. Whether you design your own exercise program or consult a physiotherapist or other expert, be sure to match your joints to the exercises that are most appropriate for them. If you have an arthritic shoulder, for example, include shoulder-stretching exercises but avoid strenuous weight lifting. If your knees are painful, then sprints are probably not in your future. By showing common sense in the exercises you choose, you can ensure that your program will improve your arthritis without causing injuries.

WARM UP. As muscles warm up, they become more supple—easier to stretch and less likely to tear. So warming up prior to a workout can be quite important for avoiding injuries. A good warm-up usually takes seven to 10 minutes—and even longer if, in the

What Studies Show

A study found that for people with RA and other forms of inflammatory arthritis, aerobic exercise seems to offer a special bonus—reducing joint inflammation. Studies have shown that RA patients who completed aerobic exercise programs had fewer inflamed joints than non-participants.

■ ■ ■ TAKING A LOAD OFF

Although exercise is the best way to protect your joints, there are aids that take the pressure off stiff joints.:

Walking stick Anyone who walks with a limp should consider using one; it protects the joints by taking weight off them and is helpful during a flare-up. Using one properly can relieve pressure on the hip joint by up to 50 percent.

Bath and kitchen tips Bath boards and elevated toilet seats with handles can take stress off joints. In the kitchen, special knives with L-shaped handles, cutting boards that hold foods firmly in place and electric can openers and jar openers can help arthritis sufferers.

past, you've injured yourself while exercising. The idea is to raise your body temperature, elevate your heart rate and loosen up the muscles and joints so that they can withstand the stresses they'll soon be confronting.

Good ways to warm up muscles include pedalling on a stationary bike, moderately fast walking or a spell of jogging on the spot.

STRETCH. Stretching is a useful prelude to exercise and also a vital form of exercise in its own right for people with arthritis. Contrary to standard wisdom, researchers have found that stretching before a workout does not decrease the risk of injury, but does help to reduce the pain and discomfort that can occur when stiff joints are made to move. People with arthritis should do stretching exercises daily or every other day. When stretching precedes other exercise, a 15- to 30-second stretch should suffice.

EASE INTO IT. For the first two weeks, maintain an easy, relaxed pace. Exercise for no more than 10 or 20 minutes at a time and no more than three or four times a week. You should expect a little muscle soreness when you embark on any exercise program.

SOFTEN THE IMPACT. Arthritis patients should be especially careful to protect sensitive joints from unaccustomed jolts. So limit yourself to low-impact exercises, such as walking, cycling or

CAUTION

Avoid "bounce stretching" —repeated brief, forceful stretches. This poor technique can actually cause damage and increase stiffness.

> ❝ *The pain in my foot kept me from wearing pretty shoes. No cute little sundresses, shorts, or capris for me, as my running shoes looked as heavy as army boots with them.*
>
> *One day I noticed a sale on Lakota Arthritis pills. I'd heard of them before, but had never tried them. I decided to give them a try. I faithfully took them each day, hoping to find pain relief, and I did. One day I tried wearing some sandals without the clunky orthotics. What a surprise: I could walk without the orthotics and the pain!*
>
> *Thanks to Lakota, I have more freedom in shoe choices and am able to complete a shopping trip without pain. I'd say that's a miracle!* ❞

Lynne Carl, Edmonton, AB

swimming, and try to work out on soft, smooth surfaces, such as grass, or cushioned surfaces in a gym. Proper footwear can be a big help in defusing the shocks of repeated impacts. If your feet underpronate (usually meaning you have high arches and need good arch support) or overpronate (meaning you probably have flat feet and need a well-cushioned sole), you may need shoes specific for your needs.

To protect your joints from further pounding, consider buying cushioned insoles for your shoes—one study found that wearing them while walking can decrease the shock measured at the knee by nearly 50 percent.

Listen to Your Senses

You can expect some muscle soreness when you first start an exercise program. But don't continue exercising if joint pain worsens, and be alert to these warning signs that you've overdone it:

- Muscle or joint pain that lasts more than two hours after you've stopped exercising
- Unusually severe fatigue
- Increased muscle weakness
- Decreased range of motion of joints
- Increased joint swelling

CAUTION

Rest is certainly advisable if you have overdone things or if you're having a flare-up of joint pain (although even then you should probably do some gentle stretching exercises). But avoid the temptation to rest your joints for long periods of time, since the inactivity may actually increase pain and stiffness. Remember that not exercising poses far more risk to arthritic joints than doing suitable exercises.

➤ FACT:

Try to exercise when joints are least likely to feel stiff or fatigued, perhaps in the late morning or early afternoon. Early mornings or late evenings are not ideal.

FEWER POUNDS, LESS PAIN

Weight loss isn't merely about vanity: It's about health. Particularly for people with arthritis, achieving a healthy weight can make all the difference in reducing pain and halting the advance of the disease. The primary reason is obvious: Carry around less weight and you put far less stress and strain on your joints.

Being overweight with arthritis can become a vicious circle. Loading joints—especially knees—with extra pounds causes more pain and decreases mobility. That typically makes you cut back on physical activity, which, in turn, contributes to even more weight gain.

If you've started getting more physical activity to build strength and endurance, you've already taken a giant step towards breaking the cycle of increasing weight, pain and disability. But diet control is an important part of losing weight as well. The most effective diet tactics are deceptively simple. Better yet, they work best when you apply them over time rather than making a drastic overhaul of your current eating habits.

Did you know?

Eliminating obesity in Canada would lower the incidence of OA of the knee by 25 to 50 percent, and reduce the incidence of OA of the hip by 25 percent or more.

Extra Weight and OA

Extra weight is now recognized as a major cause of osteoarthritis. And judging by surveys showing that more than half of all North Americans are overweight, it may be the most significant cause of all. In particular, obesity can cause OA of the weight-bearing joints—the knees and, to a lesser extent, the hips. But it is also associated with a greater risk of OA in other joints as well, including the back, ankles, big toes and hands.

THE PRESSURE OF POUNDS When you think about it, obesity's role in causing OA—or in aggravating symptoms in people who already have the disease—makes all too much sense. The protective cartilage that covers the ends of the bones in a joint is just a few millimetres thick. Years of carrying around spare pounds puts extra pressure on the knees and other weight-bearing joints, grinding down cartilage to the point that bone rubs against bone, giving rise to the pain and stiffness of OA. In people who already have OA, being overweight can speed up cartilage loss and cause the disease to worsen.

Studies have documented the overweight-arthritis link. They've followed groups of people over several years, keeping close tabs on their weight and whether they developed OA. One study involved more than 1,000 women age 45 to 64; 58 out of the 67 women with OA in one knee returned for a follow-up X-ray two years later. Of the 32 clearly overweight women, 15—or nearly half—had by then developed OA in their other knee as well; but only one of the 10 normal-weight women had gone on to develop OA in her other knee.

The evidence is clear: Too much weight is an arthritis sufferer's nemesis. But that's good news. Losing weight is easy, and is accompanied by a host of other health benefits. One warning: exercise is addictive. Once you start on the track to getting in better shape, you might become hooked.

SMALL MOVES, BIG GAINS
MEDICINE IN MOTION

Excercise is one of the pillars of good arthritis management. It is not only vital for weight loss—a boon for anyone with arthritis of the knee or hip—but is also essential to the health of your joints.

■ ■ ■ IN AN EMERGENCY: SPLINT IT

If your joint pain is suddenly too much to bear, a temporary solution is to immobilize it in a splint. Today's splints are lighter and sleeker than those of the past and are made of plastic or rubber. They can be purchased over the counter or fitted, usually by an occupational therapist. One of the simplest splints is a slip-on type used to immobilize the joints of the fingers. Splints can also be fitted to the wrist, elbow and other joints.

Splints are never worn permanently: they are designed to be put on and taken off easily, as needed, and should be used for short-term relief only, as immobility is the enemy of arthritis sufferers. Sometimes a splint is worn during the day but your doctor may recommend wearing it only at night.

GOOD MOVES FOR THE KNEES

A

SEATED KNEE EXTENSION

This is a good stretch and warmup for a strength exercise, since it uses the same basic motion without weights. You need a chair high enough to slightly elevate your heels off the floor. To give a regular chair extra height, use cushions.

A Sit in a chair, back straight, both feet flat on the floor and knees bent 90 degrees.

B Slowly straighten your right knee as far as you comfortably can, so that toes point towards the ceiling. Hold. Repeat with the other leg.

Keep your spine pressed against the back of the chair so that you don't arch your back. This movement will stretch the quadriceps muscles at the front of your thighs as well as your hamstrings.

KNEES TO CHEST

A classic for easing low back discomfort, this stretch can be done lying on a bed. It also helps your hips and knees.

A Lie on your back with legs relaxed and straight, toes pointing towards the ceiling.

B Put your hands on the back of your thighs under your knees and smoothly pull both knees as far towards your shoulders as is comfortable, stretching the extensor muscles at the back of the hips in the buttocks area. Hold.

A

MEDICINE FOR THE BACK AND SPINE

■ ■ ■ EASING MORNING STIFFNESS

For many people with arthritis, mornings are the toughest time. Even after a restful night, the morning hours bring stiffness and pain.

To deal with morning stiffness, try this sequence of exercises while you're getting out of bed: the lying total body stretch [page 63], knees to chest [page 61],; neck turn [page 64] (do this while lying down), and the seated chest stretch [page 64].

LOW BACK KNEES TO CHEST

Though similar to the knees-to-chest exercise on the previous page, this exercise keeps one foot flat on the floor, which bypasses the hip flexor muscles and provides a better stretch for the lower back.

A Lie on your back with your right leg fully extended and your left knee bent with the foot flat on the floor. Bring your right knee up to the level of your waist, keeping your left foot planted.

B Put your hands in the crook of your leg behind your right thigh and gently pull your knee towards your right shoulder. Stop when you feel a slight stretch. Hold and gently return to the starting position. Repeat on the other side.

To get the most from this stretch, keep both shoulders on the floor.

PELVIC TWIST

A Lie on your back with your knees bent, feet flat on the floor and arms extended straight out to your sides.
B Gently lower both knees to your right side until you feel a slight stretch in your left lower back and hip area. Hold and return to the starting position. Repeat on the other side.

STRETCHES

CAT STRETCH

This is a classic back stretch, often used in yoga routines.
A Get on your hands and knees. Tuck your chin towards your chest and tighten your stomach muscles to arch your back. Hold.
B Relax, raising your head so you're looking straight ahead while pushing your stomach toward the floor. Hold.

LYING TOTAL BODY STRETCH

By putting your hands over your head, this stretch (which also helps with abdominals) lengthens chest muscles in a different direction than the other stretches.
A Lie on your back on a bed or a mat with your legs extended and feet together or comfortably apart at about hip width.
B Extend your arms straight over your head and stretch your legs and toes, making your entire body as long as comfortably possible. Hold.

63

STRETCHES

If you're especially stiff in this area, have a partner assist by gently pulling your elbows back from behind the chair. When you feel a slight stretch in your chest, tell your partner to stop pulling. Or do the stretch lying on your back with knees bent and both feet flat on the floor.

SEATED CHEST STRETCH

This stretch for the upper chest and front shoulders can be done from either a standing or sitting position.
A Place your hands at the back of your head with fingers interlocked.
B Gently move your elbows backwards or behind you until you feel a stretch at the front of your shoulders and the top of your chest.

NECK SIDE BEND

A Sit up straight in a chair with your eyes looking directly ahead.
B Slowly lower your right ear towards your right shoulder, stopping when you feel a slight stretch in the muscles on the left side of your neck. Hold. Return to the starting position and repeat on the other side.

The weight of your head is sufficient to produce a good stretch for functional (but not excessive) range of motion—so there's no need to pull the side of your head down with your hand.

NECK TURN

You can do this exercise anytime, anywhere, while sitting or standing. But if your neck is sensitive or in pain, do this exercise lying down to lessen the pressure.
A Sit or stand up straight with your eyes looking directly ahead.
B Slowly and smoothly move your head to the right side until you feel a slight stretch in the muscles on the opposite side of your neck. Relax and hold. Slowly return to the starting position and repeat on the other side.

WRIST AND HAND STRETCHES

WRIST CURL

This strengthening exercise works the wrist along with the entire forearm.

A Sit in a chair with your forearms resting on your thighs and your hands extended off your knees with your palms facing downwards. Relax your hands, allowing your fingers to drop toward the floor. This is your starting position.

B Slowly bend your wrists to bring your fingers up so they point towards the ceiling as far as is comfortably possible.

C Slowly lower your fingers back to the starting position for one repetition.

Also perform this exercise in reverse, with your palms facing up.

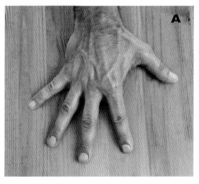

FINGER STRETCH

This is move is designed to extend your fingers' range of motion.

A Place one hand on a tabletop or your thigh with your palm facing down.

B Spread your fingers apart as far as you can and hold. Repeat with the other hand.

GENTLE FIST

A Place your right hand in a relaxed position, palm up, on a tabletop or your thigh.

B Roll your fingers in towards your palm so that you make a loose fist. Try to bring your fingers as close together as is comfortable without squeezing. Hold.

C Release and roll your fingers out to the starting position and repeat with the other hand.

THUMB TOUCH

A Place your hand, palm up, on a table with your fingers open and your hand relaxed.

B Smoothly move the tip of your thumb into contact with the tip of your index finger, lightly touching, but not pressing them together. Hold for one second. Relax and return to the starting position.

C In a similar manner, bring your middle finger to your thumb, hold and return.

D Do the same thing for the ring and pinkie fingers and repeat with the other hand.

PROTECT AND HEAL
YOUR BACK

Backaches are second only to headaches as a source of pain. With the spine's complex structure of bones, discs, nerves, ligaments and muscles, it's no wonder. Even so, there's a lot we can do to keep our backs healthy and pain-free. In these pages you'll find out about different types of back pain, which activities cause the most stress, how to minimize symptoms and therapies that can help.

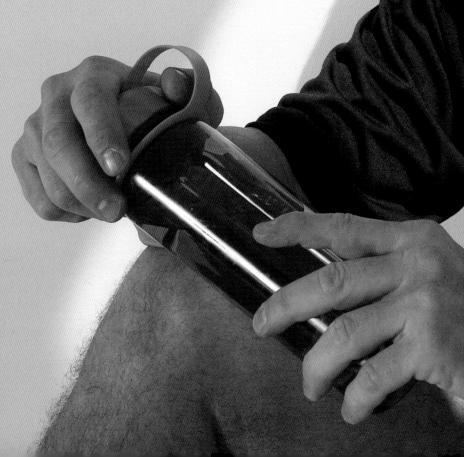

REDUCING THE STRAIN
ON YOUR BACK

Back pain is usually the result of lifestyle, aging or accident. Of these three factors, lifestyle plays a central role in how well you age and in your chances of accidental injury. Good lifestyle habits—correct posture, good lifting techniques and plenty of exercise for a strong, flexible back—will keep your risk of back pain to a minimum.

The single most important way to look after your back is to respect the natural curves of your spine. Any habitual pose that changes your back's regular curves—from an awkward sleeping position to poor driving posture—can increase the pressure on your spine.

Good posture means holding your body in its correct alignment. While it is important not to slouch, you should also be careful not to overcompensate. Holding your back too straight puts your spine under almost as much pressure as when it is too arched. Poor posture can quickly become a habit; over time, the muscles and ligaments in your back begin to lengthen or shorten, making your posture feel natural.

SLEEPING SOUNDLY

Although the weight of your upper body on your spine is considerably reduced when you're lying down, it is easy to adopt an awkward position without realizing it when you're falling asleep. In particular, try to avoid lying on your stomach with your neck twisted to one side and try not to stay in one position for too long.

Most people spend six to eight hours a day in bed, so it is well worthwhile making sure that your mattress and pillow give you the best possible support: **BIGGER IS BETTER.** A spacious bed may stop you adopting a cramped position.

■ ■ ■ SIX WAYS TO A STRONG BACK

The key to maintaining a healthy back is to be aware not only of your posture, but also of the everyday movements that place your spine and back muscles under unnecessary pressure.

1. Assess your posture regularly, both sitting and standing—it's easy to pick up bad habits without noticing. Take a good look at yourself whenever you pass a mirror.

2. Change your position regularly. If you have to stay in one position for an extended period of time—in a car or at a desk, for example—try to take a break every 20 minutes or so to move around and stretch.

3. Avoid wearing high heels for long periods. High heels accentuate the normal curve of your back and tip your pelvis, which can contribute to knee and back problems.

4. Use both shoulders when you are wearing a backpack. If you carry a heavy bag, briefcase or a suitcase, alternate the arm that you use to carry it.

5. Watch your wallet when you are sitting down. A bulging wallet in your back pocket can place pressure on the sciatic nerve.

6. Don't snooze in front of the TV; an armchair or sofa won't take pressure off your lower spine. Snoozing prevents you from shifting when your back starts to feel uncomfortable.

TRY OUT A RANGE OF BEDS. Lie on a bed for a few minutes and turn over a few times before making a decision. Especially if you're going to invest in a high-quality bed, you want one that guarantees comfort.
CHOOSE A GOOD MATTRESS. Look for a moderately firm mattress: not too hard, not too soft. Choose one that yields enough to adapt to your contours, but is not so soft that you sink into it; your spine should maintain its natural curves. Remember to flip and rotate your mattress regularly, once every two to three months.
CHOOSE A GOOD PILLOW. Your pillow should support your neck in alignment with the rest of your spine. An overstuffed pillow or too many pillows may push your head too far forward; a pillow that's too limp or flimsy may tip your head back.

GOOD POSTURE AT YOUR DESK

Poor sitting posture is a major cause of lower back problems. Sitting places much greater pressure on your spine than standing or walking. Even when you sit upright, the weight of your upper body exerts around 50 percent more pressure on your lower spine than when standing. If you sit slouched over, the pressure on your spine rises to 150 percent greater than when standing.

Good posture is particularly important if you have to spend long periods at a desk or computer. Try to get up and walk around every 20 minutes. Do neck stretches, shoulder rolls, shrugs, arms stretches, neck rolls and back stretches to loosen up your spine [see pages 82-83]. Assume other sitting positions for short periods, but try to spend most of your time in the optimal position.

GOOD POSTURE IN YOUR CAR

One UK study showed that people who drive more than 40,000 km a year take an average of 22 days a year off work with a bad back. Don't do the "banana": bring your seat forward enough so that you're not stretching to reach for the pedals and your back is fairly straight; keep your arms comfortably bent.

■ ■ ■ HOW TO SIT AT YOUR DESK

Eyes Make sure that the screen is positioned so that your eyes are level with the top of the screen.

Body Do not slouch. Keep your pelvis tucked in and make sure that your lower back is fully supported by your chair. Position the monitor and keyboard so that you don't need to twist your hips or neck.

Arms and wrists Have your work surface just lower than your bent elbows; your wrists should be level with your hands while typing. Use a wrist pad if necessary.

Legs and feet Set the seat height so that your legs are bent at right angles and your feet are flat on the floor or on a foot rest. Your legs should fit underneath the work surface so that you don't have to lean forward.

COMMON
BACK PROBLEMS

According to a 2003 study, nearly two-thirds of Canadians suffer from some form of back pain. Doctors have a good understanding of the mechanisms that cause back problems, but it is often difficult to identify the exact source of the pain.

Many episodes of back pain are trivial, if unpleasant, and tend to resolve without treatment or the need for further investigation. Nonetheless, back pain may at times be a sign of something more serious. The sooner you figure out the problem, the easier it will be to beat it; so if you're experiencing back pain, it is important to be aware of how different conditions can affect your back.

■ ■ ■ CHIROPRACTOR OR OSTEOPATH?

Chiropractors and osteopaths physically manipulate joints and tissues to relieve a wide range of musculoskeletal conditions. The two therapies take very similar approaches, although chiropractors tend to focus more closely on the spine. Osteopathy and chiropractic are complementary therapies; many conventional medical professionals recognize them as an effective way to treat many back problems. Therapists should not treat certain conditions, such as severe osteoporosis. The practice of osteopathy in Canada is somewhat restricted. Because of this, finding a practioner can be more difficult.

A session with a chiropractor or osteopath normally lasts around 20–30 minutes. The number of sessions that you will need varies considerably depending on your problem, but two to 10 sessions is normal, initially every week or so. Chiropractic services are partially covered by some provincial medicare plans, and some private insurance plans cover both types of therapy. If you feel you could benefit from visiting a chiropractor or osteopath, your doctor may be willing to refer you to a suitable practitioner. For more information contact the Canadian Chiropractic Association (www.ccachiro.org) or the Canadian Osteopathic Association (www.osteopathic.ca).

Initial consultation At your first consultation the osteopath or chiropractor will examine you to diagnose any problems and may use X-rays or other tests. An osteopath may also use touch (palpation) to identify points of weakness and problem areas and will check overall postural balance. The osteopath may ask you to remove some clothes and perform a series of movements.

Manipulation Osteopaths and chiropractors use many of the same techniques. A chiropractor will tend to focus on your back and place more emphasis on freeing up and mobilizing the spinal column. An osteopath will tend to manipulate limbs, joints and soft tissues all over your body. Neither treatment should be painful, although some people experience minor side effects such as muscle soreness.

Aftercare After manipulating or massaging your back, the osteopath or chiropractor may show you how to achieve better posture and give you advice on changing any aspects of your life that are making your problem worse. They may also teach you some simple exercises that you can do at home to relieve pain and stop problems from recurring.

SPRAINS AND STRAINS

The most frequent cause of back pain is a small injury to the soft tissues in your back, such as a muscle or tendon strain or a ligament sprain. Most strains and sprains occur during day-to-day activities such as lifting or twisting; any excessive physical demand on your back can over-stretch your tissues. Even snoozing in an armchair can place your muscles and ligaments under uneven pressure and may result in minor damage. Your lower back, in particular, is susceptible to muscular strains because it forms the pivot around which you move your upper body.

Most strains and sprains improve within a few weeks, but you may find that heat treatments, such as heat packs and baths, help to relieve discomfort.

JOINT PROBLEMS

The complexity of your spine makes it particularly vulnerable to structural problems. Each of the 26 bones that make up your spine (the remainder of your vertebrae are fused) is connected to its neighbour by three separate joints. This means that there are multiple points of wear and friction within your back.

The following conditions are problems related to joints:

SPINAL ARTHRITIS (ANKYLOSING SPONDYLITIS)

Symptoms

- Chronic back pain, especially in the lower back
- Morning back stiffness
- As disease progresses, increasing spinal rigidity and a stooped posture

What You Can Do

To ease morning stiffness and pain, take a hot shower and then do gentle back stretches.

To keep stooped posture at bay, do not slouch, and strive to maintain good posture at all times. When sitting, make sure that your chair provides good back support. In a car, adjust the headrest to provide maximum support. Tucking a pillow behind the small of your back may help relieve lower-back pain. Try to sleep flat on your back on a firm mattress and without a pillow, or sleep on your stomach with a thin pillow. The point is to sleep stretched out rather than curled into a fetal position.

HERNIATED DISC

Common Symptoms

- Back pain, usually in the lower back (lumbar)—less commonly in the neck (cervical) part of the spine—that can range from a dull ache to severe, burning or shooting pains
- Back pain that is worsened by movement, especially bending, lifting, straining, coughing, or sneezing

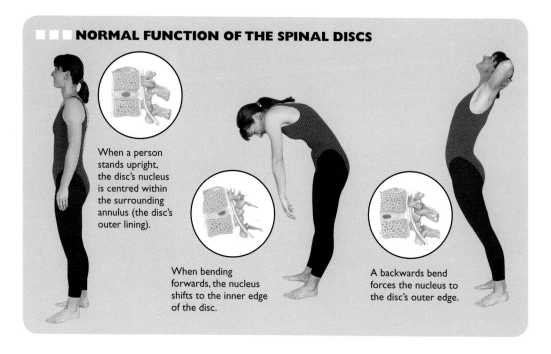

NORMAL FUNCTION OF THE SPINAL DISCS

When a person stands upright, the disc's nucleus is centred within the surrounding annulus (the disc's outer lining).

When bending forwards, the nucleus shifts to the inner edge of the disc.

A backwards bend forces the nucleus to the disc's outer edge.

- Numbness or tingling sensations that may run from the back to the buttocks and down a leg, or from the shoulder and down an arm
- Leg weakness as well as difficulty lifting a foot when walking
- Loss of nerve reflexes, such as a knee or ankle jerk

What You Can Do

A heating pad often provides relief for mild back or neck pain. Soak in a hot tub or warm whirlpool bath, if available. Sleep on a firm but not hard mattress. Properly placed pillows can ease stress on the back: a pillow under the knees for those who sleep on their backs, or one under the waist and another under the shoulder for side sleepers. Until the pain subsides, be sure to avoid lifting heavy objects, straining and bending.

Gentle stretching exercises often help. However, exercises should not be undertaken without consulting a doctor. In severe cases, a few days of bed rest may be necessary. Most experts recommend that this be limited to two or three days; longer periods of total bed rest can make matters worse by causing muscle weakness.

Maintaining physical fitness and good posture is the mainstay of prevention. When sitting—the most stressful position for the lower back—make sure the chair or car seat provides good back support. Get up frequently to stretch the back and relieve muscle tension.

LOW-BACK PAIN

Low-back pain is a very common condition: eight out of 10 Canadians will experience an episode of back pain at some point. The problem is likely to become chronic with increasing age; about half of all people over age 60 have chronic back problems.

Common Symptoms

- Acute or chronic pain in the lower back
- Diffuse pain or pain associated with specific tender points

> 66 *I work in a long-term care facility. My job is physically demanding. I try not to take pain medication because I feel it is not healthy for my other organs. The last day-shift I worked, the pain was unbearable (and believe me —I went through child-bearing!) About 10 minutes after applying Lakota to my shoulder blads and lower back, the pain was quite a bit better. I was comfortable enough to get a good night's sleep. Thanks, Lakota!* 99

Deb Haremink, Kindersley, SK

What You Can Do

If the pain is very severe, try a day or two of bed rest. Lie on your back or side on a firm surface, with your knees bent and supported by a pillow, even if you are more comfortable on your stomach. Use a heating pad, ice pack or alternating applications of warmth and cold for extra relief.

When the pain subsides, start exercises to strengthen your back. If the exercises hurt, however, stop immediately; pain is a warning that something is wrong.

How to Treat It

If symptoms persist after two weeks of self-treatment, or if they are recurring, see a doctor. Don't delay if the pain is accompanied by other symptoms, such as numbness in your legs or loss of bowel or bladder control.

Your doctor will examine your back, test your nerve reflexes and probably order X-rays. You may also have imaging studies such as CT scans or an MRI, bone density tests, and nerve and muscle evaluations.

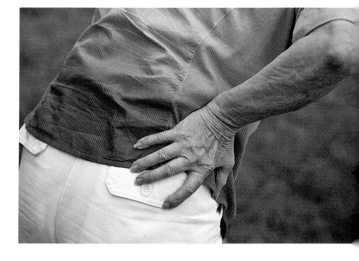

OSTEOPOROSIS

Osteoporosis is a disease in which bones lose calcium and other minerals that give them their density and strength. We build bone mass until about age 30; after that, bones slowly lose minerals. It is estimated that more than 2 million Canadians suffer from osteoporosis. The condition is most common among post-menopausal women. Men are also vulnerable to osteoporosis, although they develop it at least 10 years after women do. Other risk factors include: smoking, a sedentary lifestyle, excessive alcohol consumption, long-term use of steroid medications, high blood pressure and a diet that lacks adequate calcium and vitamin D.

❝ I suffer from chronic pain caused by a neck injury. Other than painkillers, which really don't help that much, I have constant pain in the back of my head, in the neck area. I find that Lakota is the only topical product that gives me relief. I usually apply it twice a day and whenever the pain is very bad. My wife also uses Lakota for her chronic back pain. I have recommended Lakota to many of my friends. ❞

Ted Mate, Edmonton, AB

Common Symptoms

- Mild back pain that worsens as vertebrae become increasingly compressed
- Height loss and development of a dowager's hump
- Painful bone fractures, particularly of the wrist and hip
- Sudden, severe back pain with little or no provocation

What You Can Do

A heating pad can help ease the mild back pain of osteoporosis. Daily exercise is also important, not only to maintain bone density but also to reduce pain. Bone-building and maintenance require a certain amount of stress in the form of weight-bearing exercise—walking for at least 30 minutes a day is ideal. Jogging, dancing, aerobics, stair-climbing, and racquet sports also provide weight-bearing exercise.

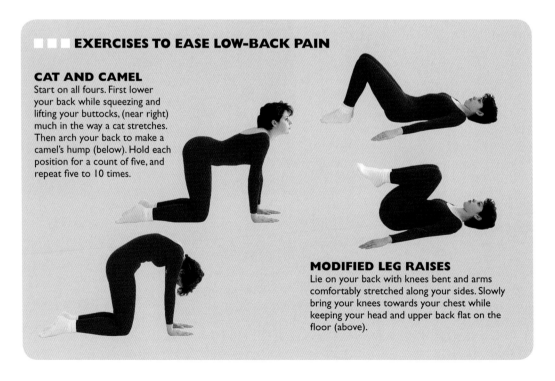

■■■ EXERCISES TO EASE LOW-BACK PAIN

CAT AND CAMEL
Start on all fours. First lower your back while squeezing and lifting your buttocks, (near right) much in the way a cat stretches. Then arch your back to make a camel's hump (below). Hold each position for a count of five, and repeat five to 10 times.

MODIFIED LEG RAISES
Lie on your back with knees bent and arms comfortably stretched along your sides. Slowly bring your knees towards your chest while keeping your head and upper back flat on the floor (above).

Remember, too, that aerobic exercise leads to increased endorphins: natural painkillers and mood enhancers. Strength training—using free weights, rubber tubing, or resistance machines—builds muscles, strengthens bones and improves balance, an important factor in preventing falls.

Make sure that your diet provides adequate calcium, vitamins and minerals.

NEURAL PROBLEMS

Because your nerves travel through your spine on their way to your brain, pain that originates in another part of your body can sometimes feel as though it comes from your back. This is known as referred pain. Conditions that can produce referred back pain include ulcers, kidney disease, ovarian cysts and pancreatitis.

This can also work the other way. Damage to the nerves in or around your spine may cause pain that seems to radiate out to other areas. Conditions that cause or result from nerve damage include the following:

SPINAL STENOSIS

Common Symptoms

- Chronic dull backache
- Occasional numbness, burning or sharp pain in the back, buttocks, or legs
- Sensation of leg heaviness or weakness when walking

What You Can Do

Try to lose excess weight and, if you have a tendency to slouch, make an effort to improve your posture. A heating pad or alternating hot and cold packs, gentle stretching and moderate, low-impact exercise—walking, swimming, cycling—may help, but check with a doctor or physiotherapist before embarking on an exercise program if you suffer from chronic back pain.

> 66 My boyfriend often gets extremely bad back pain from an injury he obtained at work. Some days he isn't even able to get up. One day he fell in the shower because his back seized up. We ran out to the store to get him something to relieve his pain, since his pain medication only does so much for him. We were referred to Lakota, and wow, what a difference! He is like a new man! His back feels so much better, and we are able to enjoy the small things in life again, like taking our children to the park and walking along the beach. Thanks Lakota!! You have saved our lives! 99

Cassie Ladouceur, Orillia, ON

SCIATICA
Common Symptoms
- Mild to severe pain in the lower back that may extend down a leg
- Burning or shooting leg pain worsened by coughing, sneezing, or bending
- Muscle weakness in the buttock, thigh, lower leg, or foot
- Numbness and tingling in the lower leg; loss of knee nerve reflexes

What You Can Do
A day or two of bed rest may ease pressure on the nerve and promote healing. A heating pad or soaking in a hot bath can also ease pain and relax muscle spasms, which worsen sciatica. Consult a doctor if the pain persists for more than a week.

STOP

CAUTION
This information can add to your knowledge, but be sure to see a doctor—or more than one —if you're experiencing pain. Self-diagnosis is a risky gamble.

How to Treat It
A doctor will test nerve reflexes in the knee and ankle and order X-rays and perhaps CT scans or an MRI to determine the source and extent of the problem. If the nerve is not seriously compressed, non-surgical treatments will be tried first. Surgery may be necessary if the nerve is compressed or if other therapies fail to relieve the pain.

ABNORMAL SPINAL CURVES/POSTURE DEFECTS
Common Symptoms
Posture defects are a common cause of chronic back pain, especially among older people. Other symptoms include:
- Kyphosis: Rounded shoulders, a hunched back, head thrust forward
- Lordosis: Arched lower back, protruding abdomen and buttocks, possible ruptured spinal disks

How They Develop
Posture defects, especially kyphosis, often develop in childhood or during adolescence; they are also common among older persons who have osteoporosis or

spinal arthritis. Mild posture defects usually do not cause pain and other uncomfortable symptoms. But as the abnormal posture becomes more pronounced, it can cause a chronic backache, ruptured discs, sciatica, and other nerve problems. Extreme kyphosis can compress the rib cage and cause breathing problems.

What You Can Do

A heating pad can help ease back pain. Stretching and exercises to strengthen the abdominal muscles, such as pelvic lifts, straight-leg raises and modified sit-ups, can improve posture and relieve back pain. Sleep on a firm mattress, preferably on your back or side. If you spend a lot of time sitting, make sure that your chair provides good back support. Wear comfortable, low-heeled shoes and avoid high heels, especially if you have lordosis.

How to Treat Them

A doctor will first determine whether the posture defect is caused by spinal arthritis, osteoporosis or another underlying disease; if so, treating it may not only relieve back pain but also correct the problem. A back brace, physical therapy and other non-surgical approaches may be recommended. In very severe cases, surgery may be necessary to realign the spine.

SCOLIOSIS

Scoliosis is an exaggerated sideways curvature of the spine.

Common Symptoms

- Back looks crooked, especially when bending over; frequent backaches
- Uneven shoulders, legs, or hips; rounded shoulder, swayback, and other postural abnormalities; a shoulder blade (scapula) that sticks out
- Sunken chest, possible breathing or heart problems

What You Can Do

Mild scoliosis—defined as a spinal curvature of 10 to 20 degrees—usually does not cause problems. A more pronounced curvature of more than 25 degrees may result in uneven shoulders or hips and a visibly crooked back. Moderate to severe scoliosis can cause posture defects and frequent backaches; if the chest cavity is deformed, serious breathing and heart problems may develop.

PERFECT POSTURE

HEAD AND NECK
The crown of your head, not your forehead, should be the highest point of your body. Keep your head and chin neutral: neither jutting out nor tucked too far in.

UPPER BACK
Lift your chest and keep your shoulders down and back, but not so far that your pose feels forced or unnatural.

UPPER BACK
Pull your stomach and your buttocks muscles tight. Try not to overarch or round your lower back.

LEGS
Keep your knees slightly bent and your toes pointing forwards. If you need to stand for long periods, rest one foot on a step to relieve pressure on your lower back and change feet every five to 15 minutes.

MINIMIZING THE SYMPTOMS OF BACK PROBLEMS

Most episodes of back pain resolve over time, but problems often recur in the long term. This may be because the immediate cause of the pain—a muscle spasm, sprain or strain, for example—is merely a symptom of a wider problem, such as muscle weakness or postural misalignment. For this reason it is important not to ignore recurring back pain.

Rest and Activity

What Studies Show

Back pain isn't a life sentence. Ninety percent of people with lower back pain get better within two months, even if they don't do a thing about it.

Doctors used to recommend bed rest for almost any back problem, and there is no doubt that rest is important. Lying down reduces pressure on your spine and prevents friction between inflamed bones and discs. However, doctors now understand that extended periods of bed rest can actually slow recovery and increase the risk of problems recurring. Complete rest may be recommended during the acute phase (the first day or so after an injury) or during painful flare-ups of chronic conditions. But as a general rule, it is vital to get mobile again as quickly as possible.

Light activity encourages circulation (which aids healing), improves flexibility and maintains strong muscles around your spine. A number of studies have found that people with back pain who return to normal activities quickly feel healthier, take fewer painkillers and are less distressed than those who limit their activities for longer periods of time.

Back Supports

You should never wear back or neck braces for extended periods unless specifically advised to do so by your doctor or specialist. Long-term use of such supports stops you from using your muscles and they will quickly start to atrophy, placing you at much greater risk of further injury.

Sports and Activities

Although exercise is a great way to relieve a painful back, certain activities do have potential risks. Sports that involve constant impact, such as jogging, can aggravate low-back pain and contact sports, such as football, can be dangerous if you have neck problems. Cycling can easily jar your back, particularly when riding over rough terrain, if your seat is set at the wrong angle or if your bike is the wrong size. On the other hand, certain activities bring real benefits. Good sports for bad backs include:

- Swimming and other water-based activities, such as water aerobics, are useful because water counteracts some of the effects of gravity, reducing compression in your lower spine. The backstroke is particularly beneficial, as it opens up the chest and shoulders.

> 66 *Wrangling horses (or just one pony) every day can lead to some very sore, tired muscles. After a long gallop, or a bucking bronco, nothing relieves an ache quite like Lakota and trust me, I've tried. Bad ponies, rambunctious horses all bow down to the superior healing power of Lakota. After a treatment with Lakota, I'm ready to get back on the horse again and ride triumphantly into the range! Lakota was made for cowgirls like me.* 99

Naomi Lindstein, O ttawa, ON

- Walking is low-impact. It helps to strengthen your back and stomach muscles without causing too much strain.
- Exercise balls can help you to target your core muscles. The ball places you in an unstable position, so you automatically engage the muscles in your abdomen, back and pelvic-girdle region—the core muscles that support your lower back and spine.
- Tai chi and yoga are both enjoyable ways to improve mobility, flexibility and muscle tone. The deliberate, flowing movements of tai chi and the controlled stretching required by yoga poses encourage good postural awareness without straining or jarring your back. [For information on yoga breathing, see page 100.]

Physical Therapy

Many of the most common causes of back pain, such as muscle spasm, muscular tension, misaligned vertebrae and some postural problems, respond well to physical manipulation. Common types of physical therapy for problem backs include:

- Massage: improves circulation, aids muscle recovery and reduces tension. If you opt for a professional massage, make sure you choose a fully qualified masseur.
- Physiotherapy: involves a range of physical and manipulative techniques that improve movement, strength and flexibility. Treatment should also address underlying factors that contribute to the physical problems..
- Osteopathy and chiropractic therapy: specialized manipulative therapies that focus on combating structural misalignments in the musculoskeletal system [see page 70 for more information.]

Back Surgery

Surgery remains a treatment of last resort for back problems. It is unlikely to be used unless other treatments have failed and, even then, the majority of back conditions are not suitable for surgery. Conditions that may benefit from surgery include pinched or compressed nerves and vertebral deformities or fractures.

EXERCISE
AND YOUR BACK

Doctors no longer recommend bed rest for back pain; the muscles, ligaments and joints in your back, like any other area of your body, need regular exercise to stay healthy. Without movement, the intervertebral discs start to dry up and shrink, your ligaments begin to lose their elasticity and the muscles around your spine grow weaker. Exercise also helps you to maintain a healthy body weight, which reduces extra strain on your spine.

" Picking up a mug of coffee from the opposite side of a table can produce as much force against your vertebral discs as lifting a 10 kg weight next to your body. "

You need strong back muscles to protect your spine. Weak muscles do not contain enough tension to brace your spine and absorb the stress of movement. It is also important to keep muscles on opposing sides of your body balanced: Having weak abdominals and strong lower back muscles is a common cause of lower back pain.

▚ ▚ ▚ LIFTING OBJECTS SAFELY

You can reduce your risk of injury by making sure that you use the correct technique. Test the weight of the object before you lift it and, if it's not too heavy, follow the guidelines below:

1. Stand with your feet hip-width apart and as close to the object as possible. Place one foot slightly in front of the other. Bend your knees and squat down, keeping a straight back and tight stomach.

3. Be careful not to twist or turn your body until you are standing up straight.

2. Hold the object close to your body as you stand up. Keep your back straight and use your legs and not your back to provide the power.

> 66 *I've struggled with back pain for a very long time. Nothing seemed to work for me. I even bought a very expensive mattress and that did nothing. I kept hearing about Lakota and thought, "What do I have to lose?" Well, I gave Lakota Roll-on a try and to my surprise, after using it every day for two weeks, my back pain was gone. I've been using Lakota for six months now and I have no more back pain. The only time I use it now is if I feel any pain in my back, which is not too often.* 99

Diane Belanger, Greenfield, NB

Physical activity isn't risk-free, but that the benefits far outweigh the dangers. To avoid potential problems, such as strained or torn ligaments, it is vital to warm up thoroughly before exercise. Always exercise within your limits, avoid sudden twisting movements of your trunk and stop immediately if anything hurts. For a program of simple exercises to increase the strength and flexibility in your neck, back and shoulders [see pages 82-87].

LIFTING AND PUSHING

Poor lifting technique is the single most common cause of acute back pain. It can also cause longer-term back problems, because it exacerbates any existing weakness. Manual workers and people whose job involves a lot of lifting are most at risk; hundreds of thousands of nurses injure their backs each year, often as a result of lifting patients. You can reduce your risk of injury by using the correct lifting techniques [see box, opposite page].

Even the best technique won't remove the risk altogether, however, so test the weight of the object before you pick it up: If you find that you're straining you may need to get someone to give you a hand. If you have to lift an object higher than your shoulders, use a stable step stool or ladder to avoid over-reaching.

Pushing and pulling heavy objects can also contribute to back problems, sprains and strains. Given the choice, always push a heavy object rather than pulling it—this puts less pressure on your lower back. Bend your knees and use your legs rather than your back for power, and be alert for sudden changes in resistance.

Everyday Strategies

Incorporate ways to prevent stressed muscles in your everyday life. Avoiding stressed muscles in the first place is even better than treating them later.

✔ Be like a cat and stretch often. Your body wants to stretch and often does so unconsciously. Stretching loosens muscles, helps your blood flow, relieves your bones and joints and refreshes your spirit.

✔ Glory in hot water; it soothes and supports the joints. Heat brings blood to your joints, muscles and skin, flushing you with nutrients. And the calmness of a soak in a tub is an unbeatable way to relax.

✔ A good massage is one of life's greatest pleasures—if you haven't experienced one, don't wait any longer. It's worth the money, and the muscle and joint relief will be substantial.

Exercises for Your Neck

Your cervical spine (the portion of your spine in your neck) supports the weight of your head and protects the nerves that travel from your head to the rest of your body. The average human head weighs 10 to 15 pounds—about the same weight as a small bowling ball—so the vertebrae in your neck are under considerable pressure, even when you're standing still. Your head is also positioned slightly forward over your spine rather than directly above, which means that your neck muscles have to work continuously to balance the weight of your head.

The muscles and joints in your neck control the nodding and rotation movements of your head and let you bend and twist your neck. Holding your head in an awkward position for any length of time can cause muscle tension and compress your neck vertebrae, which may have a secondary effect throughout your back and spine, causing pain and discomfort.

With regular practice, the simple exercises shown here will help you to maintain neck strength and mobility. If you have any existing problems, the exercises may also help you to regain loss of motion in the neck region and control pain.

Perform each movement slowly for five repetitions, resting a short time in between each set of movements.

If any of these exercises makes you feel uncomfortable or dizzy, slow down, reduce the extent of the stretch or skip the stretch altogether.

HEAD ROTATION

Rotate your head to one side until you can't turn it any further. Bring your head back to the centre point, rest a moment, then turn your head to the opposite side.

NECK FLEX/EXTENSION

Bend your head forwards until your chin touches your chest and your eyes look straight down at the floor. Bring your head back up, rest a moment, then bend it back until your eyes look directly at the ceiling.

NECK RETRACTION

Draw your head back and bring your chin down slightly. This exercise counteracts the natural tendency to poke your head too far forwards.

SIDE FLEX/EXTENSION

Keep your head facing forwards and move your ear down towards your shoulder until you feel a stretch along the opposite side of your neck. Bring your head back to the centre, rest a moment, then move your head over to the opposite side.

Exercises for Your Upper Back and Shoulders

Your thoracic spine, in your upper back, does not have such a wide range of motion as your neck or lower back, so injuries are relatively rare. However, irritation or excess tension in your back and shoulder muscles can be very painful. In particular, poor posture and hunched shoulders—common among people who sit at a desk all day—can tighten your chest muscles and overstretch the muscles in your upper back. This may compress the vertebrae in your spine and lead to areas of painful, knotted muscles and tension headaches.

The exercises below are intended to strengthen the muscles around your upper back and shoulders, open your chest and reduce tension in the muscles and ligaments. Try each movement slowly for five repetitions, resting a short time in between each set of movements.

SHOULDER BRACE

Stand with your arms relaxed by your sides. Bring your shoulders as far forward as possible and then bring them right back, pulling your shoulder blades together.

THORACIC STRETCH

1. Stand with your feet about shoulder-width apart and your knees slightly bent. Bend over from the waist and hold onto a stable support, such a chair back. Push your bottom backwards until you can feel a stretch along your upper back. Hold for a count of 15 before standing back up.

2. Sit on a chair with your feet flat on the ground. Gradually roll your upper body forwards from the waist. Reach your hands between your legs to grip the legs of the chair. Slowly curl back up.

SHOULDER SHRUG

Stand with your arms relaxed by your sides. Lift your shoulders to your ears and squeeze your shoulder blades together. Then rotate your shoulders to the back and down. Never rotate your shoulders forwards.

Exercises for Your Lower Back

The lumbar region in your lower back is the most frequently injured area of the spine. This is mainly because your lower back carries the full weight of your torso and allows for a much greater range of movement than your upper back. The majority of episodes of low-back pain (lumbago) are caused by muscle strain; back muscles—like other muscles—need exercise to maintain strength and tone.

Exercises to prevent and treat low-back pain usually focus on strengthening the spine flexors (erector spinae and gluteal muscles), spine extensors (abdominals) and the muscles along the sides of your torso (oblique abdominals). Another important group of muscles are your hamstrings, the large muscles in the back of your thighs. Tight hamstrings limit the motion in your pelvis, which can cause low-back pain.

With regular practice, the exercises shown here will help you to maintain the strength and flexibility of the muscles in your lower back. Do not strain or force the movements, and stop if you feel any discomfort. Try each movement slowly for five repetitions, resting a short time in between each set of movements.

FORWARD BEND
Stand with your feet hip-width apart. Without bouncing, slowly reach one hand down towards the opposite foot. Let your other arm swing up behind your body. Return to a standing position. Don't worry if you can't reach your toes—your flexibility should improve with practice.

KNEE ROLL
Lie on your back with your knees bent and your feet flat on the ground. Keep your knees together. Roll your knees slowly from side to side.

PELVIC TILT

Lie on your back with your knees bent and hip-width apart and your feet flat on the ground. Press your lower back down to the floor, then arch your lower back up off the floor. Let your tail bone tip down to the mat; do not lift your buttocks.

ABDOMINAL CURL

Lie on your back with your knees bent and your feet flat on the floor. Cross your hands over your chest and pull in your stomach muscles. Slowly curl your shoulders and upper back up off the floor. Try to keep your lower back in contact with the floor.

BACK EXTENDER

Lie on your stomach with your hands laced underneath your forehead. Use your lower back muscles to slowly lift your head and shoulders about 20 cm off the floor. Be careful not to strain your neck.

Exercises for Your Upper Back and Shoulders.

Your thoracic spine, in your upper back, does not have such a wide range of motion as your neck or lower back, so injuries are relatively rare. However, irritation or excess tension in your upper back and shoulder muscles can be very painful. In particular, poor posture and hunched shoulders—common among people who sit at a desk all day—can tighten your chest muscles and overstretch the muscles in your upper back. This may compress the vertebrae in your spine and lead to areas of painful, knotted muscles and tension headaches.

There are various exercises that may help with upper back and shoulder pain. The shoulder shrug: lift your shoulders to your ears and squeeze your shoulder blades together; then rotate your shoulders to the back and down.

Or try this Pilates-inspired back and neck extender exercise.

■ ■ ■ WHY PILATES

You've probably been hearing about Pilates, a system of slow, controlled exercises intended to strengthen your body's core stabilizing muscles while improving their natural flexibility. The emphasis of Pilates remains squarely on good posture and body awareness—which makes it perfect for musculoskeletal fitness. The benefits are many— hence its current popularity;

✔ Improves flexibility
✔ Improves body awareness
✔ Aids posture
✔ Tones muscles, particularly the core stabilizing muscles
✔ Increases range of motion
✔ Low impact

66 *As a graphic designer, I spend WAY too much time at the computer. I started having awful back pain, and pain meds would barely take the edge off. A friend of mine recommended Lakota. I was skeptical, but I had nothing to lose. I picked up some Lakota, and WOW! Within 20 minutes of having taken it I felt like a new person! I actually went and sat at my home computer...I was shocked that I could sit and not be in pain. Lakota has been my lifesaver!* 99

Diane Dunbrack, Bowmanville, ON

This exercise lengthens the muscles that run along the length of your spine, opening up your back. It also relieves tension in your neck. Controlled breathing helps you to focus and relax.

BACK AND NECK EXTENDER

1. Lie on your back and gently cradle your knees in your hands. Hold your knees slightly apart and in line with your hips and press your lower back flat against the floor. Pull your stomach in towards your spine and keep your abdominals tight.

2. Inhale. Then, as you exhale, gently draw your knees in towards your chest. Make sure your arms are not straining and your elbows are open and relaxed. Keep your spine flat against the floor. You should feel your chest and back begin to open out.

3. Inhale. As you exhale, slowly draw your right leg in towards your chest a little further. Inhale and release your leg, allowing it to return to the starting position. As you exhale again, slowly draw your left leg further in towards your chest. Repeat this sequence, coordinating it with your breathing, for a total of 10 times.

COMPLEMENTARY THERAPIES FOR YOUR BACK

Around a third of people in Canada use some form of complementary (or alternative) therapy and many treatments are now recognized by the medical establishment as useful additions to orthodox medicine. Approaches and training vary considerably: Some therapies, such as osteopathy, are very widely accepted; other therapies are less well regulated.

Because complementary therapies often take a holistic approach, addressing problems on a mental, emotional and physical level, they may be useful for persistent musculoskeletal problems, such as back pain. Here are some of the potentially useful therapies available:

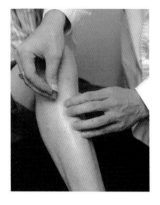

Acupuncture

This traditional Chinese therapy uses fine needles inserted into specific "acupoints" around the body in order to promote the flow of energy or "qi." Proponents believe that acupuncture can treat a range of conditions, including back pain, and a number of studies suggest that it does have genuine pain-relieving properties; brain scans on patients show that the treatment activates regions of the brain known to be involved in pain modulation.

This effect is relatively short-lived, lasting for hours or days after a session. Nevertheless, this may provide a window in which to introduce other treatments, such as physiotherapy. Acupuncture may also stimulate the nervous system and improve circulation. The therapy is now available in many clinics. Your doctor may be able to put you in touch with a qualified practitioner in your area.

Shiatsu

A Japanese massage therapy intended to stimulate energy flow through the body. The word shiatsu means "finger pressure" although practitioners also use palms, thumbs, feet and sometimes knees to apply rhythmic pressure to points around the body that correspond to the "acupoints" used in acupuncture.

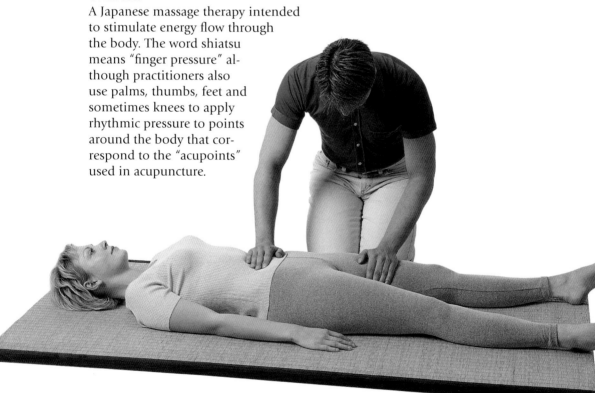

> 66 *All Lakota's products are part of my everyday life. My wife was tired of my complaints. Ever since I started teaching, I had been complaining of a sore back from long hours standing during the day and hunched over marking at my desk at night. I tried everything, but my back was sore on a daily basis. Then my wife suggested Lakota. I decided to give it a try. I have been using Lakota ever since, and I no longer have a sore back when I go to bed. I don't know who has been more thankful, me or my wife!* 99

Derrick Eaves, ON

The therapy also incorporates assisted-stretching techniques. Treatment can be fairly physical but you should feel relaxed or invigorated afterwards.

Shiatsu is deeply rooted in the language and philosophy of traditional Chinese medicine (TCM), which makes it difficult to evaluate all of the claims made for this therapy scientifically. Studies do suggest shiatsu has some genuine relaxing and pain-relieving effects and it may be a useful way to relieve muscle tension in problem backs and necks.

Reflexology

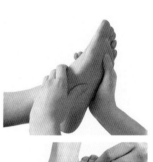

An ancient system of foot massage based on the principle that there are reflex points in your hands and feet that correspond to particular body systems and organs. Reflexologists believe that pressure on these points can reduce tension, improve circulation and remove energy blockages along the nerve pathways to particular areas of the body, such as the spine or sciatic nerve.

Many people find this type of foot massage relaxing, and this may help to relieve muscle tension and therefore pain in your back. There is little research to support the more theoretical claims on which reflexology is based, and most doctors remain largely sceptical about the therapy's wider benefits.

Chiropractic Therapy and Osteopathy

These manipulative therapies have a common origin in the traditions of bonesetting and continue to share many techniques and approaches today. Osteopathy uses manipulation, massage and stretching to improve the alignment and function of bones, joints and muscles throughout the body. Chiropractic therapy tends to focus more closely on the spine and is based on the principle that vertebral misalignments underpin most musculoskeletal disorders.

Most doctors consider the therapies to be a potentially valuable way to treat many musculoskeletal disorders.

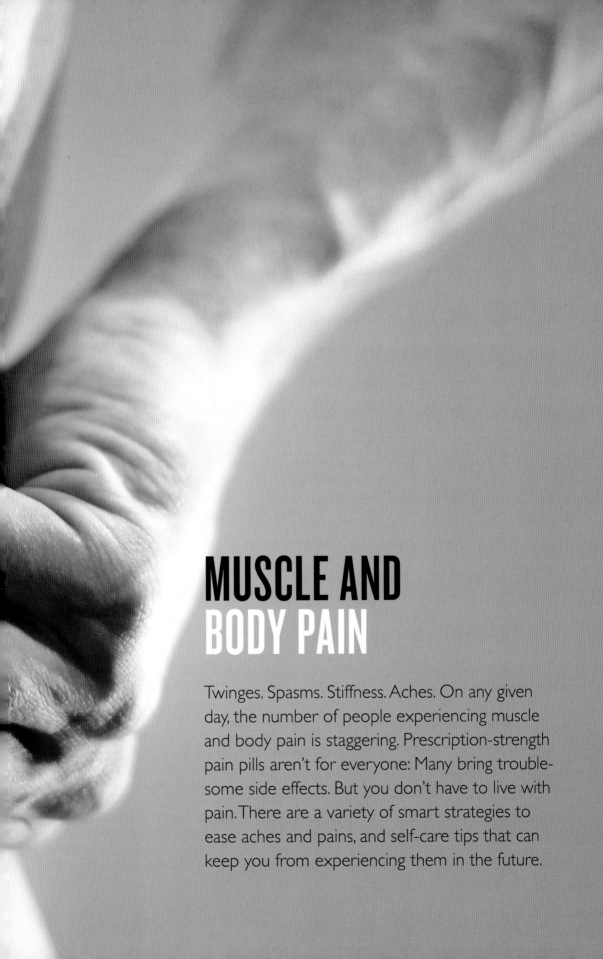

MUSCLE AND
BODY PAIN

Twinges. Spasms. Stiffness. Aches. On any given day, the number of people experiencing muscle and body pain is staggering. Prescription-strength pain pills aren't for everyone: Many bring troublesome side effects. But you don't have to live with pain. There are a variety of smart strategies to ease aches and pains, and self-care tips that can keep you from experiencing them in the future.

MANAGE YOUR
MUSCLE PAIN

Unlike other diseases, pain is invisible to everyone but the person who suffers. The first step is understanding your pain and what's causing it. From there, you can take steps to ease it, and more importantly, prevent it from coming back. This chapter is your guide to relieving, treating and, in some cases, preventing muscle pain—so you can live, work and play without constant discomfort.

TYPES OF MUSCLE AND BODY PAIN

MYALGIA AND MUSCLE CRAMPS
Symptoms

MYALGIA: Persistent muscle achiness that can be localized or widespread
MUSCLE CRAMPS: Sharp, twisting pain accompanied by hardness and temporary loss of function in affected muscle

Who Is at Risk

Almost everyone suffers muscle pain, or myalgia, from time to time. The many causes can include overuse, injuries, tension, flu and numerous other illnesses, infection and certain medications. Muscle cramps are also very common, and may be caused by dehydration, restless leg syndrome, nutritional deficiencies, overuse or extended rest and diseases such as multiple sclerosis.

How it Develops

Simple muscle aches are often brought on by overuse, especially engaging in strenuous or prolonged exercise after a period of inactivity. The achiness indicates some degree of muscle damage, such as small tears, bleeding and inflammation in the muscle fibres. Generalized muscle aches are also a symptom of many diseases, often infectious disorders such as flu, Lyme disease, malaria or polio. Excessive stress that results in constant muscle tension can also cause pain. Most muscle aches disappear, however, as healing takes place. Muscle cramps come on suddenly and usually last for only a few seconds. But they can seem to last much longer because they are acutely painful and the affected muscle cannot be used until the contraction stops. Frequent muscle cramps may be due to an electrolyte imbalance, such as a deficiency of potassium or excessive calcium circulating in the blood; dehydration can also cause cramps.

What You Can Do

Soaking in a hot tub or applying cold or hot compresses, or alternating heat and cold, may help. Gently massaging the aching muscles may also bring relief; don't, however, massage muscles or joints that are inflamed. This increases blood flow to the area and can worsen inflammation.

Slowly stretching and gently massaging a cramped muscle prompts it to relax and immediately relieves the sharp pain. A cold compress or heating pad can prevent it from cramping again. Also drink plenty of water, especially if the cramp occurs after exercising. Water helps muscles relax and contract; it can help prevent future cramping and may provide some measure of relief.

Muscle aches caused by overuse can be prevented by stretching and doing warm-up exercises before working out, and by cooling down and stretching again after each session. When embarking on an exercise program, begin slowly and gradually increase your endurance. These same measures can help prevent muscle cramps.

Don't worry about a doctor's visit: Simple muscle aches and cramps usually do not require medical treatment.

INFLAMMATORY MYOPATHIES
Symptoms

Muscle and joint pain, increasing muscle weakness, fatigue, low-grade fever, difficulty swallowing and breathing.

Who Is at Risk

Researchers think they are autoimmune disorders in which the immune system attacks body tissue—in this instance, the muscles and perhaps the skin. These disorders are most common among women aged 40 to 60.

■ ■ ■ Everyday Strategies

Exercise Exercise of any type builds muscle strength, but be sure to warm up and cool down well for long-lasting benefit.

Keep your muscles balanced Every movement you make has an opposite: push and pull, raise and lower, twist left and twist right. Exercising opposing muscles equally is the key to good posture, a strong physique and lasting mobility.

Think RICE This useful acronym stands for rest, ice, compression and elevation—these four steps provide essential and effective first-aid treatment for minor soft tissue injuries, such as ligament sprains, bruises and impact injuries and muscle tears.

Avoid repetitive movements Even very minor stresses and strains on your muscles can cause problems if performed repeatedly. If you need to perform repetitive actions, such as moving a computer mouse, try to vary your movements and take plenty of breaks.

Warm up and cool down Warm muscles are less vulnerable to injuries such as strains. It is also important to cool down and stretch following exercise—stretching helps to prevent sore, tight muscles.

Have a long soak Warm water helps to ease your aches and pains, enabling your muscles to relax and repair themselves.

Watch how you lift Try to bend your knees and not your back. Bending too far too fast, rising awkwardly or twisting badly can all put tremendous strain on your muscles.

Keep moving Fidgeting and adjusting your position while at work or play helps your muscles to avoid cramping, can relieve the symptoms of repetitive stress injury and burns calories.

Relax Stress and fatigue can lead to muscle tension and cramps and heighten your chance of tears and sprains. Take some time out to slow down and unwind—a gentle massage will relax muscles, remove painful trigger points and stimulate circulation to speed up healing of minor strains and sprains.

66 *After being a driller/blaster for over 20 years, my muscles have taken a beating. When my shoulder finally gave out while carrying a 90-pound hand drill I knew that my days as a driller were slowly coming to an end. While recuperating, I learned about Lakota from my mother-in-law and gave it a try. The Lakota Roll-on pain relievers are a welcome relief and work well for all my body's muscles. It gives me the strength to carry on.* 99

Brad Hay, BC

How it Develops

Inflammatory myopathies usually develop gradually and cause symmetrical (affecting both sides of the body) muscle weakness and pain. In one type—known as dermatomyositis—the pain is preceded by a patch of red or purplish rash on the cheeks, eyelids, nose, chest or back, as well as around the joints.

Hardened nodules, caused by calcium deposits, can also form under the skin. The muscles of the shoulders, neck, upper arms and hips are most often affected. At first, patients may notice increasing difficulty reaching overhead; as the disease progresses, walking or climbing stairs may become more difficult. Swallowing may also be affected, increasing the danger of choking. Thus, patients often need to switch to a liquid diet or one of puréed foods.

What You Can Do

Hot baths and alternating hot and cold packs can ease mild pain. It's important to maintain as much muscle strength and joint flexibility as possible. Range-of-motion exercises should be done daily; regular aerobic exercise and mild weight-training are also important. However, check with a doctor before embarking on an exercise program to make sure your chosen activities will not cause further harm.

There are no known means of preventing inflammatory myopathies. They often demand intensive medical treatment to control pain and prevent disability.

Did you know?

When doctors were asked which activities would be most likely to add healthy years to a person's life, these six responses came out on top:

1. Exercise more
2. Quit smoking
3. Eat more fruits and vegetables
4. Eat less junk food and fatty food
5. Worry less and have more fun
6. Sleep more

POLYMYALGIA RHEUMATICA

Symptoms

Persistent body aches and painful stiffness (especially of the shoulders and hips), fatigue, low-grade fever, appetite and weight loss, anemia.

Who Is at Risk

Polymyalgia rheumatica, or PMR, is a disease that combines many of the symptoms of myalgia and inflammatory arthritis. It generally occurs after age 50 and is most common among people over 70. Women are affected twice as often as men. There is a high incidence among people of northern European descent; it also tends to run in families, which suggests a possible inherited susceptibility.

How it Develops

Polymyalgia rheumatica may come on gradually, with various muscle aches, or it may begin suddenly, with flu-like symptoms. The stiffness and muscle pain range from moderate to severe. As its name suggests, the disease attacks multiple areas, most often the neck, shoulders and hips. Symptoms are most severe in the early morning and, as the disease progresses, the pain becomes constant.

What You Can Do

Self-treatment of polymyalgia rheumatica is similar to that of inflammatory myopathies. But both of these conditions also demand careful medical treatment, so if you have symptoms that suggest either, see a doctor promptly.

There are no known means of preventing polymyalgia rheumatica.

■ ■ ■ ALTERNATIVE THERAPIES

Nutraceuticals Calcium, in dosages of 1,000 to 1,500 mg a day, may help prevent muscle cramps. High doses of vitamin B-complex may also help. Up to 1,000 mg of vitamin E a day may reduce the inflammation and pain of PMR and inflammatory myopathies. Warning: Talk to your doctor before treating pain with vitamins.

Physiotherapy Therapists can ease muscle pain with a variety of techniques, including ultrasound, diathermy, hot and cold packs and whirlpool baths. They can also devise an appropriate exercise program to help maintain muscle strength and flexibility in PMR and inflammatory myopathies.

RELIEF YOU CAN COUNT ON

Still skeptical about how big a bite exercise can take out of your pain? Check out the improvements that researchers have found.

CONDITION	POTENTIAL BENEFIT FROM EXERCISE	WHAT IT TAKES
Fibromyalgia	45% reduction in pain	Walking, strength training and stretching three times per week
Osteoarthritis	24% improvement in function 30% improvement in knee pain	Aerobic exercise and strength training three times per week
Migraine	Significant reduction in migraine intensity	30 minutes of aerobic exercise three times per week
Back pain	50% reduction in pain 60% improvement in back-related function	Yoga, one hour and 15 minutes once per week
Plantar fasciitis (inflammation of tissue on sole of foot)	75% reduction in pain	Stretching the arch of the foot (pull the toes backwards towards the shins) 10 times, three times per day
Muscle and joint pain	25% reduction in pain	20 to 30 minutes of aerobic exercise three times per week

TREATMENTS:
MOVE MORE, ACHE LESS
Exercise Is Powerful Pain Medicine

Researchers now know much more about what exercise does for the body and mind. Does your pain make you grouchy? By exercising for as little as 30 minutes a day, you trigger the flow of feel-good endorphins, the body's natural painkillers that boost mood and lower stress. All that blood and oxygen pumping through your body will begin to make you feel better, happier and more in control.

Does your pain keep you from doing the kinds of things you used to do? By exercising, you have a much better chance of getting back to that go-getting self you miss. You begin to build strength, which, in turn, enables your muscles to take more stress off your bones, and flexibility, which allows greater ease of pain-free movement. Each time you take a walk to the grocery store you'll feel more energetic and, at the same time, you'll fall asleep faster at night and stay asleep, which gives you more energy to resume your life. What's more, you may notice that you're dropping a few pounds, and weight loss can also trim aches and pains.

Exercise may sound like a drag, but it's worth the effort. A Harvard study of 135 women with chronic pain found that after a 16-week regimen of walking, strength training and stretching three times a week, starting at about 30 minutes and working up to an hour, their pain was reduced by almost half, enough for them to get back to many of the activities they missed. In another study, people with knee arthritis cut their pain by 43 percent after four months of strength training. A third study found that women with fibromyalgia who entered a strength-training program twice a week for 16 weeks reduced their pain by 39 percent. A fourth study showed that people who did at least six weekly hours of aerobic exercise showed a 25 percent reduction in the aches and pain of aging, compared to a control group.

❝ *Due to a car accident eight years ago I have suffered many back pains and headaches. I have tried so many pain relief products with no success. After seeing a commercial on TV, I was intrigued and gave it a go. Now I seem to not be able to live without it. I love Lakota and the relief that it gives me. I use it on my back and neck to help alleviate headaches and muscle spasms. The effects lasted so long I was surprised and quite happy. I love you, Lakota!* ❞

Julie Reil, Orillia, ON

You don't have to be an Olympic athlete, buy new exercise clothes or even go to a gym. The important thing is simply moving your body regularly by walking or swimming, gardening or dancing—whatever feels most inviting. Getting the right type of exercise at the right intensity is a great way to ease your aches, boost your energy and even prevent future pain.

Mapping Out a Plan

The ideal exercise prescription will vary, depending on your type of pain. The key is to start with something you know you can do. Here are suggestions for getting started:

WORK WITH YOUR DOCTOR. Before you start any exercise program, check with your doctor.

START SLOW. No one expects you to sign up for a marathon. The important thing is to get started, and any activity that gets you moving fits the bill. Walk 10 minutes at lunchtime, get up from your desk every hour and do a few stretches, start lifting your groceries into the car instead of asking the bagger to do it. Whenever you have a chance to move, do it. Within a few weeks, you will feel like doing more.

THINK TIME, NOT SPEED OR DISTANCE. Initially, it doesn't matter how far or how fast you're moving, but how long. Pretty soon you'll speed up.

BE FLEXIBLE. For instance, if you can't walk at first because your knee hurts, try swimming or a stationary bike instead. And don't forget to schedule exercise on your calendar, just as you would a doctor's appointment. Beware thinking that you'll

■ ■ ■ MY ACHING MUSCLES

New exercise could make your muscles feel sore the next day. Here's how to make them feel better fast.

Gently massage your muscles. Some studies indicate that this can relieve soreness by 30 percent and also reduce swelling.

Take an Epsom salts bath. Add two cups of Epsom salts to a warm bath and soak for 20 minutes. The magnesium in the salts helps relax muscles and reduces inflammation and swelling.

Apply ice. An ice pack wrapped in a towel placed over the sore spot for 20 minutes reduces swelling. After the pain has peaked, apply a heating pad or warm towel for 20 minutes, which helps by increasing circulation.

Stretch. A few gentle stretches won't necessarily relieve soreness, but they will feel good.

Give it a rest. Go ahead and exercise the next day if you feel like it, but take it easy.

get to it at day's end; our best intentions can get lost in the shuffle.

HAVE A BAD-DAY PLAN. Some days you may that feel your pain makes it impossible to move. But don't take to bed. Instead, try to do a little something—even if it's just stretching. Most people make the mistake of thinking that pain has to vanish before starting to get active—however, as we've said throughout this book, the opposite is true.

Put Your Fears to Bed

You're in pain, and your doctor is telling you to exercise. For a moment, you suspect it's a joke. Of course, you have fears about exercising when you hurt. But it can be done, and it will help you. Here are answers to some common worries.

I'M GOING TO HURT MORE. In fact, the longer you let your muscles atrophy, the more your pain will increase. It is true that when you start exercising, your muscles may feel a little sore the next day. Strengthening muscles hurts because exercise breaks down muscles a bit. When they repair, they're more powerful. If it hurts while you're exercising, stop immediately. Step back for a moment and start again, being careful only to move within the non-painful range.

I CAN'T WALK FOR FIVE MINUTES. Unless your doctor says you're not ready, you can walk for five minutes. Tell yourself, "I'm just going to put one foot in front of the other." After you've done it once, then you'll know for sure you can do it again.

I WON'T BE ABLE TO BUILD UP TO AN HOUR. That's why you're starting with only five to 15 minutes. By adding minutes very gradually—one minute per week, three days per week—your body will become increasingly conditioned, your muscles stronger and. your breathing easier. That's how getting fit works.

I DON'T HAVE TIME. If you have time to watch television, read a book, or take a nap, you have time to exercise.

EXERCISE WILL MAKE ME TIRED. Actually, a half hour of moderate exercise usually has the opposite effect. Within the first few months of exercising, you may find you feel more energetic all the time, perhaps because you're sleeping better and your heart, lungs and muscles have an easier time doing their jobs.

Get Your Heart Pumping

One key to reducing pain is to increase your heart rate. Cardiovascular, or aerobic, exercise increases both your breathing and your heart rate, improving the flow of oxygen and nutrients to painful areas. This aids in the removal of toxins, speeding healing. Your heart works harder and, like any muscle, grows stronger so that, eventually, you will be able to do the same exercise with less effort.

■ ■ ■ CUE UP YOUR EXERCISE

It takes several weeks to create a new habit. Until exercise becomes as ingrained as brushing your teeth, and even after, use these cues to keep you glued to your exercise schedule.

✔ Put your walking shoes by the bedroom door so you see them first thing in the morning.

✔ Put a Post-it Note on your refrigerator reminding you to exercise.

✔ Ask a friend to call to remind you.

✔ Schedule your exercise as you would a dental appointment—in your calendar.

✔ Set an alarm clock for when it's time to exercise.

Exercise boosts energy and lowers stress, which are both common problems for people in pain. It releases tension, loosens tight muscles and makes falling and staying asleep easier, often a difficulty for people in pain. It strengthens muscles, which can then carry some of the burden for an aching back or hips. Stronger muscles make day-to-day activities like shopping and household tasks easier, too. You're also apt to lose weight, a boon to sore joints. A 200-pound person who stays on the same diet but briskly walks one and a half miles daily, for example, will lose 14 pounds in a year.

Giving your heart a workout also raises your spirits and sharpens your mind. It's a rare soul who returns from even 15 minutes of brisk exercise who doesn't feel a little better about themselves, who doesn't have a better perspective on the tasks and problems of the day, and who isn't in better spirits. In fact, research shows that your mood will lift after just 10 minutes of exercise and continue improving, reaching its high after about 20 minutes. Other research shows that exercise relieves depression as effectively as antidepressants and psychotherapy. The reason for the lift: Exercise releases the mood-boosting brain chemicals serotonin and dopamine, as well as endorphins that act as the body's natural painkillers.

Revved up to give your heart a workout? Here are experts' top aerobic plans for people in pain.

CAUTION

You should feel only a mild discomfort in your muscle as you stretch. Stop immediately if you feel pain or a stabbing sensation—this means you are forcing the stretch too far.

Your Walking Workout

Most people can start by walking 15 minutes. If you can't manage that, try the following: Start by walking for five minutes three days a week. The next week, walk for six minutes each of the three days. Increase each week until you reach 20 minutes, then add a fourth day.

Continue to build in that way until you are walking at least 30 minutes to an hour per day, five days a week. As your fitness improves you can speed up, walking fast enough to increase your breathing and heart rate but slowly enough so that you can still have a conversation. If your breathing and heart rate do not return to normal within 10 minutes after you stop, you're pushing too hard. Here are some ways to make walking painless.

- Walk with a friend.
- Listen to music while you walk.
- Wear breathable, loose-fitting clothing and supportive walking shoes.
- Pick a beautiful or fun spot, like a path around a lake that has benches in case you get tired. In bad weather, opt for a shopping mall.
- To protect your joints, walk on soft surfaces, such as a park trail or high school running track.

Swimming Strategies

Swimming can be especially helpful for people with joint pain. Because of the body's buoyancy, you're not thudding down on your bones. Reduced gravitational pull also makes it easier to move with less pain. At the same time, the water provides enough resistance to strengthen muscles. How to get started?

LOOK FOR A HEATED POOL. Water from 28°C to 34°C will help relax your muscles and ease your pain.

START SLOWLY. Swim using any stroke you find comfortable. Swim two or three times a week, working up to 15 to 20 minutes by the end of the first week, 25 to 30 minutes by the end of the second week. Gradually work up to 45 minutes to an hour.

KNOW WHEN TO PAUSE. If you get tired, stop and relax in the water. After your second week, begin to swim a little faster. Getting your heart working hard is key to triggering the release of pain-relieving endorphins.

MONITOR YOUR PAIN. If your pain gets worse or you feel new pain, slow down or stop.

Biking Boost

Stationary bikes are perfect for people suffering back, joint and arthritis pain. Biking builds muscle strength, keeps joints flexible, and reduces stiffness. It's also low impact, so it won't cause further pain to your joints. If you have joint or back pain, ask the gym manager whether an upright or recumbent bike would be better for you, as recumbent bikes may be better for people with back pain. If you have knee pain and you're using an upright bike, make sure the seat is high enough that your knee doesn't bend past 90 degrees but not so high that your leg is straight at the bottom of a pedal stroke. If your hips rock when you pedal, lower the seat. To avoid putting undue strain on your knees, push from your heel, not your toe.

If you're having trouble with walking, try the following program on a stationary bike:

> 66 My love of playing sports and being active has not changed from when I was young. Unfortunately my body does not always feel the same way. I often have suffered with muscle and back pain, but do not believe in taking artificial or pharmaceutical medication unless no other options are available. Lakota products have been the perfect solution. I am able to manage any pain I have, while living an active lifestyle and avoiding artificial pain supplements. 99

John Sauer, Calgary, AB

- Start with five to 15 minutes three days a week.
- Add one minute per day each week until you reach 20 minutes.
- Add a fourth day.
- Continue building the same way until you can bike for an hour five days a week.

Work Your Muscles

Your biceps don't have to look like Popeye's, but strengthening your muscles will help relieve pain, and you can do it no matter what your age or current fitness level. Stronger muscles make everyday tasks like lifting groceries, climbing out of the car and getting up stairs much easier. Mightier muscles around your joints and back help protect them by lessening strain. Think of a sturdy bridge versus a wobbly one: Which one would you rather drive your car over?

Working muscles also potentially reduces the risk of fracture. The stronger your muscles, the less chance of your falling and injuring yourself.

Working at strengthening muscles also increases your endurance and improves the functioning of your heart and lungs. It helps the body use fuel more efficiently, guards you from heart disease and simply makes you feel better about yourself. The hard part is getting started.

Getting Started

Say the words "strength training," and it's easy to picture a bodybuilder hefting gigantic barbells over his head. That image is pretty intimidating, but it's not what you need. The goal is simple: A slow, steady use of your muscles that, over time, will make you stronger. We're talking about an easy, step-by-step program. Ready to get going?

CREATE A PLAN. Begin by doing at least one session with a physiotherapist), who can create a comfortable program and show you correct postures that won't add to your pain. Your doctor should be able to refer you to someone.

Did you know?

Sitting improperly can lead to back pain. When sitting for a long time, plant both feet on the floor, with your hips slightly higher than your knees.

QUIZ
HOW DO YOU LIKE TO MOVE?

You'll have an easier time making exercise a habit if you follow your natural preferences. Ask yourself these questions:

✔ What kind of exercise do I like?
✔ Am I an indoor or outdoor person?
✔ Do I like to exercise alone or in a group?
✔ Do I like gym classes or video instruction?
✔ At what time of day do I have the most energy?
✔ Do I like to exercise all at once or in 10-minute increments?
✔ Am I someone who likes to get things done?

If walking bores you, you won't do it. If you've always been drawn to swimming, do that instead. What did you enjoy doing as a child? Skipping? Throwing a football? Roller skating? Skiiing? Find a way to tap into those natural affinities now.

1. Love the outdoors? Head to the park, walk around your neighbourhood, cultivate a garden, put up a backstop in the driveway to shoot hoops, or strap on some cross-country skis. In many cities, organizations offer outdoor fitness classes. Prefer the indoors? Go mall walking, get a home treadmill, sign up for gym classes.

2. If you prefer exercising alone, pick walking, swimming or cycling. If you like to chat while you sweat, ask a friend to join you or sign up with a trainer or for a class.

3. If you choose a class, make sure that the instructor has worked with people who have your condition. If you prefer a video, ask your physiotherapist to recommend one that is safe for you.

4. If you're a morning person, schedule your exercise then. Even if you tell yourself you'll do it later, it's much harder to get motivated to start when you're tired.

5. If you prefer to exercise in 10-minute bouts, that's fine. Try to fit three of them into your day.

6. Appeal to your practical side. You have to mail letters anyway, so why not walk to the nearest mailbox? If you want to volunteer your time for charity, why not participate in a charity walk?

WARM UP. Before you begin, walk in place for five to 10 minutes to warm your muscles.

LEAVE THE WEIGHTS FOR LATER. You can do lots of strengthening by using your body weight alone as resistance. Try slow wall push-ups or climbing stairs. Whatever exercise you do, do as many repetitions as you can until you are tired, then do two more. Don't worry if the count varies from day to day; it will, depending on what else you've done that day.

WORK YOUR MUSCLES EVERY OTHER DAY. Leave at least a day between sessions to give your muscles time to repair.

WHEN YOU ADD WEIGHTS, SKIP THE WEIGHT MACHINES. Weight machines can hide your weaknesses in a way that free weights can't; strong parts compensate for the weak parts, hiding their frailty.

Strength Moves 101

FOR OVERALL STRENGTH Any aerobics program—walking, swimming, biking—will begin to condition and strengthen you.

FOR YOUR LEGS After you're able to walk 30 minutes, add a small hill to your route. This is good for strengthening your legs and back. Or you can simply climb stairs, graduating to two stairs at a time, eventually jogging up the stairs. Step up and down on a kitchen stool. Do deep knee bends.

FOR YOUR ARMS Begin with a biceps curl. Pretend you're holding a barbell in each hand, arms by your side, hands in fists. Raise those virtual barbells to your chest, keeping your elbows tucked by your sides. Repeat until tired, plus two more. When 10 of those seem easy, start lifting a small bag of rice or a can of soup, or use hand weights. You can also do wall push-ups, which work your chest, too: Stand at arm's length from the wall. Lean forward and place your hands on the wall, slightly wider than shoulder-width apart. Exhale, bend your elbows, and lean your head and chest towards the wall, coming close but not touching it.

> 66 *I started taking a kick-boxing class in order to lose a bit of weight and start a healthier lifestyle. The day after my first class, my muscles were so sore in my back I could barely walk, and the day after that it got even worse! My fiancé suggested that I try Lakota as it helps him after work when he needs it. So he rubbed it on my back where I was sore and within an hour I already had lots of mobility compared to earlier. I felt much more relaxed and at ease. Thank you Lakota!* 99

Tara Hanley, Bowmanville, ON

Inhale then straighten your arms, pushing the weight of your body away from the wall. Repeat until you're tired.

FOR YOUR CORE Strengthening your core, the area around your trunk and pelvis, helps your posture improve, prevents back pain and simply makes it easier for you to do things with less pain, like reach for dishes on a top shelf or bend down to tie your shoes. Instead of sit-ups—the worst thing for back pain—try this: Lie down on your back on a mat, knees bent, feet on the floor. Imagine pulling your navel toward the floor without holding your breath. Bring one knee to your chest, lower it, and bring the other to your chest and repeat, doing a slow march. Your legs are your resistance, and keeping your stomach muscles tight protects your back. Keep your back flat on the floor; don't let it arch. Repeat until tired, plus two more.

Stretch Your Limits

Even those of us without chronic pain lose five percent of our flexibility every decade. Pain makes your body tighten, a normal reflex of the muscles to protect them from more pain. Even one muscle's tightness can affect us all over: A tight calf, for instance, can cause pain in your knees, shins or feet. When you don't move, tight muscles get tighter. Your goal is to reverse that process and get your body back to its former flexibility.

■ ■ ■ BE A PAIN SLEUTH

If you're not used to exercising, it can be hard to tell the difference between the good pain that can result from exercise and the bad. Here's how:

Good pain When you begin an exercise you're not used to, your muscles get sore because of tiny tears, which cause swelling and pain. A slightly sore muscle is a good thing because, as the muscle repairs, it grows stronger. Unless the soreness is severe or lasts more than a week, don't worry.

Bad pain Give your pain a number from one (no pain) to 10 (worst pain) each day before you start exercising. The number should be lower two hours after exercise or at least no worse. If you have new localized pain—in a knee or ankle, for example—that increases while you exercise, stop and have the pain checked by a doctor.

Stretching improves circulation, increasing blood flow to the areas that hurt you, speeding healing. Stretching also helps your posture, keeping your body in proper alignment so no one part is doing too much work.

Luckily, you don't have to be a rubber band to try stretching. In fact, our range of flexibility is something we're born with. If you couldn't touch your toes at age 20, chances are you'll never touch your toes. All that matters is that your muscles, ligaments and tendons are taut enough to support you but loose enough that you can move through the full range of motion you had as a young adult. Here some tips to keep in mind as you stretch.

REACH FOR TIGHTNESS, NOT PAIN. In other words, stretch until you feel resistance, but don't push so far that you feel pain.

BE SMOOTH, NOT BOUNCY. Move slowly into any stretch and hold it for five to 10 seconds. Never bounce into a stretch, which can tear muscle fibres.

STRETCH EVERYTHING. Move everything—shoulders, hips, knees, arms, neck—through their full range of motion. It's the only way to get your whole body into balance.

BE SYMMETRICAL. Whatever you stretch on one side of your body, stretch on the other.

STRETCH AFTER EXERCISE. Stretching after exercise, when your muscles are warm, is the best way to improve your flexibility.

Staying Motivated

Make exercise a habit not by thinking about abstract health improvements but by changing behaviours slowly and consistently. Set goals, keep track and build in variety—after all, the enemy of exercise is boredom. Walk somewhere different, do some yard work, have a game of badminton. There are endless possibilities.

The Where and How of Exercise

So, your new prescription is to exercise. Perhaps now you feel overwhelmed by all the choices: yoga, water aerobics or Pilates? Can you be sure the instructor can protect you from more pain?

CONSIDER A REHAB PROGRAM. Many pain and rehabilitation centres offer outpatient programs that will teach you how to begin moving. Rehab specialists can help you plan an appropriate exercise program and teach you important skills.

JOIN A GYM. Gyms offer all kinds of classes, and you can usually try all of them for the price of a membership. Most gyms have personal trainers who can help you build an individualized exercise program.

DO IT YOURSELF AT HOME. You don't have to join a gym to exercise; you can do it by yourself in the privacy of your home. Here are some exercises to get started.

BACK PAIN

WALL SQUAT
Strengthens supporting muscles (quadriceps and glutes) affected by spinal arthritis, general low-back pain, hip pain and knee pain

A Stand with your back against a wall, heels about two steps (45 cm) from the wall, shoulder-width apart.
B Pulling in your abdominal muscles, slide slowly down the wall until your knees are bent at about 90 degrees, as though you're seated. If that's too difficult, bend your knees to a 45-degree angle and gradually build up from there. Count to five and slide slowly back up the wall. Repeat 10 times.

HEEL SLIDES
Strengthens hip, hamstring and back muscles affected by general low-back pain

Lying on your back, press your lower back into the floor and hold while you slide one heel away from you along the floor until your leg is straight. Return to start. Repeat 10 times with each leg. Do three sets.

BACK PAIN

PRESS-UP ON HANDS

Increases flexibility and range or motion for those affected by disc problems and sciatica

A Lie facedown with your palms flat on the floor about level with your head. Toes can be pointed straight back or straight down onto the floor, whichever is more comfortable.
B Pushing down on your hands, straighten your arms, keeping your hips on the floor. Relax your lower back and buttocks. Hold for 10 seconds. Repeat 10 times.

KNEELING ARM AND LEG EXTENSIONS

Strengthens and stabilizes muscles affected by general lower back pain, hip pain and disc problems

A Get on all fours, hands directly below your shoulders, fingers pointing forwards, knees directly below your hips. Keep your back straight during this exercise. Pretend you're balancing a bowl of water on your back and trying to avoid spilling it, or place a broomstick along your spine lengthwise to keep your back in place.
B Tightening your abdominal muscles, raise your right arm and extend it in front of you. At the same time, raise your left leg and extend it behind you. Hold for five seconds, relax and switch sides. Do one set. (both sides) 10 times.

CARPAL TUNNEL SYNDROME

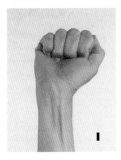

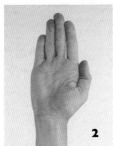

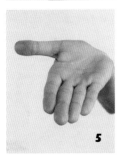

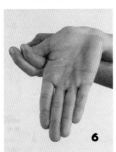

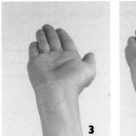

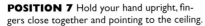

CARPAL TUNNEL STRETCH

Increases flexibility

Do each of these exercises five times. Hold each position to a count of 15. Repeat three times.

POSITION 1 Hold your hand up, wrist relaxed, and close your fingers and thumb into a relaxed fist.

POSITION 2 Extend your fingers and thumb so that they're pointing towards the ceiling.

POSITION 3 Keeping your fingers extended, bend your wrist back as if trying to make your palm face the ceiling.

POSITION 4 Repeat position 3, but move your thumb away from your fingers.

POSITION 5 Repeat position 4 with your forearm facing the ceiling, as though you're carrying a platter.

POSITION 6 Repeat position 5, but use other hand to gently stretch the thumb.

POSITION 7 Hold your hand upright, fingers close together and pointing to the ceiling.

POSITION 8 Bend the top two joints of your fingers, keeping your wrist and knuckles straight. Move slowly and smoothly to return your hand to the starting position. Repeat with other hand. Start with 10 repetitions with each hand and increase to one to three sets, as tolerated.

WALL STRETCH

Stretches your fingers, wrist, arm and chest muscles

Stand facing directly towards a wall. Place your open palm on the wall with your fingers facing backwards. Keep your shoulder relaxed and down. Turn your body away from the wall, moving your feet as needed. You should feel a stretch across your chest and down into your hand.

ELBOW PAIN

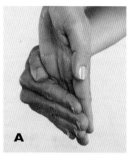

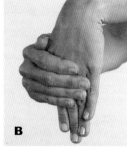

A **B**

INTERIOR AND EXTERIOR FOREARM STRETCH
Increases flexibility

A Sit with your left arm extended, palm facing up. Use your right hand to stretch the palm back by gently applying pressure until you feel a stretch in your forearm. Hold for 30 seconds and repeat three times. Switch arms.
B Sit with your left arm extended, palm facing down, wrist relaxed. Use your right hand to stretch the wrist so that your fingers point to the floor, or until you feel a stretch in the top of your forearm. Hold for 30 seconds. Repeat three times, then switch arms.

WRIST EXTENSION
Strengthens muscles

A While seated, rest your forearm on a pillow on a table, with your palm facing the floor holding a one-pound dumbbell.
B Without moving your forearm, lift the weight towards the ceiling. Do three sets of 10 repetitions with each wrist. Increase weight in increments when 10 reps become too easy.

A

B

WRIST FLEX
Strengthens muscles

A While seated, rest your forearm on a pillow on a table, with your palm facing the ceiling holding a one-pound dumbbell.
B Without moving your forearm, bend your wrist up. Return to start. Do three sets of 10 repetitions with each wrist.

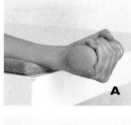

A

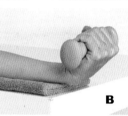

B

FOOT AND ANKLE PAIN

SIMPLE ANKLE AND FOOT STRETCH
Increases flexibility and restores range of motion

While seated, place your right ankle on your left knee. Rotate your foot clockwise 10 times, then counterclockwise. Do three sets of 10 repetitions, then switch feet.

STANDING CALF STRETCH
Increases flexibility in muscles affected by tendinitis, ankle pain and foot pain

Standing about 50 cm from a wall, place both hands on the wall. Bring your left leg forwards and your right leg back. Bend your left knee towards the wall, keeping your right foot flat on the floor. Point your right foot slightly inwards. You should feel a stretch in your right calf. Hold for 30 seconds, then switch legs.

NECK PAIN AND TEMPOROMANDIBULAR JOINT DISORDER (TMJ)

CROSS-ARM STRETCH

Stretches and increases flexibility in neck muscles and the muscles affected by TMJ

Standing up straight, bring your right arm across your chest, using your left arm to cradle and hug it toward your chest. Lean your head towards your left shoulder. Hold for 30 seconds. Return to start. Repeat three times on each side.

STANDING PEC STRETCH

Stretches and increases flexibility in neck muscles and the muscles affected by TMJ

Standing beside a wall, place your elbow on the wall at shoulder height, your forearm resting on the wall. Take a step forwards with the leg away from the wall. Lean your body forwards, but do not twist towards the wall. You should feel a gentle stretch in the front of your shoulder and chest. Hold for 30 seconds. Repeat three times on each side.

SHOULDER PAIN

CORNER STRETCH

Stretches and increases flexibility to relieve and prevent neck, shoulder and TMJ pain

Stand facing a corner and place both hands on the wall with elbows roughly at shoulder level. Lean forwards until you can feel a gentle stretch across your chest. Hold for 20 seconds, then return to starting position. Repeat two times, two sessions a day.

PENDULUM SWING

Stretches rotator cuff muscles

Stand straight, then lean forwards slightly from the hips. Keep your painful shoulder and arm relaxed and hanging straight down. Gently and slowly swing the arm back and forth, then in a circle. Continue for 30 to 60 seconds.

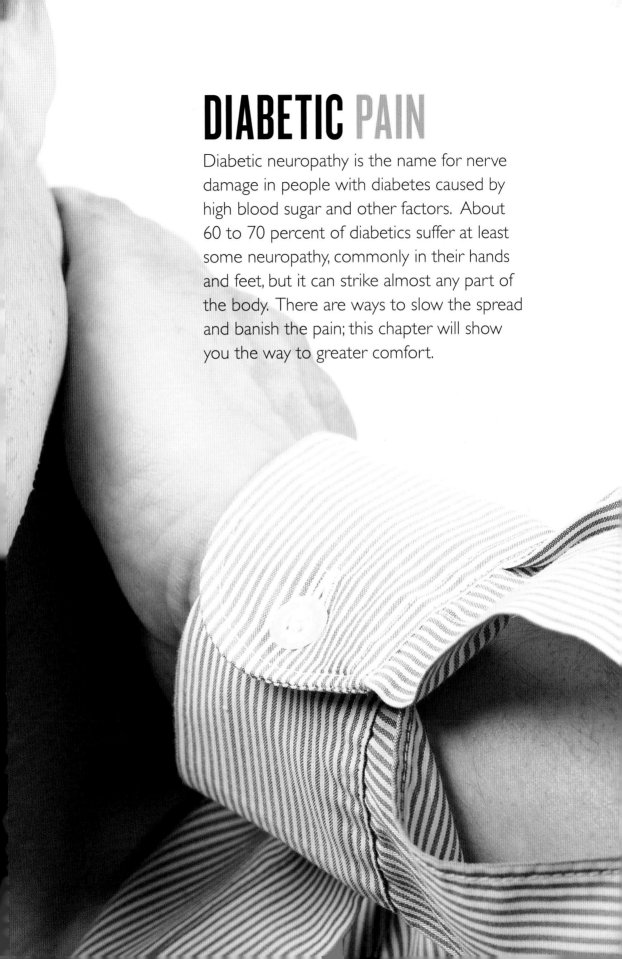

DIABETIC PAIN

Diabetic neuropathy is the name for nerve damage in people with diabetes caused by high blood sugar and other factors. About 60 to 70 percent of diabetics suffer at least some neuropathy, commonly in their hands and feet, but it can strike almost any part of the body. There are ways to slow the spread and banish the pain; this chapter will show you the way to greater comfort.

DIABETIC PAIN

The risk of neuropathy, or diabetic pain, rises with age and with duration of diabetes. So don't wait; if you're at risk, talk to your doctor and create a proactive plan to fight it, using the information below. Your priority is simple: Get your blood sugar under control, by focusing on diet and exercise.

NIPPING NERVE DAMAGE IN THE BUD

Diabetes can literally be unnerving. It's no joke: Nerve damage may be one of the most far-reaching complications of the disease because the nervous system controls or contributes to so much—everything from your sense of touch (and pain) to muscle movement, digestion and sexual function, just to name a few. Fortunately, you probably have time to prevent nerve damage, which usually develops after you've had diabetes for 10 to 15 years.

CAUTION

At the first tingle, give your doctor a jingle. If you notice tingling, burning, weakness or pain in your hands or feet, head to your doctor as soon as you can. The same goes for dizziness or changes in digestion or urination.

Doctors don't entirely understand how diabetes causes nerve damage, but likely possibilities are that high blood sugar upsets the balance of chemicals that allow nerves to transmit electrical impulses, deprives nerves of oxygen by impeding circulation and damages the nerves' protective coating (called the myelin sheath). You can breathe a sigh of relief that diabetes doesn't seem to affect the brain or spinal cord—the components of the central nervous system. Still, the rest of the body's nerves, which carry electrical impulses through what amounts to an intricate network of "wires," are vulnerable to diabetes-related signal slowdowns, miscommunication or interruptions.

There are three major types of nerve damage, or neuropathy, each of which can affect the body in many different ways. If you develop neuropathy, your doctor will determine which kind it is mostly by your symptoms and where they occur.

■■■ DO YOU HAVE DIABETES?

Many Canadians have diabetes but don't know it. Not sure if you're among them? Symptoms such as extreme thirst, frequent urination and unexplained weight loss are blatant warnings. Even if you don't have the disease, you may be at risk for developing diabetes if you:

✔ Are overweight
✔ Are age 65 or older or are younger than 65 and don't exercise regularly
✔ Ever gave birth to a baby weighing more than nine pounds
✔ Have a sibling or parent with diabetes

Go online to download the questionnaire "Are You at Risk?" on the Canadian Diabetes Association website at www.diabetes.ca.

Polyneuropathy

The most common type of nerve damage affects multiple nerves throughout the body (poly means "many"), but it mainly hits the long nerves of the peripheral nervous system that run through the arms and legs. You'll often hear this kind of nerve damage referred to as distal symmetric neuropathy, because it strikes areas away from the central nervous system (distal refers to distance from the centre) and tends to cause symptoms on both sides of the body (symmetric). Polyneuropathy generally doesn't affect movement; instead, it disrupts sensation, often causing pain, cramps or tingling in the hands or feet, and later causing numbness.

Focal Neuropathy

Far less common, focal neuropathy involves a single nerve, or set of nerves, and often affects only one area of the body—which is why it's sometimes called mononeuropathy (mono means "one"). Unlike polyneuropathy, which tends to develop gradually over time, it pops up suddenly, often causing numbness, pain or weakness in the muscles, depending on which nerves are affected. Although it can crop up anywhere, focal neuropathy often causes Bell's palsy, in which nerves lose control over muscles in the face, causing your features to droop. Focal neuropathy can make your eyes cross if it affects muscles that control eye movement, and it can cause carpal tunnel syndrome, in which compressed nerves in the wrist produce pain or weakness in the hand and forearm.

■ ■ ■ TEST OF NERVES

While it's up to you to sound the neuropathy alarm if you suspect that you have nerve damage, your doctor can confirm and fine-tune the diagnosis with subtle tests. In one, they may hold a tuning fork against body parts, such as your foot, to find out whether you can detect its vibration. Similarly, she may touch you with a hairlike wire to gauge your response to delicate stimuli, or apply heat or cold to make sure you could tell if you were being harmed by, say, scalding bathwater. If any of these tests indicate that you have nerve damage, your doctor will probably send you to a neurologist to learn the extent of the damage.

Autonomic Neuropathy

The autonomic nervous system governs the body functions that you don't normally have to think about much—such as heartbeat, digestion, sweating and bladder control—but that become more top-of-mind if nerves are damaged. Autonomic neuropathy can cause such problems as:

- Cardiovascular glitches, such as irregular heartbeat, and a condition called orthostatic hypotension, in which your blood pressure fails to quickly adjust when you stand up, making you feel faint or dizzy. Deadened nerves can also fail to transmit pain from a heart attack.
- A condition known as gastroparesis, in which muscles of the gastrointestinal (GI) tract become slow and inefficient. Sluggish digestion not only causes GI problems like nausea, vomiting, bloating, diarrhea, constipation and loss of appetite, but it makes blood-sugar patterns more difficult to predict and counter with insulin.
- Poor bladder function, in which nerves may have trouble telling when the bladder is full and don't empty the bladder completely when you void. One result is higher risk of urinary tract infections that, in turn, can accelerate kidney damage.
- Sexual dysfunction, in which men find it difficult to get or maintain an erection and women experience vaginal dryness or a tepid sexual response. Usually, however, sex drive is unaffected in both sexes.

- Dulled response to nervous symptoms of hypoglycemia, such as shakiness, sweating and anxiety, a dangerous condition known as hypoglycemia unawareness.
- Profuse sweating and poor regulation of body temperature.

KEEPING THE VERVE IN NERVES

Closely controlling blood sugar—your top priority—can reduce your risk of nerve damage by as much as 60 percent. Once neuropathy develops, treatments vary depending on how the nerve damage is affecting your body. Among the steps you can take to minimize damage and discomfort:

Get in Touch with Your Feelings

As with most diabetes complications, the sooner you pick up on nerve damage, the more you can do to keep it from escalating. Don't dismiss sensations or difficulties that disappear: In many cases, symptoms come and go or swing from mild to severe. Tell your doctor immediately if you experience:

- Tingling, numbness, burning or prickly pain in your arms, legs, hands, or feet. Stay alert: The sensations can be very subtle at first. Try to be especially aware of unusual sensations in the feet, which are often affected first, or at night, when symptoms are usually worse.
- Sensitivity to touch—even the light brushing of your sheets against you when you're in bed causes discomfort.
- Leg cramps that may come and go, especially at night.
- Difficulty sensing the position of your feet or toes, or a sense that you can't keep your balance.
- Calluses or sores on your feet.

❝ My Lakota success story begins on the day of my wedding! I spent the night at my parent's house. Unfortunately the bed was a lot softer than mine at home. I woke up with the worst back pain I have ever experienced. Luckily one of my bridesmaids had some Lakota in her purse. I was reluctant because I had never tried it before, but she swore by it. I tried it and it worked so fast, I was able to enjoy the entire day without back pain. Thankfully, my husband was able to see me smile walking down the aisle rather than frown due to pain. ❞

Ashley McIver, Thunder Bay, ON

Adjust Your Diet

Check with your dietitian to see if changes in the foods you eat might help keep some symptoms of neuropathy in check. If you're suffering from gastroparesis, try eating smaller, more frequent meals or consuming softer foods to ease digestion. Ask if you should eat less fibre, which is good for blood-sugar control for the same reason it may be bad for gastroparesis: It slows digestion. If you feel lightheaded when you stand, ask if you should consume more salt to help stabilize your blood pressure. Check with your doctor first, though, especially if you may also be at risk for hypertension, or high blood pressure.

Boost Your B's

In some cases, neuropathy is fostered by a deficiency in the vitamins B_6 and B_{12}, both of which are involved in the function of the nervous system. You can get vitamin B_6 from avocados, bananas, poultry, pork, potatoes and fish like tuna, while B_{12} is found in chicken, beef and a wide variety of seafood and fish, including oysters and sardines. Ask your dietitian or doctor if you should take supplements.

Supplement Your Nerve Health

Look online for information on alpha-lipoic acid, an antioxidant supplement that can help protect the nerves and ease the pain of neuropathy.

Talk to your doctor for advice about medication.

DROPPING POUNDS, REDUCING PAIN

If you have type 2 diabetes, your primary goal is simple; bring your blood sugar under control. There's just no better way to stave off diabetes-related complications. Best of all, you'll feel more in control of your everyday health.

A good way to shed weight is an unsurprising one: Start with what you eat. Nearly 90 percent of people with type 2 diabetes are overweight. That's no coincidence. Being overweight

What Studies Show

Smiling equals longevity: A study from 2008 of people with diabetes found that the more positive a patient's attitude, the longer his or her life is likely to be.

■ ■ ■ SECRETS OF ENJOYABLE EATING

In some quarters, the idea that you should take pleasure in food is controversial. In fact, the US Dietary Guidelines changed their instruction from "enjoy a variety of foods" to "eat a variety of foods." But Canada's Food Guide to Healthy Eating still urges Canadians to "enjoy." Should you worry that you might over-enjoy? Not necessarily. Many nutrition researchers say it's better to selectively indulge your tastes for finer (read: richer) foods than to eat a bland, boring diet you'll soon tire of. Here are some ways to increase your pleasure without overindulging your appetite;

Slow the pace. The best sensual experiences are savoured. By eating more slowly, you deepen your experience of flavours, better appreciate the social aspects of a meal, and give your body's appetite controls more time to signal that you're full, so you ultimately eat less.

Engage the senses. Pleasure doesn't have to mean calories. You can boost your enjoyment of a meal by appealing to senses other than taste. Examples: Buy a small bouquet of flowers or gather cuttings from your garden to brighten your table, dine by the light of a small votive candle or play your favourite music at suppertime.

Indulge like royalty. Choose one sinfully delicious chocolate instead of a box of fat-free cookies. The intensity and richness of the treat will make you feel satisfied, and it will actually have fewer calories than a larger portion of a "healthier" snack.

is the single most important contributor to the development of this condition—and losing weight is the single most important step in getting it under control or preventing it. It's like this: Less body fat means fewer fatty acids circulating in your bloodstream, and that means lower blood sugar.

The truth is that all you need for a radical change in your health is to make small changes in some everyday habits. In fact, losing only 10 percent of your body weight is enough to significantly reduce your blood sugar levels. Ten percent really isn't much: It's six minutes of an hour, or less than one slice of a pizza. And if you weigh 200 pounds, 10 percent is just 20 pounds.

So shoot for 10 percent—you may want to lose more, but this is a good start and provides a lot of health benefits. Best of all, you can lose 10 percent without creating a structured diet. That means no banned foods and no carb counting. Read on to learn how.

I. EAT MORE OFTEN

Start your day by eating breakfast, then go absolutely no more than five waking hours without a meal or snack.

By keeping food in your system, you avoid wild swings in blood sugar—deep valleys brought on by skipping meals or eating them late, and high peaks brought on by a surge in glucose when you finally get something in your stomach. Just as important, you keep your appetite under control by not letting hunger build to the point where you're ravenous.

Eating more often means, for starters, eating breakfast every day. This not only helps keep your blood sugar levels stable, it also helps you eat fewer calories throughout the day, according to several studies. What's more, it revs up your metabolism so that you burn more calories.

In terms of what you eat the rest of the day, if you're planning a late lunch or supper, you'll need to have a snack in between. Snacking is your friend, not your enemy. The aim is to keep your blood sugar steady and never get too hungry.

2. EAT BALANCED MEALS

Forget the question of protein versus carbohydrates—you don't have to choose. We want you to get some of both at each meal, plus at least one fruit or vegetable.

This is the best approach to controlling your blood sugar, feeling full longer, and losing weight. Sound simple? It is. Clinical experience suggests that if you're

> 66 *I was having a lot of trouble with pain in my hands and fingers. I'm a quilter and the pain was stopping me from enjoying my hobby. I started taking Lakota pills and started to notice a difference in the amount of pain I was having after only a week or so and was able to get back into quilting again. The pain continued to lessen and after about four to five weeks, I was almost pain-free. Thanks Lakota!* 99
>
> Linda Webster, Surrey, BC

overweight, that's probably not the way you're eating now. In fact, you may actually be deficient in certain nutrients despite the fact that you're taking in too many calories. Some nutritionists believe that the body's need for a variety of nutrients triggers your appetite in order to make sure you get them. If you simply eat more of what you always eat, your body never gets enough of what it really needs.

3. EAT A LITTLE LESS OF EVERYTHING BUT VEGETABLES

Portion control is essential to weight loss, but that doesn't mean you won't get enough to eat. On the contrary, you have permission to eat as much as you want— as long as it's vegetables. In fact, you should consider vegetables the ideal food: they're good sources of complex carbohydrates and smaller amounts of protein; they're generally low in fat and high in fibre; and they're rich in a variety of vitamins, minerals and other nutrients. The same is true of many fruits. That's why different forms of produce should fill at least half of your plate at any meal. To avoid getting too many sugars throughout the day, think of fruit primarily as a breakfast food and a dessert, but feel free to load up on vegetables anytime.

By adding more produce to your plate, you may actually eat more in terms of volume while still helping yourself lose weight. Plus, you'll leave less room for foods that constitute so much of the typical North American diet: highly processed and packaged foods, meats, sweets, starches and fats.

4. TRIM THE FAT

Cut back on total fat and substitute the "right" fats for the "wrong" ones.

Fat contains more than twice the calories of carbohydrates or protein, so it's an obvious target if you're trying to lose weight. Simply by eating more vegetables, you're likely to eat less fat. But don't cut all the fat from your diet. Studies show that eating a moderate amount of fat helps people stick to healthy diets, and some types of fat even help keep your blood sugar steady.

The key is to cut back on the "wrong" types of fat by consuming leaner meats and low-fat versions of dairy

What Studies Show

Research suggests the one simple habit of eating more often can confer striking health benefits. For example, a report presented to the American Heart Association in 2003 found that rates of obesity and metabolic problems, such as insulin resistance, were 35 to 50 percent lower in people who ate breakfast.

products, such as milk and cheese. That's because meat and dairy foods contain saturated fats, which contribute to insulin resistance (not to mention clogged arteries). "Good" fats, on the other hand, such as the ones in most cooking oils and in fish, actually help stabilize your blood sugar because they're digested more slowly than carbohydrates.

In one study, women trying to cut their overall fat intake discovered that their single most effective strategy was to avoid fat as a flavouring—for example, by not slathering butter on bread or potatoes. Instead, use low-fat or fat-free versions of mayonnaise, sour cream and salad dressing or try flavourful condiments such as pepper and chives. It's also crucial to put some of your favourite high-fat foods on a diet.

5. SHAKE A LEG

Start becoming more physically active by walking—just 10 minutes a day at first. Then add more time in small increments and work easy strengthening exercises into your routine.

Weight-loss experts agree that no weight-loss plan is likely to work unless it includes physical activity. Exercise burns calories and tones the muscles. It also boosts your muscle cells' insulin sensitivity, making your body more efficient at using glucose, thereby lowering your blood sugar. What's more, people who exercise have better luck keeping weight off in the long term than people who simply watch what they eat. And exercise feels good! Get your body in motion with simple activities such as walking, stretching and gentle strength training.

6. LEARN TO RELAX

Stress does more than wrinkle your brow—it raises your blood sugar as well. When you're feeling stressed, your body releases hormones that rev it up and prepare it to fight or flee. These same hormones also raise blood sugar. Research shows that you can significantly lower your blood sugar by getting stress under control. In fact, stress-reduction techniques can work almost as well as some diabetes medications.

Did you know?

"Sugar-free" isn't a sure-fire way to weight loss. Common sweeteners contain carbohydrate, which means they raise blood glucose just like sugar does. Ignore the "sugar-free" message, and read the total carbohydrate count instead.

> 66 *Before I started using Lakota, I was a couch potato. My back just burned right in the middle. I tried everything. Then a friend told me to try Lakota. I had nothing to lose so I tried some. One hour later the pain had subsided considerably. I could not believe it. Now I am as active as when I was 40. With Lakota and exercise, all the pain is now gone. I only need to take Lakota once a day with breakfast. Then I do about 15 minutes of exercises, and I feel like a new man. Thank you Lakota for saving my life!* 99
>
> Eric Grootveld, Port Alberni, BC

Manage stress, anxiety and hostility by meditating, breathing, relaxing your muscles and practicing mental imagery exercises. Keep your emotions from making you overeat and improve your mood—and your blood sugar—by getting better sleep. The satisfaction you'll get from being more relaxed is a happy bonus.

7. TRACK YOUR PROGRESS

It doesn't make sense to follow the plan without checking to see if it's working. Monitoring your progress lets you see positive results and alerts you if something's not working.

How often you need to test your blood sugar depends on several factors. You should work out a testing schedule with your doctor. As a general guideline, though, if you don't take medication or insulin and your blood sugar tends to stay in a relatively stable range between five and seven mmol/L, you may be able to test just a few times per week. Count on testing at least three times a week at the start of the program, preferably in the morning before you've had anything to eat. Your doctor may also want you to test again before supper for an idea of how your blood sugar changes during the day. If your blood sugar swings into the abnormal range, follow your doctor's advice for testing more often. If you're on insulin, medication or both, you may need to test three or four times a day, typically before meals and perhaps at bedtime.

Did you know?

Record your efforts to exercise more and eat better. Studies show that people who write down what they eat are more likely to consume fewer calories. And something tells us that people who track their exercise efforts are more likely to stick to a get-moving plan.

THE LINK BETWEEN
PAIN AND SLEEP

Pain interferes with sleep, and sleep deprivation compounds pain—the two can form a disturbing cycle. Studies have found that disturbed sleep alters some pain control mechanisms, making chronic pain worse. And then there's the simple fact that being low on sleep drags down your spirits.

The first thing to do about sleeplessness is understand its source: Pain? Anxiety? Stress? Once you know what's causing it, make easy lifestyle changes, such as adjusting your diet—skip the caffeine, for instance—and your sleep habits.

SLEEP PROBLEMS

It's no surprise that pain can affect how you sleep. And it's logical that lack of sleep can make any health condition feel that much worse. That's why this chapter focuses on ways to become a master of shut-eye. Try a variety of these approaches and you're more likely to get a good night's rest and feel ready to take on other health problems during the day—and get back to enjoying the good things in life.

Aging and Losing Sleep

Sleep patterns alter as we age, and insomnia becomes a sadly common experience. After age 55, sleep patterns change radically; the body clock decides to reset itself to a different time zone and levels of important sleep hormones drop. For many, sleep changes start much earlier, after you've reached your thirties, but they may happen so gradually that you don't notice them for decades.

But sleep doesn't have to be a problem, even if you're well into your golden years. Studies have shown that men and women in their eighties who are healthy and active are able to get enough rest to allow them to lead the lives they want to lead. That isn't to say that they sleep the same way they did when they were younger. They wake up more frequently and stay awake for longer. They might wake up earlier in the morning. But by adapting, they're able to get enough sleep to feel awake and refreshed.

So what are their secrets to overcoming—or sidestepping—the pressures of insomnia risks that evolve with the passing years? Everything from exercising in sunlight and saying no to an evening cocktail to working with doctors to mini-

mize the effects of health issues and medications on their sleep schedules. One thing is certain; poor sleep is not something you need to put up with. If you're feeling drained and unable to do the things you want to do, it's time to start figuring out how to improve your sleep. Sleep deprivation can frustrate your efforts to feel good, and it can worsen any other health issues you're dealing with.

■ ■ ■ SICK AND TIRED

Without question, poor health affects how you sleep.

One study found that those with four or more medical conditions were five times more likely to be sleepy during the day and four times more likely to say they slept poorly than people with no major health concerns. Health conditions and sleep disorders often go hand in hand—therefore, they should be treated at the same time.

Here are examples of health conditions known to affect sleep:

Pain A bad back, an arthritic knee, a pulled shoulder muscle, heartburn—any type of ongoing pain has the power to keep you awake or pull you out of a deep sleep. Talk with your doctor about pain treatments that can ensure you get a proper night's rest. Also, review any prescriptions you might have with your doctor—codeine, demerol, morphine and steroids can disturb your sleep, as can migraine relievers that contain caffeine.

Allergies People with allergic rhinitis—the most common form of allergies resulting from ubiquitous dust, pollen and animal dander—are much more likely to experience insomnia, wake up during the night, snore, and feel fatigued when they do get up. The French researchers who discovered this also found that those with allergic rhinitis are more likely to sleep fewer hours, take longer to fall asleep and feel sleepier during the day than those without the condition.

Gastroesophageal reflux disease (GERD) Pennsylvania State University researchers found a significant relationship between GERD, a particularly severe form of heartburn, and daytime sleepiness, insomnia, and poor sleep quality.

ADJUST TO SLEEP-PATTERN CHANGES. Your first step? Understanding and accommodating the way your body and mind sleep. Accept the fact that the timing and quality of your sleep does change over time. Just as you will never have the body shape and weight you did 30 years ago, you will not have the sleep patterns you once had. Be sensitive to the changes. Are you tired earlier or more sensitive to morning light? Monitoring changes and adjusting to them is half the battle.

Tired at 8 p.m.? Turn in. Lower levels of melatonin, the hormone that helps control your sleep/wake cycles, are one reason you may feel sleepier early in the evening than you used to. Just accept the change and go to bed earlier. Your goal, just as it was when you were younger, is to get seven to eight hours of quality sleep each night.

Can't drop off to sleep in an instant? Be patient—you'll get there. Taking longer to fall asleep is a natural part of aging. Older people may take 20 minutes or more to fall asleep; younger people may only need five to 10 minutes. (Read on for ways to feel sleepier at bedtime and to tell your brain it's time to doze.)

Waking up three or four times a night is normal now. Once asleep, older people go through the cycles of sleep more quickly than younger people—and wake up between cycles more frequently. Researchers suspect that lower levels of growth hormone in your system may help explain why you spend less time in the deepest, most restorative sleep stage, called stage 4 by researchers.

Wide awake at 5 a.m.? Get up! Your body clock may have shifted to an early-to-bed, early-to-rise schedule. Turning in earlier will help ensure that early waking isn't a rude awakening.

What Studies Show

Don't be stoic about sleeplessness; it's a problem that has very profound effects. Research shows that after going 17 to 19 hours without sleep, your brain activity is similar to that of someone with a blood alcohol content of 0.05.

123

CONSIDER DAYTIME NAPS. Napping is a controversial solution for people struggling with insomnia. There is evidence that a short daytime nap doesn't have much impact on nighttime sleep, so you probably won't have to worry about "saving up" your resting hours for later. But if you do find that a 30- to 45-minute afternoon nap keeps you awake too long at night, it may not be right for you. You may have to choose the method that works best for you. Once you decide, treat it like a regular program. If you are going to nap, do it at the same time every day to get in the habit. Your body will adjust and your energy levels will be steadier.

To Improve Your Nightly Sleep

RESERVE YOUR BED FOR SEX AND SLEEP. Avoid watching TV or paying bills in bed. Any activities that keep you awake or cause stress are strictly verboten.

CREATE A CLUTTER-FREE SANCTUARY. Your brain deserves the balm of a soothing, organized, pleasant environment free of worrisome reminders like baskets filled with laundry that needs to be folded, stacks of magazines to be sorted or bills to be paid. Consider painting the walls a soothing colour, too. How about sage green or a luminous, pale purple-blue?

BLOCK THE LIGHT. Moonlight, street lights, late sunsets and early dawns can all interfere with the circadian rhythm changes that determine your sleep patterns. If dawn comes too soon, or sunset too late, buy heavy curtains or blackout blinds to block the light.

NESTLE ON A NEW PILLOW. If yours is more than six months old, or if you wake up in the morning with a sore neck and shoulders or a stuffy nose, it may be time for new head support. What's best? It depends on you, but here are some pointers:

Did you know?

Eating before bed is bad news for insomniacs. Allow at least three hours between supper and bedtime. The brain doesn't sleep well on a full stomach. This might take some planning ahead— try having your big meal at lunchtime and have a lighter meal early in the evening.

- Neck pain? Go for a thinner pillow or look for a special "neck pillow." In one Swedish study, a neck pillow—rectangular with a depression in the middle—enhanced sleep. The ideal neck pillow is soft and not too thick.
- Always turning your pillow over to find the cooler side? Invest in natural cool. Natural fibres—and natural-fibre pillowcases—stay cooler. In studies, "cool pillows"—some were water-filled, and others used a mix of sodium sulfate and ceramic fibres—enhanced sleep.
- Stuffy or allergy-prone? Go hypoallergenic—and invest in an allergen-reducing pillowcase, too.

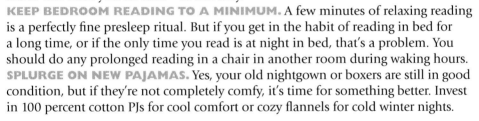

MOVE YOUR BED. Outside walls and windows in your bedroom mean more noise. Locating your sleeping spot along an inside wall could improve things, a Spanish study suggests.

TURN YOUR DIGITAL CLOCK TO THE WALL. When you think about it, why would anyone want a luminous clock shining on them continuously during the time when you most want darkness and peace? They can really interfere with sleep and they can cause extra stress as well. How? You may wake for a moment at 2 a.m., drift back to sleep, then wake again at 2:30—and think you've been awake the whole time. The solution: Turn the clock around and stop worrying. The alarm will wake you on time—so rest easy.

KEEP BEDROOM READING TO A MINIMUM. A few minutes of relaxing reading is a perfectly fine presleep ritual. But if you get in the habit of reading in bed for a long time, or if the only time you read is at night in bed, that's a problem. You should do any prolonged reading in a chair in another room during waking hours.

SPLURGE ON NEW PAJAMAS. Yes, your old nightgown or boxers are still in good condition, but if they're not completely comfy, it's time for something better. Invest in 100 percent cotton PJs for cool comfort or cozy flannels for cold winter nights.

> 66 *Last year when I was visiting my family while pregnant with my son, I had some serious back pain that would not go away. I tried everything. Exhausted, and in total pain, I finally found Lakota and rubbed it on. That kicked in fast and lasted long enough to let me get some sleep which was a good thing because I was actually in labour...a MONTH EARLY! My first time and I had no idea what was really going on. Thank you so much for helping me get some sleep, because once that nap was over I was on an adrenaline kick for about 24 hours, with a healthy, happy son!* 99

Michelle Ortlieb, Windsor, ON

AND SLIP ON SOME TOE-TOASTING SOCKS. Got cold feet? Wear warm socks to bed. Swiss researchers found that when blood vessels in the feet dilate late in the evening, the body can effectively cool down and prepare for sleep. Putting on socks can help make that happen by provoking the blood vessels to widen and radiate heat.

SCENT YOUR SHEETS WITH LAVENDER. Place a single drop of lavender essential oil on your pillow or spray your sheets with lavender water before you turn

in. Studies at the University of Leicester in England and the Smell and Taste Research Center in Chicago found that this soothing botanical can work as well as sleeping pills for quelling insomnia and tension.

OR, INFUSE YOUR BEDROOM WITH JASMINE. Other studies suggest that a faint jasmine aroma may work better than lavender for helping you drift into peaceful sleep and stay more alert the following day. Try a scented oil stick or place a few drops of jasmine essential oil in a cup of hot water by your bed.

INTERVIEW YOUR PARTNER. Ask whether you stop breathing, jiggle your legs or wiggle your body while you sleep. Millions of people have obstructive sleep apnea, which causes brief interruptions in breathing all through the night. Over time, sleep apnea can raise your odds of developing high blood pressure and heart disease. Wiggly legs or thrashing in your sleep could be signs of restless legs syndrome or another movement disorder. If there are signs of a medical problem, it's probably time to get yourself referred to a sleep clinic.

KICK FLUFFY AND FIDO OUT OF YOUR SLEEPING ZONE. A 2002 study found that one in five pet owners sleep with their pets—or, more accurately, don't sleep, because their pets are on the bed or in the room. It could be that sneeze-provoking kitty dander, those midnight potty runs to the backyard or the patter of little poodle feet, but the study found something more incriminating; 21 percent of the dogs and seven percent of the cats snored!

After breaking my back nine years ago, I went through narcotics and painkillers like they were candy. When those stopped working, I combined chiropractics and physiotherapy. Soon after that, I was in such pain I could hardly take care of myself or my family. One day I went to the local pharmacy to pick up some painkillers and found a display of Lakota. I grabbed a box of Back Pain Triple Action and have never looked back! Thank you Lakota for giving me my life back!

Keri J., Abbotsford, BC

To Live a Sleep-Friendly Lifestyle

Take a walk after lunch, then read the paper on the patio. Exercise cuts stress, and getting exercise in the sun can help keep your body's circadian rhythms calibrated. You need about two hours of daily exposure to bright sunlight to help your body stay in sync. If you can't get outdoors, consider buying a light box—a fixture that radiates light that mimics the brightness and wavelengths of natural sunlight.

Or try tai chi on the lawn. In China, people rise at dawn to perform this series of ancient, gentle, dancelike movements in local parks. It's gained a lot of popularity in North America in the past few decades. The sleep bonus: Tai chi beat a low-impact exercise class for improving sleep in a study of 118 women and men ages 60 to 92 in one US-based study. People who did tai chi three times a week for six months fell asleep 18 minutes faster and slept 48 minutes longer each night than other exercisers.

Schedule worry-time during the day, in the kitchen! We're not kidding. If your mind is accustomed to revving up sleep-robbing anxiety in bed, retrain your brain by moving your worry session to another place and time. Try midmorning at the kitchen table—grab a notebook and pen, and take 10 minutes to write out your worries. This will clear your mind and break the association between bed, night, and worry. If thoughts keep cropping up, try keeping a pad by your bed and write your thoughts and worries down so that you can think about them later.

Make herbal tea or water your drink of choice after lunchtime. Nix coffee as well as other caffeine sources like chocolate; colas and other soft drinks; and black, green or white tea. People can become more sensitive to caffeine as they age, and even small amounts may keep you up late. Caffeine blocks a brain chemical called adenosine that helps us to feel drowsy and fall asleep, and the effect may last longer in older people, whose livers don't filter caffeine as effectively. Instead, sip some chamomile tea, which contains ingredients proven to calm the nervous system and, at bedtime, can help to induce sleep.

127

Instead of an evening cocktail, have a glass of wine with an early supper. Drinking before bed may help you fall asleep, but as the alcohol wears off you're likely to suffer light, easily broken sleep. If you enjoy a drink, have it at least a few hours before bed.

Drink more water during the day and less in the evening. If you have diabetes, an enlarged prostate, incontinence or even garden-variety "tiny bladder syndrome" (the bladder shrinks with age), you may get up frequently to urinate, then have trouble falling back to sleep. Try drinking more water during the day so you don't feel thirsty in the hour or so before you turn in. That way, you may ensure fewer slumber interruptions without risking dehydration.

To Soothe Yourself Before Bed

SOFTEN THE MOOD. An hour before bedtime, switch on the answering machine, turn off the television or computer, pull on your softest PJs, and cue up your favourite relaxing sounds. One study, whose subjects were women over 70, showed that those who listened to quiet music fell asleep faster and had fewer middle-of-the-night awakenings than before they started scheduling listening time. The best music? Whatever soothes you, whether it's Frank Sinatra, the Bee Gees, mellow jazz, or classical Debussy.

TRY PROGRESSIVE RELAXATION. Sit in a comfortable chair with both feet on the floor or lie on the sofa or your bed. Inhale and exhale naturally. After a few minutes, systematically tighten a muscle group as you inhale, then relax it completely as you exhale. Progressively tighten and loosen both feet, your lower legs and upper legs, then work your way up to your back, arms, neck, shoulders and even your face. Then continue to breathe naturally, feeling any remaining tension ebb away.

Next, combine progressive relaxation with music. A study had a group of women and men with sleep problems listen to soft, slow music while they performed a relaxation exercise. Their heartbeats and breathing rates slowed—and they slept better and longer. Music is one of the greatest natural mood-adjusters,

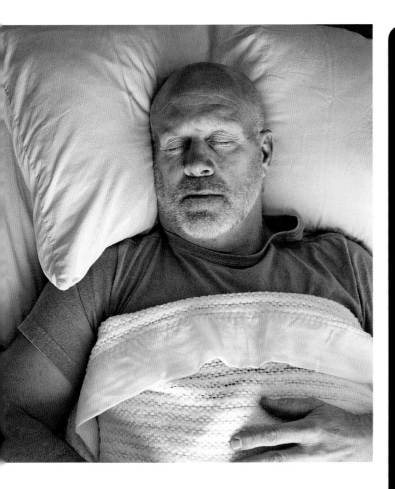

■ ■ ■ HOW TO FIX A SNORER

Bedding down with a chronic snorer is bad for your sleep and worse for your hearing. Loud snorers can generate 80 decibels of noise, as loud as rush-hour traffic, report researchers from Queen's University in Kingston—and their bed partners suffered hearing loss as a result. If you can't or won't sleep in separate rooms, try these remedies.

✔ Store-bought foam or silicone rubber earplugs can screen out about 32 decibels, which is often enough to let you fall asleep.

✔ An audiologist can make you custom-fitted ear plugs that filter more noise. They are expensive, but worth it.

✔ A white noise machine, which creates a steady, soothing layer of sound, can help mask the snoring.

✔ Present your partner with a box of anti-snoring strips, which work by pulling the nostrils open wider. A Swedish study found they significantly reduced snoring.

✔ If all else fails, ask your mate to make an appointment at a sleep centre. He or she may be a candidate for a test called polysomnography, which detects sleep apnea.

perfect for shifting you into the right gear and breaking you out of a stress tailspin.

SOAK IN A HOT BATH. Immersing yourself in warm water an hour or two before bed helps blood vessels dilate so that your body can release heat—part of the natural cooling down that precedes sleep.

POP A CHILL PILL. Take a supplement with 500 mg of calcium and 300 mg of magnesium. Magnesium is a natural sedative—even a slight shortfall can leave you lying in bed with your eyes wide open—while calcium helps regulate muscle movements. Getting plenty of both minerals can cut your risk of nighttime leg cramps. Take a supplement right before bed.

ENJOY A SLEEPYTIME SNACK. Have a handful of walnuts, a banana or a glass of milk—all rich sources of the sleep-inducing amino acid tryptophan. (Bananas also pack melatonin, the sleep hormone.) If incontinence or frequent bathroom visits aren't a problem, have a glass of water—but not juice. In one study, people who drank juice just before bed became extra alert due to the high sugar content of their drinks and needed an extra 20 to 30 minutes to fall asleep.

AVOID ANTACIDS. Take antacids right after dinner, not before bed. Antacids contain aluminum, which may interfere with sleep.

RECIPES
FOR PAIN RELIEF

There's a new frontier in medicine.
Researchers at the forefront say the key
to a longer, healthier life is an idea that's
radical yet simple: A healthy diet can
help heal what ails you. That is, putting
the right foods on your table and
steering clear of the wrong ones
can help you lose weight, bolster
your body's defenses against
disease and even slow
the aging process.

You Are What You Eat!

Highly processed foods are filled with chemicals, salt, and sweeteners. Natural foods like fresh fruits and vegetables have nutrients that work wonders on your body. The choice is easy. Make sure to eat 5 to 10 servings every day.

FOOD
FOR THOUGHT

The studies are piling up fast, and they're impossible to ignore: Choose wisely in your grocer's produce section, the data show, and you may spend less time in line at the pharmacy. Get to know your local fishmonger, and you may never meet a cardiologist. Start thinking about food in a novel way—as a kind of therapeutic and preventive medicine—and you may need a lot less of the kind of medicine that comes in pill form. A healthy diet that provides the right nutrients and keeps your weight down is the best way to prevent all kinds of health problems, and it's a great start for relieving body pain.

THE NEW FOOD FRONTIER

Perhaps you've already make occasional forays into this new frontier. Maybe you skipped steak and potato for salmon and a green salad. Or made breakfast toast with dense, chewy slices of whole-grain bread instead of nutrient-challenged white bread. Or snacked on a granola bar and finally switched to skim milk.

Taking simple measures such as these can have profound effects on your health and the way you feel. Sparing your body from a lot of unhealthy stuff, such as saturated fat and refined sugar, gets you off to a running start. On top of that, exciting new studies have confirmed healing wisdom known for thousands of years: The healthiest foods are packed with beneficial chemicals that can promote well-being and protect your body from the ravages of disease.

The idea of nutrition therapy goes all the way back to the beginning. "Let food be thy medicine and medicine be thy food," said Hippocrates, the ancient Greek who is widely regarded as the father of modern medicine. True to his word, Hippocrates prescribed a grocery list of edible cures. This chapter follows his example. You'll find lots of healthy recipes that please the palate and map a direct route to better health.

You probably already know that foods are good sources of vitamins, minerals and nutrients. But you may not realize that fruits, vegetables and other plant foods also contain thousands of newly discovered compounds, known as phytochemicals or phytonutrients, that scientists are still busy cataloguing. These chemicals provide flavour and colour, yet cutting-edge research suggests that many of them are also important—some scientists say essential—to your health.

In short, foods are nutritional powerhouses bursting with compounds that have health benefits. They have another advantage: You won't find many reports in the medical literature of broccoli overdoses, and the only way a banana can hurt you is if you slip on the peel—which isn't something you can say about those medicines you store in a cabinet over the bathroom sink.

Changing your diet won't guarantee that you'll never need drugs or get sick, of course. But, according to health experts, if North Americans ate the right foods (and exercised regularly), our health and weight would improve.

The recipes on the following pages are filled with lots of the right foods—foods that will help to lengthen your life, reduce belly fat and cool inflammation. So go ahead and enjoy these delicious, nutritious dishes.

Huevos Rancheros

SERVES 4

For a fun weekend brunch, serve this perfectly balanced Mexican-style dish of poached eggs, warm tortillas and a fresh tomato-and-chili salsa, topped with low-fat, grated cheese and sour cream, scallions and fresh cilantro.

PREP TIME 10 MINUTES + MARINATING   **COOK TIME** 10 MINUTES

SALSA

5 medium tomatoes, finely chopped

1 mild fresh red chili pepper, seeded and finely chopped

1 small red onion, finely chopped

1 small garlic clove, finely chopped

2 tbsp finely chopped fresh cilantro

1 tbsp olive oil

2–3 tbsp lime juice

Pepper

EGGS

4 x 25 cm whole wheat flour tortillas

1 tsp vinegar

4 eggs

60 g coarsely grated low-fat cheddar cheese

6 tbsp low-fat sour cream

4 scallions, chopped

Chopped fresh cilantro

Lime wedges

1 | To make salsa: Place chopped tomatoes in bowl and stir in chili, pepper, red onion, garlic and cilantro. Add oil and lime juice to taste. Set aside to marinate for about 30 minutes, then season lightly with pepper to taste.

2 | Preheat oven to 180°C (350°F). Wrap stacked-up tortillas in foil and put in oven to warm for 10 minutes.

3 | Meanwhile, half-fill large skillet with water. Heat until just starting to simmer, then reduce heat so water does not boil. Add vinegar. Break eggs into water, one at a time, and poach for 3 minutes. Toward end of cooking, spoon water over yolks. When cooked, remove eggs with slotted spoon and drain on plate lined with paper towels.

4 | Place warmed tortillas on plates. Spoon on some salsa, then put eggs on top and season with pepper to taste. Let everyone help themselves to remaining salsa, grated cheese, sour cream and scallions, plus chopped cilantro for sprinkling over the top and lime wedges for squeezing.

PER SERVING (WITH ½ CUP SALSA): 422 cals, 16 g fat (5 g sat), 200 mg chol, 51 g carbs, 3 g fibre, 19 g protein

Cherry-Oatmeal **Muffins**

Most store-bought muffins today should be ashamed—they're oversized, lacking in fibre, loaded with fat and sugar. These tender golden muffins are bundles of whole grains that will please your heart and your palate.

PREP TIME 15 MINUTES   **COOK TIME** 40 MINUTES

1 cup old-fashioned rolled oats
3/4 cup all-purpose flour
3/4 cup whole wheat flour
1/3 cup toasted wheat germ
1/3 cup plus 1 tbsp sugar
1 tsp baking powder
1/2 tsp baking soda
1/2 tsp salt
1 1/3 cups buttermilk
3 tbsp olive oil
1 large egg
1 tbsp grated orange zest
3/4 cup dried cherries, cranberries or raisins

1 | Preheat oven to 190°C (375°F). Line a muffin pan with paper liners. Toast oats on a cookie sheet until golden brown and crisp, about 10 minutes, stirring occasionally. Transfer to large bowl and let cool to room temperature.

2 | Add all-purpose flour, whole wheat flour, wheat germ, ⅓ cup of sugar, baking powder, baking soda and salt to oats, stirring to combine. Whisk together buttermilk, oil, egg and orange zest in small bowl until blended.

3 | Make a well in centre of dry ingredients and pour in buttermilk mixture. Stir with a wooden spoon just until dry ingredients are moistened. Fold in cherries.

4 | Spoon batter into muffin cups. Sprinkle top of each muffin with ¼ tsp sugar. Bake until golden brown and a toothpick inserted in centre of a muffin comes out clean, about 30 minutes. Remove muffins from pan to wire rack to cool.

PER SERVING: 194 cal, 5 g fat (1 g sat), 32 g carbs, 5 g protein, 4 g fibre, 16 mg chol, 230 mg sodium, 55 mg calcium

Whole-Grain **Pancakes** with Fresh Fruit and Yogourt MAKES 12

A combination of wheat germ, rolled oats and whole wheat flour make these delicious pancakes high in fibre, iron and B vitamins. Berries add lots of antioxidants to the mix.

PREP TIME 15 MINUTES   **COOK TIME** 25 MINUTES

1 cup whole wheat flour
1/4 cup rolled oats
1 tbsp toasted wheat germ
2 tbsp brown sugar
2 tsp baking powder
1/4 tsp salt
1 cup low-fat (1%) milk
1 1/4 cups plain nonfat yogourt
2 egg whites
2 cups raspberries or blueberries

1 | In large bowl, mix flour, oats, wheat germ, sugar, baking powder and salt. In another bowl, beat milk and ½ cup yogourt with egg whites. Add to flour mixture and stir quickly just to moisten dry ingredients.

2 | Spray non-stick skillet with cooking spray and heat until hot. *Do not use cooking spray near flame.* Measure ¼ cup of batter for each pancake and pour into hot skillet, making 3 or 4 pancakes at a time.

3 | When bubbles show on top, lift pancakes with a spatula. If browned underneath, flip over and cook until other side is golden brown.

4 | Transfer pancakes to heated platter. Serve with raspberries and remaining yogourt. If not serving at once, cover, and keep warm in low oven.

PER PANCAKE: 83 cal, 1 g fat (0 g sat), 16 g carbs, 4 g protein, 3 g fibre, 2 mg chol, 173 mg sodium, 84 mg calcium

Western **Omelette** SERVES 2

This omelette is made with the same peppers and onions called for in the original, but egg whites replace some of the whole eggs and red-skinned potatoes stand in for the ham—making a less salty, less fatty version.

PREP TIME 10 MINUTES   **COOK TIME** 18 MINUTES

1 medium red-skinned potato, chopped (about 3/4 cup)
1 medium onion, chopped
1/2 cup chopped green bell pepper
1/2 cup chopped red bell pepper
2 large eggs
3 large egg whites
1/2 tsp hot red pepper sauce
Pinch of salt
2 slices whole wheat bread, toasted

1 | Preheat oven to 200°C (400°F). Coat 20 cm ovenproof non-stick skillet with cooking spray and set over medium heat. Sauté potato until soft, about 5 minutes.

2 | Stir in onion and green and red peppers. Sauté until soft, about 5 minutes. Remove skillet from heat. Remove vegetables. Coat skillet again with cooking spray and return to heat.

3 | Meanwhile, whisk eggs, egg whites, red pepper sauce and salt in medium bowl. Pour into hot skillet. Cook until set on bottom, lifting up edge with heatproof spatula to let uncooked portion flow underneath.

4 | Spoon vegetables over half of omelette and fold omelette over filling. Transfer skillet to oven and bake until eggs are completely set, about 3 minutes. Cut omelette in half and serve with toast.

PER SERVING: 247 cal, 5 g fat (1 g sat), 34 g carbs, 17 g protein, 6 g fibre, 180 mg chol, 358 mg sodium, 63 mg calcium

Summer **Spinach Scramble**

Leafy green vegetables, such as kale and spinach, contain calcium, folic acid and fibre. These are key nutrients for a healthy heart.

PREP TIME 10 MINUTES   **COOK TIME** 10 MINUTES

2 cups shredded fresh spinach or kale, stems removed

5 large eggs

5 large egg whites

1/4 tsp ground cumin

1/4 tsp salt

1/3 cup chopped lean ham

2 scallions, trimmed and thinly sliced

1 | Cook spinach in a large pot of boiling salted water until tender, 3 to 5 minutes. Drain. Rinse under cold water. Drain well.

2 | Whisk eggs, egg whites, cumin and salt in a large bowl.

3 | Coat a large non-stick skillet with non-stick cooking spray. Heat over medium heat. Add egg mixture; stir until eggs start to thicken slightly, 2 to 3 minutes. Stir in spinach, ham and scallion. Cook, stirring occasionally, until eggs are soft-scrambled, 2 to 3 minutes.

PER SERVING: 145 cals, 15 g protein, 7 g fat (2 g sat), 270 mg chol, 5 g carbs, 1 g fibre, 385 mg sodium

Grilled Turkey **Caesar Salad**

SERVES 4

Caeser salad is a mouth-watering classic that has a bad reputation, health-wise. This tasty version uses the traditional romaine, fresh lemon and cheese, but skips the egg and uses less oil.

PREP TIME 20 MINUTES   **COOK TIME** 10 MINUTES

2 garlic cloves, peeled

2 anchovy fillets, rinsed and minced (optional)

3 tbsp fresh lemon juice

2 tbsp non-fat sour cream

1 tbsp olive oil

500 g boneless, skinless turkey breast

1/4 tsp salt

1/2 tsp pepper

8 cups torn romaine lettuce

1 cup garlic-flavoured croutons

30 g chunk Parmesan cheese

1 | Preheat grill or broiler. With side of chef's knife, mash garlic cloves and anchovies (if using) until a paste forms. Put garlic paste, lemon juice, sour cream and oil into jar with tight-fitting lid and shake until blended.

2 | Sprinkle turkey with salt and pepper and lightly coat with non-stick cooking spray. Grill until cooked through, 4 to 5 minutes on each side. Slice turkey across grain 1 cm thick.

3 | Toss together romaine, croutons and turkey until mixed. Divide evenly among plates. Shave strips of Parmesan with a vegetable peeler evenly over salads. Shake dressing to mix. Serve dressing on the side.

PER SERVING: 288 cal, 8 g fat (2 g sat), 13 g carbs, 40 g protein, 3 g fibre, 102 mg chol, 400 mg sodium, 167 mg calcium

Radiatore **Salad Giardiniera**

SERVES 6

This pasta salad takes its name from the Italian word meaning garden—and indeed the freshest picks from the vegetable patch provide it with a wonderful mix of colours, flavours and nutrients. Serve as a supper side dish, or double the recipe to tote to a picnic or potluck.

PREP TIME 30 MINUTES + MARINATING   **COOK TIME** 25 MINUTES

¾ tsp salt

1/2 tsp pepper

3 cups broccoli florets

1 large red bell pepper, cut into thin strips

1 medium yellow squash, thinly sliced

1 small red onion, chopped

3 cups radiatore, fusilli or rotini pasta

1 cup yellow or red grape tomatoes, halved

2/3 cup cider vinegar

1/4 cup extra-virgin olive oil

3/4 cup finely chopped parsley

2 tbsp finely chopped fresh dill

1 | Set out large bowl of ice water. Bring a large pot of water, ¼ tsp salt, and ¼ tsp pepper to a boil over high heat. Put broccoli, red pepper, squash, and onion in perforated liner or large strainer. Blanch just until colours brighten, about 2 minutes. Quickly transfer to colander; plunge into ice water.

2 | Cook pasta in the boiling water according to package directions. Rinse with cold water and drain; put in large pasta bowl. Drain vegetables and add to pasta; add tomatoes and toss.

3 | Put vinegar, oil, parsley, dill and remaining salt and pepper in jar with tight-fitting lid and shake until combined. Pour over salad and toss to coat. Cover and refrigerate at least 8 hours, or overnight. Toss again before serving.

PER SERVING: 303 cal, 11 g fat (1 g sat), 43 g carbs, 8 g protein, 7 g fibre, 0 mg chol, 318 mg sodium, 60 mg calcium

Cantaloupe Salad with Raspberry Vinaigrette

SERVES 4

This sweet salad supplies vitamin C, soluble fibre and several potent antioxidants. But the real focus is on its fabulous flavour—fragrant fruits are tossed with a spicy raspberry-balsamic dressing for a pleasing tang, and pumpkin seeds add a toasty, nutlike taste.

PREP TIME 10 MINUTES   **COOK TIME** 5 MINUTES

1 tbsp hulled pumpkin seeds

1/4 cup seedless raspberry all-fruit spread

1 tbsp balsamic vinegar

2 tsp fresh lemon juice

1/4 tsp cinnamon

1/4 tsp pepper

1 large cantaloupe, cut into wedges

1 cup blueberries

1 | Toast pumpkin seeds in small, heavy skillet over medium heat until they begin to pop, about 5 minutes. Set aside to cool.

2 | Whisk together raspberry spread, vinegar, lemon juice, cinnamon and pepper in large bowl.

3 | Add cantaloupe and blueberries to bowl and toss to combine. Serve salad sprinkled with toasted pumpkin seeds.

PER SERVING: 144 cal, 2 g fat (0 g sat), 33 g carbs, 3 g protein, 3 g fibre, 0 mg chol, 34 mg sodium, 23 mg calcium

Barley, Black Bean and **Avocado Salad**   SERVES 4

We think of barley as a soup ingredient, but it's also a delicious "dinner grain," served hot or cold. Barley is an excellent source of cholesterol-lowering soluble fibre and, when combined with black beans, adds up to a salad that could hardly be more healthy.

PREP TIME 10 MINUTES   **COOK TIME** 20 MINUTES

1 cup carrot juice

1/2 tsp thyme

1/8 tsp cayenne

1/2 cup quick-cooking barley

3 tbsp fresh lemon juice

1 tbsp olive oil

1 can (540 mL) black beans, rinsed and drained

1 cup diced tomatoes

1/2 cup diced avocado

1 | Combine carrot juice, thyme, salt and cayenne in medium pot. Bring to a boil over medium heat, add barley, and reduce to a simmer. Cover and cook until barley is tender, about 15 minutes.

2 | Meanwhile, whisk together lemon juice and oil in large bowl. Transfer barley and any liquid remaining in pot to bowl with lemon-juice mixture; toss to coat.

3 | Add beans and tomatoes, and toss to combine. Add avocado and gently toss. Serve at room temperature or chilled. For best flavour, remove from the refrigerator 20 minutes before serving.

PER SERVING: 272 cal, 7 g fat (1 g sat), 43 g carbs, 9 g protein, 10 g fibre, 0 mg chol, 448 mg sodium, 66 mg calcium

White Bean, Bacon and **Wilted Spinach Salad**

SERVES 6

We love spinach when it's neither entirely raw nor cooked but just wilted by a warm dressing. In the fight to purge processed food, this salad is a real winner, with lean turkey bacon, beans and plenty of vitamin-rich vegetables.

PREP TIME 15 MINUTES   **COOK TIME** 15 MINUTES

1 tbsp olive oil

3 slices turkey bacon, cut crosswise into 1 cm wide strips

375 g fresh shiitake mushrooms, stems removed and caps thinly sliced

1 can (540 mL) white beans, rinsed and drained

1/2 cup low-sodium mixed vegetable juice

2 tbsp red-wine vinegar

1 tbsp Dijon mustard

Pinch salt

1/4 tsp black pepper

12 cups spinach leaves

1 yellow bell pepper, cut into small squares

1 large red onion, halved and thinly sliced

1 | Heat oil in large non-stick skillet over medium heat. Add bacon and cook until crisp, about 5 minutes. With slotted spoon, transfer bacon to paper towels to drain.

2 | Add shiitake mushrooms to skillet and cook until tender, about 5 minutes. Add beans and cook until heated through, about 3 minutes.

3 | Whisk vegetable juice, vinegar, mustard, salt and black pepper in small bowl. Add to mushroom mixture in skillet and bring to a boil.

4 | Meanwhile, combine spinach, bell pepper, red onion and bacon in large bowl. Add hot mushroom mixture to bowl and toss to combine.

PER SERVING: 171 cal, 5 g fat (1 g sat), 23 g carbs, 10 g protein, 7 g fibre, 13 mg chol, 452 mg sodium, 112 mg calcium

Fruit Boats with Orange-Balsamic Glaze

SERVES 4

Fresh melon boats, carved in only minutes and overflowing with tart kiwis, ripe berries and juicy melon balls, are the perfect refresher. They're low in calories and have only one gram of fat per serving.

PREP TIME 20 MINUTES   **COOK TIME** 5 MINUTES

1/4 cup balsamic vinegar

1/4 tsp grated orange zest

2 tbsp fresh orange juice

2 tsp brown sugar

I large cantaloupe

2 cups strawberries, hulled and quartered

I cup blueberries

I cup raspberries

2 kiwis, peeled, halved, and cut into thin wedges

1 | Combine vinegar, orange zest, orange juice and brown sugar in microwavable dish. Microwave on high until syrupy, 2 to 3 minutes. Or, cook over medium-high heat in a small pot, 4 to 5 minutes. Set glaze aside.

2 | Make cantaloupe boats: Cut cantaloupe lengthwise in half, and cut each half in half again, crosswise to form triangular "boats." Discard the seeds. Scoop out cantaloupe with a melon baller, putting the balls in a large bowl, and leaving a thin layer of flesh on the rind.

3 | Put strawberries, blueberries, raspberries and kiwi into the bowl with the melon balls.

4 | Drizzle fruit with glaze. Toss to coat evenly. Spoon into cantaloupe boats and serve immediately.

PER SERVING: 171 cal, 1 g fat (0 g sat), 42 g carbs, 3 g protein, 7 g fibre, 0 mg chol, 40 mg sodium, 53 mg calcium

Crab and Grapefruit Salad

SERVES 4

Crab and grapefruit are surprisingly great partners for a quick, no-cook salad posh enough for company and low-fat and high-protein enough for the most fitness-conscious member of the family.

PREP TIME 25 MINUTES   **COOK TIME** 0 MINUTES

4 grapefruits

2 tbsp low-fat mayonnaise

I tbsp finely chopped mango chutney

2 tsp Dijon mustard

I tsp sesame oil

1/8 tsp salt

1/8 tsp pepper

375 g lump crabmeat, picked over to remove any cartilage

2 cups watercress, tough stems trimmed

I Belgian endive, cut crosswise into I cm wide strips

I head Bibb or Boston lettuce, separated into leaves

1 | With small paring knife, peel grapefruit. Working over a large bowl to catch juice, separate grapefruit sections from membranes; reserve any juice that collects in bowl.

2 | In medium bowl, whisk together mayonnaise, chutney, mustard, sesame oil, salt, pepper and 3 tbsp reserved grapefruit juice.

3 | Add crabmeat, tossing to combine. Add watercress, endive and grapefruit sections, and toss. Serve salad on a bed of Bibb lettuce.

PER SERVING: 236 cal, 5 g fat (1 g sat), 31 g carbs, 21 g protein, 5 g fibre, 63 mg chol, 433 mg sodium, 156 mg calcium

Roast Salmon with Red Potato Salad

SERVES 4

This elegant entrée is what the French would call a salade composée, a salad whose elements are arranged separately on the plate. Here, fresh salmon shares the spotlight with a light potato salad and a healthy helping of greens.

PREP TIME 30 MINUTES   **COOK TIME** 30 MINUTES

375 g salmon fillet (in one piece)

1/4 tsp salt

680 g small red-skinned potatoes, unpeeled

3 shallots, minced

1/3 cup white vinegar

2 tbsp Dijon mustard

1/2 tsp pepper

1/2 cup minced fresh dill

2 cups radishes, cut into thin matchsticks

6 cups mixed salad greens

1 | Preheat oven to 230°C (450°F). Place salmon skin-side down in baking dish and sprinkle with ⅛ tsp of salt. Roast until just cooked through, 10 to 15 minutes. Let cool to room temperature. Remove skin.

2 | Meanwhile, in large pot of boiling water, cook potatoes until fork-tender, about 20 minutes. Drain potatoes and set aside. When cool enough to handle, slice potatoes crosswise.

3 | Combine remaining ⅛ tsp salt, shallots, vinegar, mustard and pepper in large bowl. Add warm potatoes to bowl with shallot mixture, tossing to combine.

4 | Just before serving, add dill and radishes to potatoes, and toss to combine. Slice salmon on the diagonal into 8 pieces. Arrange potato salad, salmon and greens on each plate.

PER SERVING: 312 cal, 10 g fat (2 g sat), 35 g carbs, 19 g protein, 5 g fibre, 39 mg chol, 383 mg sodium, 75 mg calcium

Grilled **Portobello Mushroom Sandwiches** SERVES 4

If you have yet to explore the cooking possibilities of portobellos, get ready for a treat. These meaty-textured mushrooms are like a juicy slice of sirloin when grilled, but they're virtually fat-free.

PREP TIME 15 MINUTES   **COOK TIME** 15 MINUTES

2 tbsp water

1 tbsp olive oil

Pinch salt

1/2 tsp pepper

4 large portobello mushrooms
(10 cm diameter)

4 kaiser rolls

2 garlic cloves, peeled and halved

2 tsp grainy mustard

2 cups arugula leaves

4 plum tomatoes, thickly sliced

30 g Parmesan cheese, in a chunk

1 | Preheat grill or broiler. In small bowl, whisk together water, oil, salt, and pepper. Remove stems from mushrooms. Brush tops of mushrooms with olive-oil mixture. Grill mushrooms until tender, about 7 minutes per side.

2 | Cut rolls in half horizontally. Place rolls on grill or under broiler, cut side down, and grill until just toasted, about 1 minute. Rub toasted faces of rolls with garlic; discard garlic.

3 | Brush rolls with mustard. Top with arugula, sliced tomatoes and mushrooms. Use a vegetable peeler to shave off curls of Parmesan. Top mushrooms with Parmesan and tops of rolls.

PER SERVING: 266 cal, 8 g fat (2 g sat), 38 g carbs, 11 g protein, 3 g fibre, 6 mg chol, 450 mg sodium, 176 mg calcium

Tuna Provençale on a Baguette

SERVES 4

Flavourful, savoury, and full of heart-smart nutrients, this French-inspired sandwich is sure to become a favourite. It's a variation of the classic pan bagnat, a baguette bursting with tuna, olives and garden-fresh veggies.

PREP TIME 20 MINUTES + STANDING   **COOK TIME** 0 MINUTES

2 large tomatoes, peeled and chopped

5 black olives, pitted and finely chopped

1/8 tsp salt

1 baguette (175 g, about 60 cm long)

1 1/2 tbsp extra-virgin olive oil

1 large onion

1 large green bell pepper

2 cans (170 g each) no-salt water-packed albacore tuna, drained

2 tbsp white-wine vinegar

2 garlic cloves, minced

1/4 tsp anchovy paste

1 | Mix tomatoes, olives and salt in medium bowl then let stand until juicy, about 15 minutes.

2 | Meanwhile, cut bread almost in half, lengthwise (do not slice completely through). Open like a book, being careful not to separate bread. Pull out about ½ cup of the crumb (soft centre) with your hands. Using ½ tbsp oil, brush cut sides of bread. Then spread on tomato mixture and any juices that have collected in bowl.

3 | Cut onion in half through stem end, then cut crosswise into thin semicircles. Cut green pepper in half, and then cut crosswise into thin semicircles. Layer onion, green pepper and tuna over tomato mixture. Whisk vinegar, garlic, anchovy paste and remaining oil in small bowl. Drizzle over tuna.

4 | Wrap stuffed loaf tightly in plastic wrap. Weigh it down with heavy skillet and let stand at room temperature until ingredients have soaked into bread, about 30 minutes. Cut diagonally into 4 equal sandwiches.

PER SERVING: 324 cal, 9 g fat (1 g sat), 35 g carbs, 27 g protein, 4 g fibre, 36 mg chol, 455 mg sodium, 42 mg calcium

Chunky Gazpacho with Garlic Croutons

SERVES 4

Whirl up this traditional soup from Andalusia, in southern Spain. A delicious concoction of tomatoes, garden-sweet peppers, cool cucumbers, a hint of garlic—all high in what's good for you and low in fat and calories.

PREP TIME 20 MINUTES   **COOK TIME** 15 MINUTES + CHILLING

2 garlic cloves, peeled

4 slices French bread (2.5 cm thick)

1 tsp pepper

1/4 tsp salt

1/2 cup coarsely chopped red onion

3 cups (750 mL) no-salt-added tomatoes

1/4 cup seasoned dry bread crumbs

1/4 cup chopped parsley

3 tbsp red-wine vinegar

1 tbsp olive oil

2 medium cucumbers, peeled and chopped

2 medium green bell peppers, chopped

2 medium red bell peppers, chopped

1 | Preheat oven to 180°C (350°F). Cut 1 garlic clove in half and rub cut sides on inside of large bowl and on both sides of bread slices. Tear bread into 2.5 cm pieces. Put in the large bowl and lightly coat with non-stick cooking spray. Sprinkle with ½ tsp pepper and ¼ tsp salt. Toss to coat and transfer to a baking sheet. Bake croutons until golden, about 15 minutes. Cool completely.

2 | Pulse onion and remaining garlic in food processor or blender until finely chopped. Add half of tomatoes and all their juice. Purée. Add bread crumbs, parsley, vinegar, oil and remaining pepper and salt. Process just until blended and pour into large nonreactive bowl.

3 | Chop remaining tomatoes. Stir into tomato mixture with half of chopped cucumbers and half of green and red peppers. Refrigerate until chilled, about 1 hour. Ladle into bowls and top with remaining cucumber, green and red peppers and croutons.

PER SERVING: 251 cal, 5 g fat (1 g sat), 44 g carbs, 9 g protein, 6 g fibre, 0 mg chol, 474 mg sodium, 104 mg calcium

Chilled Cream of **Zucchini Soup**

SERVES 8

This lovely green soup makes a delightful summer lunch or a beautiful beginning to a summer dinner. It's kept low-fat and good for you by using non-fat yogourt, low-fat milk and a minimum of oil.

PREP TIME 20 MINUTES   **COOK TIME** 25 MINUTES

1 tbsp olive oil

1 large onion, coarsely chopped

2 cloves garlic, finely chopped

13/4 cups vegetable stock

1 cup all-purpose potatoes, peeled and diced

500 g zucchini, trimmed and thinly sliced

1 1/2 cups parsley leaves

1 cup low-fat (1%) milk

1/8 tsp salt

1/8 tsp pepper

1 cup non-fat plain yogourt

1 | In large pot, heat oil over moderate heat. Add onion and garlic, then about ¼ cup stock. Sauté until softened but not browned. Add potatoes and stir to coat. Pour in remaining stock and bring to a boil.

2 | Add zucchini and simmer, partially covered, until all vegetables are very tender, about 10 minutes.

3 | Remove from heat and stir in parsley. Strain soup into large bowl; purée vegetables in a blender or food processor until very smooth.

4 | Stir purée into stock and allow to cool. Stir in milk, salt and pepper then chill soup until ready to serve. Before serving, spoon a large spoonful of yogourt on top of each bowl of soup. With the tip of the spoon, gently draw yogourt out in a spiral to make a swirl.

PER SERVING (1 CUP): 103 cal, 3 g fat (1 g sat), 17 g carbs, 5 g protein, 2 g fibre, 2 mg chol, 287 mg sodium, 119 mg calcium

Peach Soup with Almonds

SERVES 4

Although this thick creamy soup tastes like a dessert, it's actually low-calorie, low-fat, rich in fibre and vitamins and contains 7 grams of protein per serving. Kids and adults alike will love this cold fruit soup as part of a summer meal.

PREP TIME 20 MINUTES + CHILLING   **COOK TIME** 20 MINUTES

750 g (2 or 3) fresh peaches or 600 g frozen and thawed

Zest of 1 lemon, cut in wide strips

2 tbsp sugar

2 cups buttermilk or low-fat (1%) milk

Pinch of ground nutmeg

1 cup peach nectar

1/4 cup sliced almonds

1 | Bring large pot of water to a boil. Add a few peaches and return to a boil. Transfer peaches to a bowl of cold water. When cool enough, peel peaches with a small knife and cut into chunks; discard pits. Poach and peel remaining peaches, working in batches.

2 | Bring 1 cup water, lemon zest and sugar to a boil, then add peaches. Cover and simmer, stirring occasionally, until very soft, 5 to 8 minutes. Remove pot from heat; discard lemon zest.

3 | Pour 1 cup buttermilk into a food processor or blender. Reserving peach syrup, add peaches and purée. Transfer to a large bowl. Add remaining buttermilk, nutmeg and peach nectar. Stir in reserved syrup. Cover and refrigerate for at least 1 hour.

4 | Preheat oven to 180°C (350°F). Spread almonds on a cookie sheet; toast until golden, about 10 minutes. Cool almonds and sprinkle on soup before serving.

PER SERVING (1 CUP): 209 cal, 5 g fat (1 g sat), 40 g carbs, 7 g protein, 4 g fibre, 5 mg chol, 133 mg sodium, 170 mg calcium

Shrimp **Chowder**

SERVES 4

Why should clams have all the fun? Shrimp also go well in a classic chowder broth, made with tomatoes, corn and chunks of potato. Fennel seed and orange zest add a wonderful extra layer of flavour.

PREP TIME 15 MINUTES   **COOK TIME** 20 MINUTES

2 tsp olive oil

1 medium onion, finely chopped

4 cloves garlic, minced

375 g potatoes, diced

1 cup bottled clam juice

1 cup water

1/2 tsp fennel seed

1 tsp grated orange zest

1 can (540 mL) no-salt stewed tomatoes, chopped with their juice

Pinch salt

1/2 tsp hot red pepper sauce

250 g medium shrimp, peeled, deveined, and cut into bite-size pieces

1/2 cup frozen corn kernels

1 | Heat oil in large non-stick pot over medium heat. Add onion and garlic to pot and cook, stirring frequently, until onion is softened, about 7 minutes.

2 | Stir in potatoes, clam juice, water, fennel seed and orange zest. Bring to a boil. Reduce to a simmer, cover and cook until potatoes are almost tender, about 10 minutes.

3 | Stir in tomatoes, salt and hot pepper sauce. Return to a boil. Add shrimp and corn. Cover and cook until shrimp are just opaque and corn is hot, about 3 minutes.

PER SERVING: 191 cal, 3 g fat (0 g sat), 29 g carbs, 11 g protein, 5 g fibre, 73 mg chol, 495 mg sodium, 109 mg calcium

Mexican **Shrimp Sauté**

SERVES 4

This delectable dish features everybody's favourite shellfish, snappily seasoned with turmeric and ground coriander, and sautéed with corn and peppers. Shrimp is a great source of protein that is impressively low in saturated fat.

PREP TIME 15 MINUTES   **COOK TIME** 10 MINUTES

2 tsp olive oil

1 green bell pepper, cut into thin strips

1 jalapeño, seeded and minced

3 cloves garlic, minced

1500 g large shrimp, peeled and deveined

2 tsp turmeric

3/4 tsp ground coriander

1 package (300 g) frozen corn kernels, thawed

1/4 cup chopped cilantro

1 tbsp fresh lime juice

1 | Heat oil in large non-stick skillet over medium heat. Add bell pepper, jalapeño and garlic and cook until bell pepper is tender, about 5 minutes.

2 | Add shrimp. Sprinkle with turmeric and coriander and toss to combine. Add corn and cook until shrimp are cooked through and corn is tender, about 3 minutes.

3 | Stir in cilantro and lime juice.

PER SERVING: 164 cal, 4 g fat (0 g sat), 18 g carbs, 15 g protein, 3 g fibre, 107 mg chol, 552 mg sodium, 66 mg calcium

Greek-Style **Shrimp Skillet**

This quick dish is packed with vitamin C—thanks to the tomatoes and bell peppers—and protein from the shrimp. Rinse the black olives before adding them if you're watching your sodium intake.

PREP TIME 10 MINUTES   **COOK TIME** 20 MINUTES

500 g medium shrimp, peeled and deAttveined

3 cloves garlic, minced

1 medium onion, chopped

1 can (540 mL) low-sodium diced tomatoes

1 tsp dried oregano

12 black olives, halved and pitted

1 large yellow or green pepper, diced

Small handful fresh parsley, chopped

1/2 cup crumbled feta

1 tbsp olive oil

1 | Pour olive oil into large skillet over medium-high heat. Stir-fry onion and pepper until tender-crisp, about 2 to 3 minutes. Add garlic and stir for 1 more minute.

2 | Add tomatoes, oregano and olives and mix thoroughly. Bring to a boil, reduce heat, cover and simmer for 5 minutes.

3 | Add shrimp and cook, uncovered, until done, about 3 to 5 minutes. Divide equally among 4 bowls. Sprinkle feta and parsley on top and garnish with a lemon slice, if desired. Serve with a crusty whole-grain or multi-grain bread or dinner roll.

PER SERVING: 276 cals, 30 g protein, 11 g total fat (4 g sat), 13 g carbs, 2 g fibre, 207 mg chol, 526 mg sodium

Lemon-Glazed **Sole Fillets**

SERVES 4

Here's a smart dinner solution—grill fish fillets on top of fresh lemon slices, then top with a light citrus sauce. It's a tasty way to get more seafood into your diet. And best of all, it's ready in less than 25 minutes.

PREP TIME 15 MINUTES   **COOK TIME** 8 MINUTES

5 large lemons

6 large fresh basil leaves

1 tbsp olive oil

1 garlic clove, minced

4 sole fillets (125 g each), or any firm white fish, fresh or frozen and thawed

1/4 tsp salt

1/4 tsp pepper

1/2 cup reduced-sodium chicken broth

1 1/2 tsp cornstarch

2 tsp sugar

1 | Roll 1 lemon on countertop to get juice flowing; grate zest from this lemon and squeeze juice. Cut 3 lemons into twelve 5 mm slices. Slice remaining lemon into 8 wedges. Make basil chiffonade: Stack basil leaves and roll up tightly (to resemble a cigar). Slice across the roll, making cuts about 1 mm apart. Set aside for garnish. Heat oil in small pot over medium heat. Add garlic and cook until golden, about 2 minutes. Whisk in lemon juice then remove from heat.

2 | Coat grill rack or broiler pan with non-stick cooking spray. Preheat grill to medium or preheat broiler. Lightly brush both sides of fish with garlic mixture and sprinkle with salt and pepper. Place 3 lemon slices on grill or broiler pan and put 1 fish fillet on top. Repeat with remaining lemon slices and fish. Grill or broil fish, without turning, until just opaque throughout, about 6 minutes. Cook lemon wedges alongside until browned, about 2 minutes on each side.

3 | Meanwhile, blend broth and cornstarch in a cup until smooth. Whisk cornstarch mixture, sugar and ¼ tsp lemon zest into remaining garlic mixture. Bring to a boil over medium-high heat and cook until sauce thickens, about 1 minute.

4 | Transfer fish to plates, lemon slices down. Spoon sauce over fish and sprinkle with basil chiffonade and remaining lemon zest. Garnish with grilled lemon wedges.

PER SERVING: 150 cal, 6 g fat (1 g sat), 10 g carbs, 15 g protein, 1 g fibre, 51 mg chol, 497 mg sodium, 55 mg calcium

Baked Fish on a Bed of Broccoli, Corn, and Red Pepper SERVES 4

Baking fish fillets on top of cut fresh vegetables creates an easy and nutritious one-dish meal that is high in protein, vitamins and minerals but low in fat and calories. You can change the vegetables depending on what is in season.

PREP TIME 15 MINUTES   **COOK TIME** 50 MINUTES

4 sole fillets (125-175 g each), or any firm white fish, fresh or frozen and thawed

2 tbsp fat-free Italian dressing

1 tbsp fine dry plain bread crumbs

1 tbsp grated Parmesan cheese

1/4 tsp paprika

1 tbsp olive oil

2 cups broccoli florets

1 cup fresh or frozen corn kernels, thawed

1 sweet red pepper, cut into thin strips

1 small red onion, thinly sliced

2 tbsp chopped parsley

1 tbsp chopped fresh basil

Pinch salt and pepper

1 | Place fish in shallow baking dish and brush lightly with Italian dressing. Cover and refrigerate. In small bowl, combine bread crumbs with Parmesan cheese and paprika until blended.

2 | Preheat oven to 220°C (425°F). Brush 4 individual or one ovenproof dish with oil. In a large bowl, combine broccoli, corn, red pepper, onion, parsley, basil, salt and pepper.

3 | Divide vegetable mixture evenly among dishes. Cover with aluminum foil and bake until vegetables are just tender, about 35 to 40 minutes.

4 | Uncover dishes and top vegetables with fish fillets. Cover again and bake until fish is barely cooked and still moist in thickest part, about 8 to 10 minutes. Uncover dishes, sprinkle with bread crumb mixture, and continue to bake, uncovered, until topping is golden, about 2 to 3 minutes.

PER SERVING: 185 cal, 7 g fat (1 g sat), 14 g carbs, 18 g protein, 3 g fibre, 52 mg chol, 466 mg sodium, 71 mg calcium

Italian Sausage with Lentil Salad

SERVES 4

Who on earth makes homemade sausage? Maybe you—because you won't find such health-smart sausage in the supermarket, and it takes only minutes to prepare. Lentils are a healthy companion to Italian sausage.

PREP TIME 15 MINUTES   **COOK TIME** 40 MINUTES + COOLING

2/3 cup lentils

1 small onion, finely chopped

2 carrots, finely chopped

2 tbsp tomato paste

1/4 tsp salt

2 cups water

3 tbsp fresh lemon juice

4 tsp Dijon mustard

1 tbsp olive oil

375 g well-trimmed pork tenderloin, cut into 1 cm cubes

1/2 cup fresh basil leaves

2 slices whole-grain sandwich bread, crumbled

1/4 cup low-fat (1%) milk

2 tbsp grated Parmesan

1 | Combine lentils, onion, carrots, tomato paste, 1/8 tsp salt and water in large pot. Bring to a boil over medium heat. Reduce to a simmer, cover and cook until lentils are tender, about 30 minutes. Drain off any remaining liquid.

2 | Whisk together lemon juice, mustard and olive oil in large bowl. Add warm lentils and toss to combine. Cool to room temperature, then refrigerate lentil salad until serving time, up to a day ahead.

3 | Meanwhile, combine remaining 1/8 tsp salt, pork and basil in food processor and pulse until pork is coarsely ground and ingredients are well combined. Transfer to medium bowl. Add bread, milk and Parmesan; mix to combine. Divide mixture into 8 portions and mold into 4 to 10 cm long sausage shapes. (No casings are used. If make a day ahead, refrigerate.)

4 | Preheat broiler. Broil sausages 10 cm from heat until lightly browned and cooked through, about 7 minutes, turning them over halfway through cooking. Slice sausages and serve on bed of lentil salad.

PER SERVING: 301 cal, 7 g fat (2 g sat), 33 g carbs, 28 g protein, 9 g fibre, 58 mg chol, 494 mg sodium, 138 mg calcium

Grilled Chicken and Red Pepper **Pizzas**

Rounds of Middle-Eastern "pocket bread," or pita, make a perfect base for mini-pizzas topped with grilled chicken, feta cheese, red onions and bell peppers. Because feta is so flavourful, you only need a small amount.

PREP TIME 20 MINUTES   **COOK TIME** 25 MINUTES

250 g skinless, boneless chicken breast

1/8 tsp salt

1/8 tsp black pepper

2 medium red onions, cut into thick rings

2 red bell peppers, cut lengthwise into flat panels

4 whole wheat pita breads (10 cm)

60 g feta cheese, crumbled (scant 1/2 cup)

3 tbsp chopped fresh mint

1 | Spray grill rack or broiler pan with non-stick cooking spray. Preheat grill to medium or turn on broiler. Sprinkle chicken with salt and black pepper. Grill until just cooked through, about 4 minutes per side. When chicken is cool enough to handle, pull into shreds.

2 | Place onions and bell pepper pieces, skin side down, on grill or under broiler. Cook until onions are tender and peppers are charred, about 10 minutes. When cool enough to handle, peel peppers and thickly slice.

3 | Top pitas with onion rings, peppers, shredded chicken and feta. Grill until pita is crisp, about 4 minutes. Sprinkle mint over tops.

PER SERVING: 213 cal, 5 g fat (3 g sat), 25 g carbs, 18 g protein, 4 g fibre, 49 mg chol, 489 mg sodium, 109 mg calcium

Savoury **Chicken Parcels**

SERVES 4

This colourful dish shows how easy it can be to make a healthy entrée without sacrificing flavour—or slaving over a hot stove. Foil pouches bake for 30 minutes, and that's it: a super-healthy, nutrient-rich supper is ready!

PREP TIME 15 MINUTES   **COOK TIME** 30 MINUTES

4 boneless, skinless chicken breast halves (680 g)

120 g mushrooms, sliced

2 carrots, cut into 4 cm matchsticks

2 zucchini, cut into 4 cm matchsticks

1 tbsp olive oil

1 tbsp chopped basil

2 tbsp lemon juice

1/8 tsp salt

1/8 tsp pepper

1 | Preheat oven to 190°C (375°F). Cut 4 sheets of aluminum foil, about 30 cm square. Place 1 chicken breast on each; arrange a quarter of vegetables on top.

2 | Prepare seasoning mixture: In small bowl, whisk together oil, chopped basil, lemon juice, salt and pepper until combined. Spoon a quarter of seasoning mixture evenly over each chicken and vegetable mound.

3 | With chicken and vegetable mound crosswise on foil, fold 2 sides over both ends of chicken breast. Fold nearest edge over chicken; then fold farthest edge towards you over whole parcel so that the end folds underneath.

4 | Bake parcels in baking dish for about 30 minutes. Unwrap each parcel and transfer chicken, vegetables and their juices to plates.

PER SERVING: 265 cal, 8 g fat (2 g sat), 8 g carbs, 39 g protein, 2 g fibre, 109 mg chol, 330 mg sodium, 37 mg calcium

Tandoori **Chicken**

SERVES 4

Spices are turning out to be surprising sources of heart-protecting phytochemicals—good reason to be generous with the seasoning in the marinade for this classic Indian chicken dish, cooked under the broiler in less than 10 minutes.

PREP TIME 10 MINUTES + MARINATING   **COOK TIME** 10 MINUTES

1/2 cup plain low-fat yogourt

1 1/2 tbsp chili powder

1 tbsp coriander

2 tsp cumin

3/4 tsp ground ginger

1/2 tsp salt

1/2 tsp pepper

1/2 tsp cinnamon

3 cloves garlic, peeled

4 skinless, boneless chicken breast halves (150 g each)

1/4 cup golden raisins

2 tbsp slivered almonds, toasted

1 | Combine yogourt, chili powder, coriander, cumin, ginger, salt, pepper, cinnamon and garlic in a blender and purée until smooth.

2 | With a chef's knife, make several shallow slits on one side of each chicken breast half. Place in a shallow plastic container that will hold chicken in a single layer. Pour yogourt mixture over chicken, turning to coat well. Cover and refrigerate at least 6 hours or up to overnight.

3 | Preheat broiler. Spray broiler pan with non-stick cooking spray. Reserving marinade, remove chicken and place on broiler pan. Broil 10 cm from heat for 4 minutes. Turn chicken over, brush with reserved marinade, and broil until chicken is cooked through, about 4 minutes. Discard any remaining marinade.

4 | Serve chicken with raisins and almonds sprinkled on top.

PER SERVING: 253 cal, 6 g fat (1 g sat), 14 g carbs, 33 g protein, 2 g fibre, 93 mg chol, 483 mg sodium, 106 mg calcium

Grilled Jamaican **Jerk Chicken**

The saucy seasoning mixture that adds spark to Jamaican-style "jerk" meats is a uniquely Caribbean blend of spicy, sweet and hot. For a healthfully varied meal, we've added bell pepper, pineapple and scallions to the dish.

PREP TIME 15 MINUTES + MARINATING   **COOK TIME** 15 MINUTES

1 tbsp ground allspice

4 cloves garlic, minced

1 tbsp minced fresh ginger

1 large pickled jalapeño pepper, minced

1/4 cup white-wine vinegar

11/2 tbsp light-brown sugar

11/2 tbsp olive oil

11/4 tsp black pepper

3/4 tsp salt

4 skinless, boneless chicken breast halves (150 g each)

8 scallions

2 large red bell peppers, cut into 32 chunks

24 canned pineapple chunks (about 11/2 cups)

1 | Combine allspice, garlic, ginger, jalapeño, vinegar, brown sugar, oil, black pepper and salt in large bowl. Measure out 2 tbsp of mixture and set aside. Add chicken to mixture remaining in bowl and turn to coat on all sides. Refrigerate for 1 hour. (Don't leave chicken longer than 1 hour or ginger and vinegar will start to break down the fibre of chicken.)

2 | Trim scallions leaving just a small portion of tender green. Cut each scallion into 3 pieces.

3 | Preheat grill to medium. On each of 8 long skewers, alternately thread 3 pieces of scallion, 4 pieces of bell pepper, and 3 pieces of pineapple.

4 | Lift chicken from marinade and place chicken on grill. Brush reserved 2 tbsp spice mixture over skewers and place on grill. Grill, turning chicken and skewers once, until chicken is cooked through and vegetables are crisp-tender, 5 to 10 minutes for the skewers, 10 to 15 minutes for the chicken.

PER SERVING: 293 cal, 8 g fat (1 g sat), 23 g carbs, 33 g protein, 4 g fibre, 91 mg chol, 322 mg sodium, 74 mg calcium

Grilled **Flank Steak** Argentine

SERVES

Juicy slices of beef and crispy potatoes are topped with a tangy green chimichurri sauce, a favourite condiment in Argentina. Make extra sauce for use later in the week on vegetables, chicken or fish!

PREP TIME 15 MINUTES + MARINATING   **COOK TIME** 26 MINUTES

1/3 cup reduced-sodium chicken broth

1 tbsp extra-virgin olive oil

2 tsp fresh lemon juice

2 large garlic cloves, minced

1 tbsp chopped fresh oregano or 1 tsp dried

1/2 tsp crushed red pepper, or to taste

1 small onion, finely chopped

1/2 cup finely chopped flat-leaf parsley

500 g beef flank steak (2.5 cm thick)

1/2 tsp salt

1/2 tsp pepper

4 medium baking potatoes, scrubbed

1 | Put broth, oil, lemon juice, garlic, oregano, red pepper, onion and parsley in large ziplock bag. Seal bag tightly and shake to mix chimichurri sauce. Rub steak on both sides with ¼ tsp salt and ¼ tsp black pepper, and then put steak into bag and close. Refrigerate at least 30 minutes, or up to 2 hours, turning bag once.

2 | Meanwhile, place a wire cooling rack over paper towels. Cut potatoes lengthwise (do not peel) into 1 cm thick slices. Bring potatoes, remaining salt and pepper, and enough water to cover to a boil in large pot over high heat. Reduce heat to medium and simmer until potatoes are almost tender, about 10 minutes; transfer potatoes to rack. Lightly coat potatoes on both sides with non-stick cooking spray (preferably olive oil).

3 | Remove steak from sauce. Boil sauce vigorously in small pot 3 minutes, stirring constantly; remove from heat and cover to keep warm. Meanwhile, coat grill pan with non-stick cooking spray and set over medium-high heat. Cook steak and potatoes until steak is done to taste (3 to 4 minutes on each side for medium-rare, 4 to 5 minutes for medium) and potatoes are crispy, about 4 minutes per side.

4 | Thinly slice steak across the grain. Divide potato and steak slices among 4 plates. Spoon about 2 tbsp warm chimichurri sauce over each serving.

PER SERVING: 317 cal, 10 g fat (3 g sat), 29 g carbs, 28 g protein, 3 g fibre, 70 mg chol, 364 mg sodium, 76 mg calcium

Blue Cheese-Stuffed **Burger**

SERVES 4

WHAT?!? A cheeseburger on a healthy diet? Once in a while, you just gotta give in! For the sake of your healthy diet, use extra-lean ground beef and a variety of cheese so strong you only need a little bit for lots of flavour.

PREP TIME 10 MINUTES   **COOK TIME** 15 MINUTES

340 g extra-lean ground beef

1 cup quick-cooking oats (uncooked)

2 tbsp ketchup

2 tsp Dijon mustard

1/4 tsp black pepper

4 tsp crumbled blue cheese

4 hamburger rolls

4 romaine lettuce leaves

1 firm, ripe tomato, sliced

1 small red onion, sliced

1 | Preheat broiler or barbecue. Mix beef, oats, ketchup, mustard and pepper in large bowl until well blended. Divide into eight equal pieces and flatten into thin patties.

2 | Place 1 tbsp of crumbled cheese in the centre of each of 4 patties. Top with remaining patties and pinch edges to seal completely.

3 | Cook 10 cm from the heat until well done—4 to 6 minutes on each side. Serve burgers on rolls with lettuce, tomato and red onion.

PER SERVING: 338 cal, 8 g fat (3 g sat), 41 g carbs, 26 g protein, 4 g fibre, 47 mg chol, 469 mg sodium, 103 mg calcium

Shepherd's Pie

SERVES 4

This version of the two-fisted, one-dish super is made with ground sirloin rather than the traditional lamb. That means less fat in the dish, as does replacing some of the meat with fibre-rich kidney beans. Juicy tomatoes keep the mixture moist.

PREP TIME 20 MINUTES   **COOK TIME** 35 MINUTES

2 tsp olive oil

4 scallions, thinly sliced

6 cloves garlic, minced

1 large green bell pepper, chopped

170 g extra-lean ground sirloin

1 tbsp chili powder

11/2 tsp ground coriander

11/2 tsp ground cumin

11/2 cups canned tomatoes, chopped with their juice

1 can (540 mL) red kidney beans, rinsed and drained

750 g all-purpose potatoes, peeled and thinly sliced

1/3 cup chopped cilantro

1 | Heat oil in large non-stick skillet over low heat. Add scallions and half of garlic and cook, stirring frequently, until tender, about 2 minutes. Add bell pepper, increase heat to medium and cook, stirring, until pepper is crisp-tender, about 5 minutes.

2 | Stir in beef, chili powder, coriander and cumin and cook, stirring occasionally to break up beef, until beef is no longer pink, about 2 minutes. Stir in tomatoes and beans, and bring to a boil. Reduce to a simmer, cover, and cook until mixture is thick and flavourful, about 10 minutes.

3 | Meanwhile, cook potatoes and remaining garlic in medium pot of boiling water until tender, about 10 minutes.

4 | Reserving ¼ cup of potato cooking liquid, drain off remaining liquid and keep potatoes and garlic in pot. Return reserved cooking liquid to pot. With potato masher, mash potatoes and garlic until not quite smooth, leaving some texture. Stir in cilantro.

5 | Preheat oven to 220°C (425°F). Spoon meat mixture into 22 cm deep-dish pie plate. Spoon mashed potatoes over top. (Recipe can be made ahead to this point. Cover and refrigerate. Return to room temperature before baking.) Bake until filling is bubbling, about 15 minutes.

PER SERVING: 367 cal, 5 g fat (1 g sat), 64 g carbs, 20 g protein, 12 g fibre, 23 mg chol, 463 mg sodium, 114 mg calcium

Picadillo with Rice

SERVES 4

Want some excitement for supper? Simmer up a Latin-style skillet of freshly-ground pork tenderloin with the tantalizing flavours of chilies, raisins and olives. Served over rice, picadillo is a hearty and healthy one-dish supper.

PREP TIME 10 MINUTES   **COOK TIME** 45 MINUTES

21/2 cups water

1/4 tsp salt

1 cup brown rice

300 g pork tenderloin, cut into chunks

2 tsp olive oil

1 large onion, finely chopped

3 cloves garlic, minced

1 can (680 mL) no-salt tomato sauce

1/2 cup raisins

1/4 cup pitted green olives, coarsely chopped

1 jalapeño, minced

1/2 tsp oregano

1 | Bring water to a boil in medium pot. Add ⅛ tsp of salt and rice. Reduce to a simmer, cover, and cook until rice is tender, about 45 minutes.

2 | Meanwhile, place pork in food processor and pulse until coarsely ground.

3 | Heat oil in large non-stick skillet over medium heat. Add onion and garlic and cook, stirring frequently, until onion is soft, about 5 minutes.

4 | Add pork and stir until no longer pink, about 3 minutes. Add remaining ⅛ tsp salt, tomato sauce, raisins, olives, jalapeño and oregano. Cook, stirring frequently, until pork is cooked through and sauce is flavourful, about 10 minutes. Serve picadillo over rice.

PER SERVING: 422 cal, 7 g fat (1 g sat), 68 g carbs, 22 g protein, 6 g fibre, 46 mg chol, 469 mg sodium, 60 mg calcium

Scallop and Cherry Tomato **Sauté**

SERVES 4

Scallops are infinitely adaptable in the kitchen, and are notably low in fat and cholesterol. Here, they are sautéed with cherry tomatoes, seasoned with garlic and basil, and enlivened with a vermouth-based sauce.

PREP TIME 5 MINUTES   **COOK TIME** 10 MINUTES

500 g sea scallops

4 tsp cornstarch

2 tsp olive oil

3 cloves garlic, minced

1 pint cherry tomatoes

2/3 cup dry vermouth, white wine or chicken broth

Pinch salt

1/3 cup chopped fresh basil

1 tbsp cold water

1 | Dredge scallops in 3 tsp cornstarch, shaking off excess. Heat oil in large non-stick skillet over medium heat. Add scallops and sauté until golden brown and cooked through, about 3 minutes. With slotted spoon, transfer scallops to bowl.

2 | Add garlic to pan and cook 1 minute. Add tomatoes and cook until they begin to collapse, about 4 minutes. Add vermouth, salt and basil to pan. Bring to a boil and cook for 1 minute.

3 | Meanwhile, stir together remaining 1 tsp cornstarch and cold water in small bowl. Add cornstarch mixture to pan and cook, stirring, until sauce is slightly thickened, about 1 minute.

4 | Return scallops to pan, reduce to a simmer, and cook just until heated through, about 1 minute.

PER SERVING: 165 cal, 3 g fat (1 g sat), 12 g carbs, 15 g protein, 1 g fibre, 27 mg chol, 452 mg sodium, 36 mg calcium

Broiled Beef with Mustard-Glazed Potatoes

SERVES 4

Here's steak and potatoes "with heart"—lean eye round in a honey-mustard marinade, and potatoes that are boiled first, then tossed in the marinade and broiled alongside the meat. Both are served on a bed of peppery watercress.

PREP TIME 15 MINUTES + MARINATING **COOK TIME** 35 MINUTES

1/4 cup Dijon mustard

1 tbsp honey

1 tbsp cider vinegar

2 cloves garlic, minced

Pinch salt

1/4 tsp pepper

500 g well-trimmed beef eye round

680 g small red-skinned potatoes

1 large onion, cut into 8 wedges

1 bunch watercress, tough ends trimmed

1 | Combine mustard, honey, vinegar, garlic, salt and pepper in large bowl and stir to combine.

2 | Place beef in shallow bowl. Measure out 2 tbsp of mustard mixture and rub all over beef. Marinate beef 30 minutes at room temperature or up to overnight in the refrigerator.

3 | With a vegetable peeler, remove strip of skin from around each potato. Drop potatoes in large pot of boiling water and cook until firm-tender, about 20 minutes.

4 | Drain potatoes well. Add to bowl of mustard mixture, tossing to coat. With slotted spoon, transfer potatoes to broiler pan. (Leave room on broiler pan for onion wedges and beef.)

5 | Add onion to mustard mixture in bowl, turning wedges to coat. Add to broiler pan with potatoes.

6 | Preheat broiler. Add beef to potatoes and onion on broiler pan. Broil 10 cm from heat for 8 minutes, turning beef, potatoes and onion over midway through cooking. Let beef stand 5 minutes before slicing. Serve on bed of watercress.

PER SERVING: 316 cal, 4 g fat (1 g sat), 40 g carbs, 30 g protein, 4 g fibre, 67 mg chol, 472 mg sodium, 88 mg calcium

Pesto-Coated **Pork Chops**

SERVES 4

Pork chops fit just fine in a healthy diet, thanks to their general leanness. To keep these chops svelte but succulent, top them with a layer of oh-so-healthy pesto. The olive oil in the pesto helps seal in the pork juices.

PREP TIME 15 MINUTES **COOK TIME** 8 MINUTES

170 g no-egg noodles

2 cups fresh basil leaves

3 garlic cloves, peeled

1/2 tsp salt

1/2 tsp freshly ground black pepper

2 tbsp plain dry bread crumbs

2 tbsp extra-virgin olive oil

4 center-cut pork loin chops (1 cm thick, about 125 g each)

1 | Prepare noodles according to package directions. Drain and keep hot. Meanwhile, preheat broiler.

2 | Put basil, garlic and a pinch each of salt and pepper in food processor. Pulse until roughly chopped. Add bread crumbs and process 30 seconds until incorporated. With motor running, slowly add oil through feed tube until puréed. Set aside.

3 | Coat large heavy ovenproof skillet and broiler rack with non-stick cooking spray. Set skillet over high heat until very hot but not smoking. Sprinkle both sides of chops with remaining salt and pepper. Sauté chops until browned, about 1 minute on each side. Remove from heat. Spread chops on both sides with pesto and transfer to broiler pan.

4 | Broil chops until pesto is slightly darker and juices run clear, about 2 minutes on each side. Divide noodles evenly among 4 plates and top with a pork chop.

PER SERVING: 395 cal, 12 g fat (2 g sat), 38 g carbs, 32 g protein, 1 g fibre, 78 mg chol, 390 mg sodium, 76 mg calcium

Snow Peas and Apples with Ginger

SERVES 4

Slices of firm apple, briefly stir-fried, have the same crunch as water chestnuts, so they partner well with crisp, fresh snow peas. And the two are complementary from a nutrition sense; apples are loaded with fibre, snow peas with vitamin C.

PREP TIME 10 MINUTES   **COOK TIME** 10 MINUTES

2 tsp olive oil

2 tbsp finely slivered, peeled fresh ginger

3 cloves garlic, minced

500 g snow peas, strings removed

2 crisp red apples, unpeeled, cut into thin wedges

1/2 tsp salt

1 | Heat oil in large non-stick skillet over low heat. Add ginger and garlic and cook until tender, about 2 minutes.

2 | Add snow peas, apples and salt to skillet and cook, stirring frequently, until peas are crisp-tender, about 7 minutes.

PER SERVING: 126 cal, 3 g fat (0 g sat), 23 g carbs, 4 g protein, 5 g fibre, 0 mg chol, 297 mg sodium, 64 mg calcium

Orange Beef Stir-Fry with Broccoli and Red Pepper SERVES 4

Recipes for beef and broccoli stir-fries may be commonplace, but this one stands out. Stir-frying orange zest with fresh ginger gives the sauce extraordinary fragrance and flavour. This dish provides a generous quantity of vegetables balanced with lean protein, providing excellent nutritional value for the calories.

PREP TIME 10 MINUTES   **COOK TIME** 10 MINUTES

1/2 cup orange juice

2 tbsp low-sodium soy sauce

1 tbsp oyster sauce

1 tbsp rice vinegar

1 1/2 tsp chili-garlic sauce or hot red pepper sauce

1 1/2 tsp cornstarch

1 tbsp canola oil

340 g flank steak, trimmed, halved lengthwise and cut into 5 mm thick slices

1 tbsp minced fresh ginger

2 tsp freshly grated orange zest

3 garlic cloves, minced

1 cup sliced onion

450 g broccoli crowns, cut into 2.5 cm florets (about 4 cups)

1 red or yellow bell pepper, cut into 5 cm by 5 mm slivers

1 | In small bowl, whisk together orange juice, soy sauce, oyster sauce, vinegar, chili-garlic sauce (or hot sauce) and cornstarch; set aside.

2 | Heat 1 tsp oil in large non-stick skillet or stir-fry pan over high heat. Add half of steak and cook, without stirring or turning, until browned on underside, about 1 minute. Stir and turn slices, then cook just until browned on other side, about 30 seconds. Transfer to plate. Add another 1 tsp oil, repeat with remaining steak and transfer to plate.

3 | Add remaining 1 tsp oil to skillet, then add ginger, orange zest and garlic and stir-fry until fragrant, 10 to 20 seconds. Add onion and stir-fry for 1 minute. Add broccoli and bell pepper and stir-fry for 30 seconds. Add ¼ cup water, cover and cook just until crisp-tender, about 1½ minutes. Push vegetables to outside of pan. Stir reserved sauce, pour into centre of pan, and cook, stirring, until glossy and thickened, about 1 minute. Stir vegetables into sauce, return steak to skillet and turn to coat. Serve with brown rice.

PER SERVING (1 ½ cups): 247 cals, 25 g protein, 17 g carbs, 3 g fibre, 9 g fat (3 g sat), 34 mg chol, 655 mg sodium

Vegetable **Tart Provençale**

This tart brims with the sunny flavours of southern France; it is perfect for a luncheon or light supper. The crust is easy to assemble and scented with thyme; rows of vegetable slices are beautiful to behold, yet easy to prepare.

PREP TIME 20 MINUTES   **COOK TIME** 47 MINUTES

2 large sweet Vidalia onions, sliced

1 1/2 cups all-purpose flour

1 1/2 tsp chopped
fresh thyme

1/2 tsp salt

1/3 cup ice water

2 tbsp olive oil

2 medium zucchini (250 g each)

4 medium tomatoes, cut into
5 mm slices

2 tbsp freshly grated Parmesan
cheese

1 | Coat large non-stick skillet with non-stick cooking spray and set over medium-high heat until hot. Reduce heat to medium-low and sauté onions until very soft and golden, 20 minutes. Transfer to plate.

2 | Preheat oven to 200°C (400°F). Mix flour, thyme and ¼ tsp salt in large bowl. Stir in water and oil just until soft dough forms. Lightly sprinkle work surface with flour and pat out dough into 25 x 40 cm rectangle or 32 cm round. Fold in half and transfer to 30 x 15 cm tart pan or 22.5 cm round tart pan with removable bottom. Trim edges.

3 | Cut zucchini on diagonal into long slices 3 mm thick. Lightly coat skillet again with cooking spray and set over medium heat. Sauté zucchini until golden, 5–7 minutes.

4 | Arrange zucchini, tomatoes and onions in rows on pastry, standing them up and overlapping them slightly. Sprinkle with remaining salt and Parmesan. Bake until crust is golden, about 20 minutes. Serve hot, warm or at room temperature.

PER SERVING: 320 cal, 9 g fat (2 g sat), 52 g carbs, 9 g protein, 5 g fibre, 2 mg chol, 362 mg sodium, 100 mg calcium

Five-Way **Chili**

SERVES 4

"Five-way" chili is spaghetti topped with beef chili, kidney beans, tomatoes, chopped onions and shredded cheddar. Our lightened version is made with lean beef, spinach linguine and so many richly flavourful seasonings that we could skip the cheese.

PREP TIME 15 MINUTES   **COOK TIME** 25 MINUTES

2 tsp olive oil

2 large onions, finely chopped

3 cloves garlic, minced

225 g lean ground top round

2 tbsp chili powder

1 tsp cinnamon

1 1/2 cups canned tomatoes, chopped with their juice

1 can (540 mL) red kidney beans, rinsed and drained

1/4 cup water

3 tbsp tomato paste

2 tsp brown sugar

2 tsp unsweetened cocoa powder

Pinch salt

250 g spinach linguine

4 scallions, thinly sliced

1 | Heat oil over medium heat in large non-stick skillet. Add onions and garlic and cook, stirring frequently, until onions are golden brown, about 10 minutes.

2 | Stir in beef, chili powder and cinnamon and cook, breaking up beef with spoon, until no longer pink, about 5 minutes.

3 | Stir in tomatoes, beans, water, tomato paste, brown sugar, cocoa and salt, and simmer until chili sauce is flavourful, about 10 minutes.

4 | Meanwhile, in large pot of boiling water, cook pasta according to package directions. Drain and transfer pasta to large bowl. Add chili sauce and scallions and toss to combine.

PER SERVING: 461 cal, 6 g fat (1 g sat), 77 g carbs, 28 g protein, 15 g fibre, 27 mg chol, 477 mg sodium, 144 mg calcium

Persian Rice Pilaf with Dried Fruits and Almonds
SERVES 6

Pilaf always begins with a grain, often rice. But the ingredients can vary: One day add dried fruits and sweet spice... another, savoury vegetables and herbs. With every bite, a pilaf makes an ordinary meal extraordinary!

PREP TIME 15 MINUTES **COOK TIME** 40 MINUTES + STANDING

12 dried apricot halves

1 tbsp trans fat-free margarine

1 medium onion, chopped

1 cup jasmine or white rice

1/4 tsp ground cardamom

1/4 tsp salt

1/4 tsp pepper

21/2 cups reduced-sodium chicken broth

1/2 cup golden raisins

1/3 cup slivered almonds, toasted

Fresh rosemary sprigs for garnish

1 | Snip apricots with kitchen shears into small slivers (you need about ⅓ cup).

2 | Melt margarine in large non-stick pot over medium heat. Sauté onion, rice, cardamom, salt and pepper until rice is toasted, about 8 minutes.

3 | Stir in broth, raisins, almonds and apricots and bring to a boil. Reduce heat to medium-low. Cover and simmer until broth is absorbed, about 25 minutes. Remove from heat and let stand 5 minutes. Fluff with fork. Garnish with rosemary sprigs.

PER SERVING: 256 cal, 5 g fat (1 g sat), 48 g carbs, 6 g protein, 4 g fibre, 0 mg chol, 146 mg sodium, 53 mg calcium

Polenta with Meat and Mushroom Sauce
SERVES 4

Polenta—cornmeal mush—is a staple in northern Italy. Comforting and adaptable, polenta can be cooked spoonably thin or sliceably thick. Here, a small amount of extra-lean beef adds big flavour to the sauce.

PREP TIME 10 MINUTES + SOAKING **COOK TIME** 20 MINUTES

1 cup dried shiitake mushrooms

2 cups boiling water

1 tsp olive oil

2 cloves garlic, minced

115 g extra-lean ground beef

1 can (540 mL) crushed tomatoes

1/2 tsp salt

1/2 tsp cinnamon

1/2 tsp pepper

3/4 cup yellow cornmeal

2 tbsp grated Parmesan cheese

1 | Combine mushrooms and boiling water in medium ovenproof bowl. Let stand 20 minutes or until softened. With slotted spoon, scoop mushrooms from liquid and strain liquid through fine-meshed sieve; reserve liquid. Thickly slice mushroom caps.

2 | Heat oil in large non-stick skillet over medium heat. Add mushrooms and garlic and cook, stirring frequently, until garlic is tender, about 2 minutes.

3 | Add beef and stir until meat is no longer pink, about 3 minutes. Add ⅓ cup mushroom soaking liquid, tomatoes, ¼ tsp salt, cinnamon and pepper. Bring to a boil, reduce to a simmer, and cook, uncovered, until sauce is slightly thickened, but still of pouring consistency, about 5 minutes. Remove from heat.

4 | Combine cornmeal and remaining mushroom soaking liquid in medium bowl, stirring until smooth. Bring 2 cups water and remaining ¼ tsp salt to a boil in medium pot over high heat. Reduce to a gentle simmer and stir in cornmeal mixture. Cook, stirring, until polenta is thick but still pourable, about 5 minutes.

5 | Reheat sauce if necessary. Spoon polenta into shallow bowls and top with sauce and Parmesan.

PER SERVING: 300 cal, 5 g fat (1 g sat), 45 g carbs, 20 g protein, 8 g fibre, 18 mg chol, 500 mg sodium, 90 mg calcium

Sunny Risotto with Carrots

SERVES 4

One bite of this rich-tasting, aromatic risotto will make you question how low-fat and low-calorie it can really be. The secret to its incredibly appealing texture is the starch in the rice, which makes each forkful creamy as it absorbs the liquid.

PREP TIME 15 MINUTES   **COOK TIME** 35 MINUTES

2 tsp olive oil
1 small onion, finely chopped
2 large carrots, cut into 5 mm dice
1 cup arborio rice
1/2 cup dry white wine
2 cups reduced-sodium chicken broth
1 cup carrot juice
1/4 tsp salt
1/4 cup grated Parmesan cheese
1/4 tsp pepper

1 | In medium non-stick pot, heat oil over moderate heat. Add onion and sauté until tender, about 5 minutes. Add carrots and sauté until crisp-tender, about 4 minutes. Add rice, stirring to coat.

2 | Add wine and cook, stirring occasionally, until evaporated by half, about 2 minutes. In medium bowl, combine broth, carrot juice, ½ cup water, and salt. Add broth mixture, ½ cup at a time, to rice and cook, stirring, until absorbed, before adding the next ½ cup. (Total time will be about 20 minutes.)

3 | Remove from heat. Stir in Parmesan cheese and pepper.

PER SERVING: 310 cal, 5 g fat (1 g sat), 56 g carbs, 9 g protein, 3 g fibre, 4 mg chol, 322 mg sodium, 87 mg calcium

Nutted **Lemon Barley**

SERVES 8

Although barley is a staple food in the Middle East, Canadians have traditionally consigned it almost exclusively to soups. Cooked in a spicy broth, as it is here, barley makes a welcome change from potatoes or rice to accompany meat.

PREP TIME 10 MINUTES   **COOK TIME** 55-60 MINUTES

2 tbsp olive oil
2 onions, finely chopped
3 stalks celery, finely chopped
1 cup pearl barley, rinsed
2 1/2 cups low-sodium canned chicken stock
1 tsp finely grated lemon zest
1/2 tsp dried oregano
1/8 tsp salt
1/8 tsp pepper
2 tbsp sunflower seeds
1 tbsp fresh lemon juice
1/4 cup golden raisins
2 tbsp chopped parsley

1 | In a wide heavy pot, heat oil over moderate heat. Add onions and celery and sauté, stirring, until softened and lightly browned, about 7 minutes. Stir in barley until coated with oil. Pour in stock and add lemon zest, oregano, salt and pepper.

2 | Bring stock to boil, then reduce heat; cover pan and simmer, stirring occasionally, until barley is nearly cooked through and almost all liquid is absorbed, about 40 minutes.

3 | Meanwhile, toast sunflower seeds in dry non-stick skillet over moderate heat, stirring frequently or shaking pan until golden brown. Remove from heat and transfer to plate.

4 | Stir lemon juice and raisins into barley mixture and cover pot. Remove pot from heat and allow mixture to stand about 5 minutes, then gently stir toasted sunflower seeds and chopped parsley into barley until just mixed.

PER SERVING: 167 cal, 5 g fat (1 g sat), 26 g carbs, 5 g protein, 6 g fibre, 0 mg chol, 96 mg sodium, 37 mg calcium

Linguine with No-Cook Sauce

SERVES 6

Of all the ways to dress linguine, this quick and easy sauce is bound to become the most-requested in your house. Bursting with fresh flavour, it's full of tomatoes, olive oil and fresh herbs, including mint (what a surprise!).

PREP TIME 20 MINUTES + STANDING   **COOK TIME** 12 MINUTES

1,500 g fresh plum tomatoes, seeded and chopped

2/3 cup chopped fresh basil

1/4 cup extra-virgin olive oil

1/4 cup chopped flat-leaf parsley

2 tbsp chopped fresh mint

2 tsp grated orange zest

3 garlic cloves, minced

1/2 tsp salt

1/2 tsp pepper

375 g linguine

1/4 cup Parmesan cheese

1 | Mix tomatoes, basil, oil, parsley, mint, orange zest, garlic, salt and pepper in bowl. Let stand at least 30 minutes or up to 2 hours at room temperature.

2 | Cook pasta according to package directions. Drain well and put into a large pasta bowl. Top with sauce and sprinkle with Parmesan.

PER SERVING: 356 cal, 12 g fat (2 g sat), 53 g carbs, 12 g protein, 5 g fibre, 3 mg chol, 262 mg sodium, 95 mg calcium

Chocolate **Snacking Cake**

MAKES 36 SQUARES

Craving a little chocolate? Each of these luscious little gems has only 77 calories and 1 gram of fat. And because these treats are low in saturated fat, you can satisfy that craving while your heart and conscience thank you.

PREP TIME 15 MINUTES   **COOK TIME** 35 MINUTES + COOLING

1 1/3 cups sifted self-rising flour

1 cup plus 2 tsp unsweetened cocoa powder

1/4 cup buttermilk

1 tbsp instant espresso powder

1 cup granulated sugar

1/2 cup packed light brown sugar

1/2 cup unsweetened applesauce

2 tsp vanilla

2 large egg whites

1/2 cup mini chocolate chips

1 | Preheat the oven to 180°C (325°F) . Line a 20 cm square baking pan with foil, leaving a 2.5 cm overhang all round. Sift the flour and 1 cup cocoa powder into a small bowl. Heat the buttermilk and espresso powder in a small pot over low heat until the espresso is dissolved.

2 | Mix the granulated and brown sugars, applesauce, buttermilk mixture and vanilla in a medium bowl. Stir in the flour mixture, just until blended. Beat the egg whites in a large bowl with an electric mixer set on high, just until soft peaks begin to form. Fold the egg whites into the batter and stir in the chocolate chips.

3 | Scrape the batter into the baking pan with a rubber-tipped spatula and smooth the top. Bake for 35 minutes or just until the batter sets (do not overbake). Let the cake cool in the pan on a wire rack for 15 min.

PER SQUARE: 77 cal, 1 g fat (0.5 g sat), 0 mg chol, 15 g carbs, 1 g fibre, 8 g sugars, 1 g protein.

Marble **Cheesecake**

A classic cheesecake is made from a couple of pounds of cream cheese, a stick of butter and three or more eggs. Now read the ingredients and the "numbers" on this chocolate-swirled beauty, and get baking!

PREP TIME 15 MINUTES   **COOK TIME** 55 MINUTES + CHILLING

90 g low-fat honey graham crackers (6 whole crackers)

1/2 cup toasted wheat germ

1 tbsp plus 1 cup sugar

2 tbsp extra-light olive oil

500 g silken (or soft) tofu, well drained

500 g light cream cheese

3 tbsp flour

1 large egg plus 2 large egg whites

1 tsp vanilla

1/4 cup chocolate syrup

1 | Preheat oven to 180°C (350°F). Combine graham crackers, wheat germ and 1 tbsp sugar in food processor and process to fine crumbs. Add oil and process until moistened. Place mixture in 22 cm springform pan and press into bottom and partway up sides. Bake until set, about 10 minutes.

2 | Add drained tofu, remaining 1 cup sugar, cream cheese, flour, whole egg, egg whites and vanilla to food processor (no need to clean bowl) and process until smooth and well blended.

3 | Measure out 1 cup tofu mixture, place in small bowl, and stir in chocolate syrup. Pour remaining plain tofu mixture into crust in springform pan.

4 | Pour chocolate mixture in a ring on top of batter and swirl it in with a knife. Bake 45 minutes. Turn off oven and leave in oven 45 minutes undisturbed. Cool to room temperature before chilling overnight.

PER SERVING: 234 cal, 5 g fat (1 g sat), 34 g carbs, 11 g protein, 1 g fibre, 20 mg chol, 319 mg sodium, 190 mg calcium

Key Lime **Pudding Parfaits**

SERVES 6

This lush, layered dessert is made with puréed cottage cheese and low-fat evaporated milk—a miraculous ingredient for healthy cooks because it's improbably thick, rich, and velvety.

PREP TIME 15 MINUTES   **COOK TIME** 5 MINUTES + CHILLING

11/2 cups low-fat evaporated milk

1/2 cup light (1%) cottage cheese

2 tbsp cornstarch

2 tsp grated lime zest

2/3 cup fresh lime juice

1/2 cup plus 2 tsp sugar

1/4 tsp salt

5 whole graham crackers

1/4 cup toasted wheat germ

1 | Combine ½ cup evaporated milk and cottage cheese in food processor or blender and puree until very smooth.

2 | Place cornstarch in a medium pot. Stir in remaining 1 cup evaporated milk, lime zest, lime juice, ½ cup sugar and salt. Stir in cottage cheese mixture. Cook pudding over medium heat, stirring constantly, until mixture comes to a boil. Cook, stirring, until thick, about 1 minute.

3 | Transfer pudding to bowl, let cool to room temperature, then refrigerate until completely chilled, about 2 hours.

4 | Meanwhile, place graham cracker squares in a food processor and pulse until coarse crumbs form. Combine graham cracker crumbs, remaining 2 tsp sugar, and wheat germ in small skillet. Cook over medium heat, stirring frequently, until graham cracker crumbs are lightly toasted, about 5 minutes. Cool to room temperature.

5 | Dividing evenly, alternate layers of graham cracker mixture and pudding in 6 parfait glasses, beginning and ending with graham crackers. Refrigerate until serving time.

PER SERVING: 192 cal, 2 g fat (0 g sat), 37 g carbs, 8 g protein, 1 g fibre, 11 mg chol, 264 mg sodium, 185 mg calcium

Lemon **Angel Food Cake** with Strawberries

SERVES 12

Whipped up from a dozen egg whites—but no yolks—this lofty dessert delight is confected with no shortening at all. The vividly colourful fruit sauce makes the cake worthy of a festive occasion.

PREP TIME 20 MINUTES   **COOK TIME** 50 MINUTES + CHILLING

1 bag (600 g) frozen strawberries, thawed

1/2 cup orange juice

12 large egg whites, at room temperature

11/4 tsp cream of tartar

1/2 tsp salt

11/4 cups sugar

3 tbsp grated lemon zest

1 tsp vanilla

1 cup flour

1 | Combine strawberries and orange juice in large bowl. Refrigerate.

2 | Preheat oven to 160°C. Beat egg whites, cream of tartar and salt in large bowl with electric mixer until foamy. Gradually beat in sugar, 2 tbsp at a time, until thick, soft peaks form. Beat in lemon zest and vanilla.

3 | Gently fold flour into egg-white mixture, ¼ cup at a time, until incorporated. Spoon into ungreased 25 cm angel food or tube pan. Bake until top springs back when lightly pressed, about 50 minutes.

4 | Invert cake pan to cool. If angel food pan does not have legs, hang pan over the neck of a bottle. Cool cake completely. Run metal spatula around edges and centre of pan, then invert onto cake platter. Serve with strawberries and their juice.

PER SERVING: 159 cal, 0 g fat (0 g sat), 35 g carbs, 5 g protein, 1 g fibre, 0 mg chol, 152 mg sodium, 14 mg calcium

Double Raspberry **Sorbet**

Go ahead raspberry lovers, take a bite. This velvety smooth sorbet and rich sauce give you a double dose of your favourite fruit—and you can make it from frozen berries any time of year.

PREP TIME 25 MINUTES + FREEZING   **COOK TIME** 8 MINUTES

1 cup sugar

4 packages (375 g each) frozen raspberries, slightly thawed

1 tbsp fresh lemon juice

1 | Bring sugar and 1 cup water to a boil in medium pot over medium-high heat, stirring until sugar dissolves. Boil gently 5 minutes; remove from heat.

2 | Combine raspberries and lemon juice in food processor and process until smooth. Press raspberries through sieve set over large bowl. Discard seeds.

3 | Stir sugar syrup into raspberry purée. Cover and refrigerate until chilled, about 1 hour. Reserve ½ cup for sauce and refrigerate until ready to serve.

4 | Freeze sorbet mixture in ice cream maker according to manufacturer's directions. Transfer to freezer-safe container. Cover and freeze until ready to serve. Let sorbet stand at room temperature 10 minutes before scooping ½ cup into each of 8 dessert dishes. Drizzle each serving with 1 tbsp raspberry sauce.

PER SERVING: 171 cal, 0 g fat (0 g sat), 46 g carbs, 1 g protein, 7 g fibre, 0 mg chol, 0 mg sodium, 25 mg calcium

HOME REMEDIES

Long before drugs were synthesized in laboratories, people shared home remedies and techniques for dealing with pain and other health problems. Many of them stand the test of time. This chapter offers a range of home remedies shared by Lakota customers. Give them a try—you could be surprised by their effectiveness.

HOME REMEDIES

You don't have to run to the doctor for every bruise, backache, cut or cold. Chances are the solution you need is right at hand. Some of these tips are far from new, but that doesn't mean they're not valuable today.

JOINT PAIN

When I get pain in my finger joints I rub them vigorously for a few minutes, apply some ice and then slowly squeeze a tennis ball several times to loosen the joints. I also repeatedly squeeze a tennis ball several times a day in order to strengthen my wrists and fingers. I find that my grip and finger pain is relieved by this exercise.

Wilfred Kotzer, Toronto, ON

For joint pain, I make fruit smoothies every morning for breakfast. I mix in ginger, cinnamon, black poppy seeds, flax, hemp nuts and three different kinds of fresh fruit with a bit of water. We have been drinking these smoothies for over a year now.

Wendy McLean, Cameron, ON

For arthritis aches and pains try this recipe: into 2 cups of water add 3-4 tablespoons of apple cider vinegar and 3-4 tablespoons of raw honey. Mix well and store in a closed bottle in the fridge. Every morning take 2 tablespoons.

Jill Steeves, Fall River, NS

Cherries are a good remedy for knee pain caused by arthritis (especially gout pain). Eat 20.

K.M. Shiu, Scarborough, ON

This is a simple way that I utilize Lakota. I put Lakota in the fridge and cool it down. I then apply the chilled Lakota in the affected achy location and, as the Lakota activates and reacts with my skin, the stiffness and pain disappears! I really like the feeling! Simple, yet effective!

Michael Montague, Elora, ON

For arthritis, have a bath in Epsom salts. Epsom salts have high magnesium content, which is good for arthritis.

Tracey Linisky, Gilbert Plains, MB

I use ground flaxseed in many ways while cooking to help keep symptoms of arthritis and joint inflammation in check.

Shepherd Campbell, McKellar, ON

BACK PAIN

My favourite home remedy for back pain is: two cups of rice in a sock, sewn shut, then heated. You can position it however you want, and it's much more comfortable than sleeping/relaxing on a water bottle!

Diane Dunbrack, Bowmanville, ON

Ever wake up in the morning with a stiff back? What I find helps is to stand with your feet shoulder-width apart and try touching your toes. Bend down slowly and stretch as far as you can. Some mornings I can touch my toes; other mornings I can't. Hold this position for 20 seconds and slowly straighten up.

David R. Nafziger, Kitchener, ON

For help with your neck or back pain, take a pillowcase and throw in a tennis ball or hard ball of some kind—a soft spongy one doesn't work. Then, back yourself up to a wall and roll the ball up and down your neck and back for a do-it-yourself massage.

Carol Anne Carstensen, West Vancouver, BC

MUSCLE PAIN

My home remedy for sore muscles is stretching. It sounds simple, but make sure you get up and stretch every couple of hours. It really goes a long way!

Tara Hanley, Bowmanville, ON

I find bath salts and a few drops of peppermint or eucalyptus in a warm bath will slowly melt away the pain and tiredness I feel in my joints and muscles.

Jennifer Hebert, Thunder Bay, ON

I take white pearl barley, pour it into a microwave-safe bag and heat if for about 1 minute. When I remove it from the microwave, I wrap it in a soft flannel receiving blanket used for babies. I place this on the back of my neck and the heat and the barley seem to relieve the stiffness. Try it, it works great!

Holly Quaiscer, Calgary, AB

For relief of muscle tension, I use a bath soak recipe of: 2 tablespoons fresh ginger root, 1 oz fresh rosemary, 20 drops rosemary oil, 20 drops lavender oil, 1 cup rose water. Put the fresh rosemary and ginger root in a cotton bag, and add the rest of the ingredients to the water. Swirl around so that they mix together and get in the tub and soak for 20 minutes.

E. Liddell, Mississauga, ON

A home remedy I like to use for muscle pain is to have some hot green tea. This relaxes you and, in turn, relaxes tight shoulder and back muscles.

Anthony Bucci, Mississauga, ON

When you've twisted an ankle, strained your back or simply overused a limb, try putting ice cubes in a Ziploc bag and wrap it in a damp tea towel. Apply to the sore area for 10 minutes on and 10 minutes off. This helps kill the pain and reduces inflammation.

Tracey Hoey, Burlington, ON

STOMACH AND RELATED AILMENTS

I have found that anything with mint helps with nausea.

Brenda Hunka, Vegreville, AB

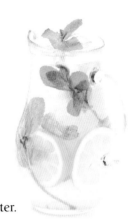

For bouts of upset stomach, settle it with ginger ale (one containing REAL ginger). It's good on bad days.

Sean Cuthill, Victoria, BC

When your stomach is upset, drink water with a little of baking soda, and it helps you feel better.

Katheryn Rivas, Mississauga, ON

Apple cider vinegar works for heartburn. Drink 1 tablespoon and your heartburn will be gone in less than 10 minutes.

Mary Bosley, Parry Sound, ON

To alleviate bloating and stomach cramps, I take a hand towel and wet it in water as hot as I can stand, then wring out the towel and drape it across my stomach.

Tammie Banks, Saint John, NB

This is a simple remedy for heartburn pain. It works every time and has never failed me. Take a spoonful of mustard and eat it. Heartburn will be gone before you know it.

Richard Dezso, London, ON

For vomiting, make rice water (put dry rice in a glass with lots of water, stir until cloudy); you can add sugar for taste and energy. Sip on the rice water.

Ruby Pisko, Lethbridge, AB

I suffer from frequent nausea, and one of the ways to make it bearable is to run cold water over the inside of my wrists. An ice pack to the back of the neck also helps.

Andrea Oliver, St. John's, NL

When I have bad pain from acid reflux I take a few spoonfuls
of any kind of yogourt and it calms it right down.

Stacey Napier, Prince George, BC

In case of diarrhea drink a very strong black tea with no sugar.

Jacqueline Hollinger, Oshawa, ON

MOSQUITO AND OTHER BITES

For mosquito bites, make a paste with water
and baking powder and apply to bite.

Stanley Pijl, Fort Erie, ON

In our house we use toothpaste to help stop the itching of
mosquito bites; the best is peppermint. Usually the itch w
disappear within minutes of application on the bite.

Natalia Kucaba, Ontario, ON

I relieve the pain from mosquito bites by using a damp washcloth
soaked in plain white vinegar on the bites. The swelling goes down
and the painful itch subsides. It works very well for me.

Tyler Hill, Chatham, ON

For spider bites, my neighbour told me to get some dirt out of the
garden and mix it with a little water until it was thick mud, then rub
a layer of it over the bite and swollen area of my arm, let it dry for 30
minutes, then wash it off. The inflammation and the swelling had gone
right down and all I could see were the puncture marks of the bite.

Irene Rothwell, St. Catharines, ON

I immediately apply honey to bee stings. The relief is
almost instantaneous!

Dave Donatelli, Abbotsford, BC

To take the sting out and prevent a bee sting from swelling up,
cut an an onion in half and place it on the sting. It will relieve
the pain and prevent swelling.

Sharon McIntyre, Prince George, BC

SORE THROAT

My home remedy: If I have a sore throat I put a teaspoon of honey in
a cup of hot water along with the juice of half a lemon. I sip on this
before I go to bed and I am usually fine in the morning.

Patricia Mitchell, Lanark, ON

When a sore throat hits, gargling with warm salt water will help kill the bacteria.

Pat Vanthuyne, Delhi, ON

My home remedy is to suppress a cough that hurts your throat. Mix 2 tablespoons of molasses with a ¼ teaspoon of ginger. This remedy has always helped me as a child and now as an adult to sooth my throat and help suppress that annoying hacking cough.

Joanne Hughson, Sussex, NB

HEADACHES

I don't know what it is about stimulating the scalp, but having someone run their fingers through my hair is the perfect remedy when I feel a migraine coming on. It provides immediate relief.

Sarah Corner, Brockville, ON

With the type of headaches I get, the best solution is often a home remedy. Lay down with a cool washcloth on my forehead and covering my eyes. The cool and dark often does the trick.

Kirsten Yee, Burnaby, BC

Whenever I have a headache, I try this first: A cold pack on the back of my neck and maybe another one on my forehead. After 15 minutes of relaxing with the ice packs I generally feel well enough to carry on with my regular routine.

Shirley Hill, Chatham, ON

If you have a headache drink two glasses of water in the first hour and one every hour after until it is gone.

Breanna Sherk, Caledonia, ON

SUNBURN

If you are suffering with pain from a severe sunburn, try pouring vinegar on the burnt area. It will draw the heat right out. This is well worth the trade off of smelling like a pickle.

Bruce Chartrand, Kingston, ON

TOOTHACHE

If you ever have a toothache or a cracked tooth and can't get to a dentist right away: Crush up some cloves and make a paste and place on your tooth. The cloves will ease the pain.

Mike Woelk, AB

RELIEVING STRESS

Take deep breaths and push your stomach out when inhaling.
Do this for a minute and then relax.

Courtney Jones, Calgary, AB

For pain or stress: Run a very warm bath before bedtime.
Add 1 tablespoon of your favourite shampoo. Next,
add 1 teaspoon of mineral oil, or any other kind
of non-fragrance oil. Last, add several dashes of your
favourite perfume. Relax and enjoy for about 20
minutes, adding hot water as needed. I guarantee this
remedy will give you the best sleep in the world.

Marcia L. Theriault, Quebec City, QC

A good night of deep sleep, if you can get it, is the best healing
potion out there.

Karen Hiebert, Abbotsford, BC

PIMPLES

Use toothpaste on your pimples while you sleep to dry them out quicker.

Robin Millar, Edmonton, AB

EAR PAIN

For ear pain, nuke some olive oil in the microwave. Wait until it has
sufficiently cooled down. Then take a Q-Tip and gently dab the now
warm olive oil in your ear, proceed to take some cotton and put it in
your ear so the oil does not run out. Take a warm cloth, place it on top
of the ear that hurts with the olive oil in it, lie down and try to relax.

Jennifer Borges, Hamilton, ON

My family has used this home remedy for generations;
it seems to work no matter what the ailment. Homemade
chicken soup. It is still the best home remedy for all types
of illnesses.

Joanne Lavoie, Lethbridge, AB

OTHER TIPS

Hiccups!! A spoonful of peanut butter always works!
In less than a minute the hiccups should be gone.

Nathalie Lapierre, Falconbridge, ON

After years of pain I was told about Lakota and all I can say is, oh my—
it has eliminated all of my pain. I was scheduled for surgery and I even
cancelled it because of this fantastic product.

Heather Harris, Lewis Mountain, NB

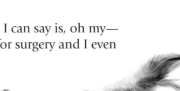
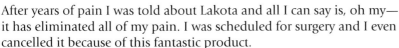

APPENDIX: LAKOTA PRODUCT GUIDE

Since its inception over 10 years ago, Lakota has developed a range of formulas that fight different kinds of pain. Once you try them, these products will speak for themselves— which is why Lakota remains Canada's number one pain reliever. Read on for information on Lakota products.

RELIEVES JOINT PAIN & ARTHRITIS SYMPTOMS
SOULAGE LES DOULEURS ARTICULAIRES

Joint Care
Arthroformule

120 CAPSULES
NPN 80032766

■ JOINT CARE FORMULA

Joint Care Formula is the original Lakota joint health supplement. It's the product we recommend first to anyone with Joint or Arthritis Pain. It is made with a combination of traditional herbal ingredients and modern scientifically produced ingredients. The traditional herbal ingredients are based around the White Willow Bark pain reliever. White Willow Bark was used by indigenous peoples for centuries to relieve pain.

The key pain reliever in White Willow Bark is a compound called salicin, which is the basis of aspirin. What makes aspirin a poor substitute for White Willow Bark is the side effects. Aspirin replaces salicin with acetylsalicylic acid, which is hard on the stomach lining. Natural-source salicin, however, converts to salicylic acid in the stomach, preventing the harmful, damaging effect of aspirin.

The White Willow Bark used in the Joint Care Formula is a unique variety that meets special potency standards. Most White Willow Bark available in Canada is not potency tested, so it is impossible to know how much of the active compound it contains. The White Willow Bark used in Joint Care Formula, however, has the highest potency of salicin available anywhere in the world.

Lakota Joint Care Formula also contains Devil's Claw, an effective pain reliever, especially when used in conjunction with the White Willow Bark. Only the root of Devil's Claw is used in the Lakota formulations. This is important because only the root contains the active harpagosides, which are natural anti-inflammatories and pain relievers.

Another ingredient is boswellia. Related to the ancient frankincense plant, boswellia produces a sticky resin that has an anti-inflammatory effect.

Collagen type II is one of the modern ingredients used in the Joint Care Formula. It is made from chicken sternum cartilage. Collagen type II is the type of collagen found in synovial fluid (joint fluid).

Lakota Joint Care Formula also has a daily dose of glucosamine, a building block of joint cartilage. On its own, glucosamine has limited effectiveness, but together with the natural anti-inflammatories and pain relievers it provides additional joint lubrication.

A new addition to the original Joint Care Formula is Lumanite, a medicinal mineral. Lumanite contains copper, manganese, selenium and pantothenic acid. Trace amounts of these mineral compounds aid in rebuilding the building blocks of joints.

Lakota Joint Care Formula has become the number one joint health formula available in Canada. Millions of bottles have been sold in Canada alone. That's no surprise: a great many arthritis sufferers are living a more active and fulfilled life since taking the Lakota Joint Care Formula.

The best way to use the Joint Care Formula is to take two pills in the morning and two at night. When first starting out, it often helps to take an extra two pills at lunchtime to speed up the pain-relieving effects. Once the pain has subsided, you can try to move to a maintenance dose of two pills per day. If the pain increases, move back to two in the morning and two at night.

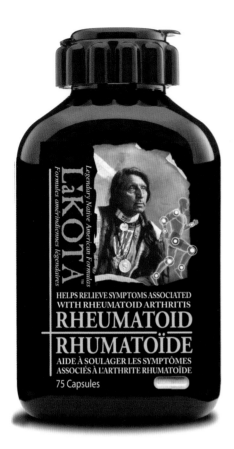

■ RHEUMATOID FORMULA

The Lakota Rheumatoid Formula was formerly called the Rheumatoid-Osteo Formula. It consists of collagen type II together with L-proline, an amino acid that helps transport the collagen type II to the joint cartilage. The formulation has both bovine and chicken collagen to provide the optimal molecular composition.

The Rheumatoid Formula is especially effective with rheumatoid arthritis. Rheumatoid arthritis is an autoimmune disorder that results in the body beginning to reject its own cartilage. Several clinical studies have examined the role of a collagen type II supplement in rheumatoid arthritis. One important study, from Harvard, found that collagen type II can be effective in relieving rheumatoid arthritis pain, even in small doses.

Although the product is called Rheumatoid Formula, we recommend taking it as a joint supplement for anyone who puts a lot of strain on their joints: runners, gardeners, construction workers and anyone who does a lot of bending and lifting.

The recommended use of Lakota Rheumatoid Formula is to take two capsules every morning with breakfast. Taking four capsules for the first month may speed up the recovery process. Rheumatoid Formula has almost no interactions with other medications, so it is generally safe to take together with Lakota Joint Care or Extra Strength Arthritis or a glucosamine supplement.

■ EXTRA STRENGTH ARTHRITIS

Lakota Extra Strength Arthritis is an entirely new formulation based around ASU. ASU (Avocado Soybean Unsaponifiables) is a natural extract from avocado and soybean oil. This natural extract takes two months to become fully effective; but once it is working, the pain relief lasts. It is one of the leading formulations available anywhere in the world. Based on clinical research, ASU is one of the most effective products for arthritis.

This formula is a good choice if you have severe joint or arthritis pain and the Joint Care Formula does not seem to provide sufficient relief.

The recommended way to use the Extra Strength Arthritis Formula is to take two tablets every morning with breakfast. It must be taken for two months to show a beneficial effect.

■ LAKOTA PM

Lakota PM was added to the Lakota product lineup in 2007. At the time it was introduced, no other pain reliever-sleep aid combinations were available in Canada.

Like many of the Lakota pain-relieving supplements, Lakota PM contains a special variety of White Willow Bark, carefully prepared to preserve the high level of salicin from the original plant. This special variety of White Willow Bark is the most potent form available anywhere.

In combination with pain relief, Lakota PM offers a gentle, natural sleep aid. It contains a combination of valerian, passion flower, hops and melatonin. Like many of the other ingredients used in Lakota products, the specific preparations are unique. The valerian used in the Lakota PM is processed using patented equipment that make it possible to reduce the cellulose plant matter, making it much more potent than any off-the-shelf variety. This vale-rian, combined with the other natural sleep aids, improves sleep without causing unpleasant, groggy mornings.

Many people who try Lakota PM are surprised at how well they sleep—often they get the first good sleep they've had in weeks. Lakota PM can be used together with the other Lakota pain relievers.

The recommended use of Lakota PM is two tablets about an hour before bedtime. This allows the natural pain relievers and sleep aids to work their way into your system. It can be taken in combination with other Lakota products. Because of the natural sleep aids in the product, we don't recommend taking more than two per day. Never operate machinery of any kind after taking Lakota PM.

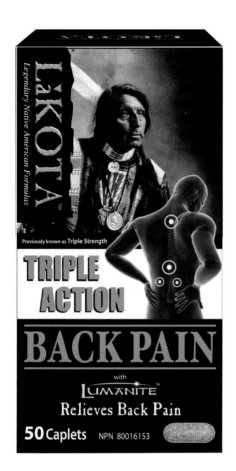

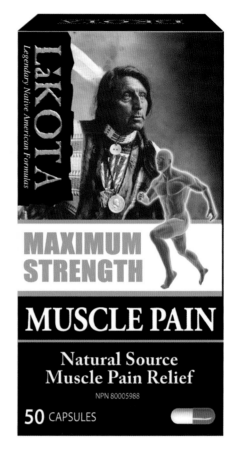

■ TRIPLE ACTION BACK PAIN

Lakota Triple Action Back Pain is a world-renowned natural pain-relieving tablet specifically for upper and lower back pain. For pure pain relief, there is nothing stronger. It's our most potent pain-relieving formula. It features the two specially processed extracts: White Willow Bark and Devil's Claw. Both are made from world-class sources and careful processing to get the maximum natural pain relief in a tablet.

There is no product comparable to Triple Action Back Pain. Not only does it have the two strong natural pain relievers working together, it also has natural muscle relaxants. Often back pain is related to muscle tension. Lakota Triple Action Back Pain addresses muscle tension with a tailored valerian extract and with black cohosh.

Triple Action Back Pain also contains Lumanite, a medicinal mineral. Lumanite contains copper, manganese, selenium and pantothenic acid. This mineral combination works on restoring the connective tissues that are vital to back health.

Relieving pain, relaxing muscles, rebuilding connective tissue—Lakota Triple Action Back Pain is back pain medicine that works.

To use the Lakota Triple Action Back Pain, take two tablets every four hours up to a maximum of six tablets daily or as directed by a health care practitioner. Take additional caution when combining this with the Lakota PM as both products produce a potent natural relaxing effect. Can be used for both chronic and acute back pain.

■ MAXIMUM STRENGTH MUSCLE PAIN

Lakota Maximum Strength Muscle Pain is a herbal pain reliever for sore and overworked muscles. Combining White Willow Bark and Devil's Claw root, common to most Lakota pain relievers, it adds a large dose of processed boswellia extract that is more potent than any other available. Maximum Strength Muscle Pain is a combination herbal product that takes a multifactor approach to pain. It adds yucca, sarsaparilla root and feverfew leaf and is packaged in a gelatin capsule. The gelatin capsule speeds up the delivery of these multifactor pain relievers.

Lakota Maximum Strength Muscle Pain is best used immediately after overuse or intense exercise. We even recommend taking it before intense exercise when you know you're likely to be in pain later. Pain from muscle overuse is primarily due to inflammation from micro-tears in muscle fibres. By limiting inflammation right from the start, muscle pain is inhibited before it begins.

LAKOTA ROLL-ONS AND SOFT TOUCH

What makes Lakota Roll-on pain relievers so effective?

Lakota Roll-on and Soft Touch pain relievers have a unique natural ingredient: an extract from the pepper plant, known as capsaicin. Capsaicin is the element that gives heat to peppers. In the past, it was used by indigenous peoples as a pain reliever. More recently, scientists in turn have "discovered" the natural pain relieving properties of capsaicin.

A form of capsaicin has been on the market for some time, available in specialty stores. But it has remained unpopular; its effectiveness as a pain reliever is limited. That's because the capsaicin you find on shelves is almost always synthetic capsaicin. Synthetic capsaicin passes the basic required lab test to be called capsaicin, and it's cheaper and easier to work with. But it doesn't work like natural capsaicin. Synthetic capsaicin is missing at least two of the pain-relieving compounds found in natural capsaicin.

Lakota Roll-on and Soft Touch pain relievers use a natural extract of capsaicin— that's what makes the products so effective. But it isn't easy to make. Just as vegetables from the garden vary in sizes, texture or taste from one year to the next, the capsaicin produced in peppers is subject to extreme fluctuations. Natural capsaicin varies from batch to batch.

So, in order to use the natural extract, every batch produced by Lakota must be made with a slightly different formula. Few companies are willing to put up with a production process that varies from batch to batch, but that's what we do at Lakota. In order to get the best possible product, each batch is tailored by hand to meet our specific standards.

In fact, you may even have noticed that the colour of the Roll-on or Soft Touch varies slightly depending on the batch. That's because the orange colour of the peppers, which comes from the natural colour of the peppers, can vary. Rather than worry about colour consistency, we have rigorous

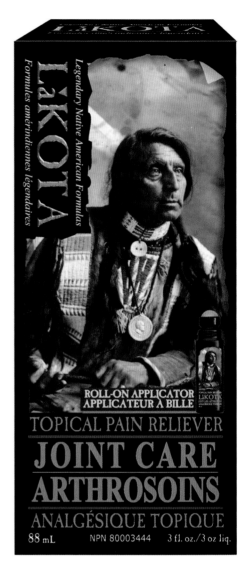

■ **JOINT CARE ROLL-ON**
Joint Care Roll-on was the original natural roll-on pain reliever that launched Lakota. Its formula combines the unique natural capsaicin extract with herbal additives. In addition to capsaicin, it has juniper-berry oil, Canada balsam, yarrow extract and birch oil. These tree oils help the Lakota Joint Care Roll-on absorb easily into the skin to provide maximum anti-inflammatory action right in the joint.

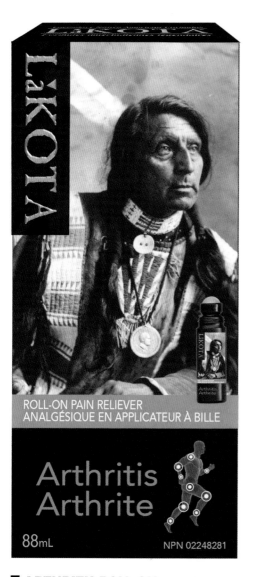

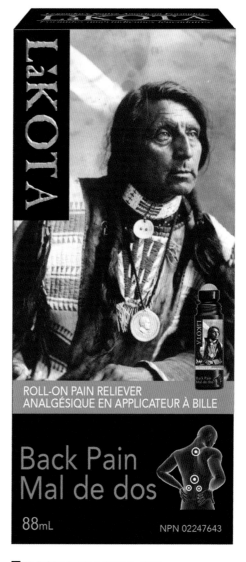

■ ARTHRITIS ROLL-ON

Lakota Arthritis Roll-on is a pure natural capsaicin extract formulation without the added herbal oils of the Joint Care Roll-on. Some customers prefer this easy-to-apply, odourless formulation to all others. Try it first for joint and arthritis pain. It can be used on knees, hands, ankles, hips, shoulders, wrists and back.

■ BACK PAIN ROLL-ON

Lakota Back Pain Roll-on was introduced in 2007. It is based on the same natural capsaicin extract, but with added menthol. The menthol provides instant cooling relief, and the natural capsaicin extract provides longer-term pain management. The roll-on applicator makes it possible to apply this to your back on your own. The applicator also works as a massaging tool, providing the pressure that fingers are often too weak to give. Can be used on lower back pain, pain around the spinal area and shoulder pain.

standards for pain-relieving efficacy, and so we allow the natural orange colour to vary slightly. We know that our customers care less about consistent colour than about consistent pain relief.

Natural capsaicin in Lakota also works in a unique way. It doesn't simply cover up pain with heat—it actually blocks the chemicals that transmit pain signals. When the Lakota Roll-on or Soft Touch is applied to the painful area, the capsaicin is absorbed and selectively binds to pain sensors. These nerve sensors are the same nerves that sense heat, so a sensation of heat is produced. Activating the pain sensors depletes the receptors of substance P— the chemical that transmits pain signals— greatly reducing the sensation of pain. To make a long story short: Lakota Roll-on and Soft Touch pain relievers don't mask pain: They actually stop pain at the source.

Using Lakota Roll-on and Soft Touch products

To use the Lakota Roll-on or Soft Touch pain relievers, shake the container to bring the thick gel to the applicator-end of the bottle. Tap the bottle on your palm lid-down, while the lid is still on; this helps bring all the gel into contact with the roller ball or sponge. If you're using the Roll-on container, roll the ball over the painful area, covering it with the pain-relieving gel. Some people like to apply pressure with the ball to massage the painful area.

Allow a few minutes for the pain-relieving gel to absorb before covering with clothing. Some people prefer to use their hands to massage the Lakota into the skin to speed up absorption. This is not required, but it may help. Be sure to wash your hands after you touch the pain-relieving gel, as it can sting your eyes.

Similarly, to apply Lakota with the Soft Touch sponge, squeeze the tube while the sponge is on the painful area and massage the gel into the skin with the sponge. This works great as a pain-free massage.

Apply four times per day or as often as needed. The Lakota can last up to 24 hours, and often people feel it warm up again in

■ MUSCLE PAIN ROLL-ON

The Lakota Muscle Pain Roll-on is an odourless formula designed with the weekend warrior in mind. Like the other Lakota rubs, it features the natural capsaicin extracted from specially selected pepper plants. The muscle rub also has added herbal oils to provide additional soothing relief. It's meant for those days when overuse or injury has made muscles stiff and painful. We recommend using the roll-on applicator as a massaging tool to loosen muscles as you apply the pain-relieving gel.

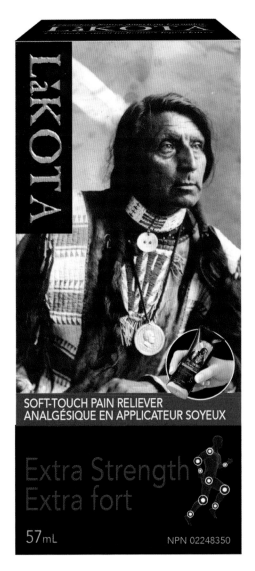

SOFT-TOUCH PAIN RELIEVER
ANALGÉSIQUE EN APPLICATEUR SOYEUX

Extra Strength
Extra fort

57mL   NPN 02248350

■ **EXTRA STRENGTH SOFT TOUCH**

Lakota Extra Strength Soft Touch is currently the best selling of the Lakota Roll-on and Soft Touch pain relievers. It has a stronger dose of the special capsaicin extract, as well as a menthol enhancer. This is the formula to use on the toughest pain. Some may find it too powerful!

Unique to the Extra Strength is the Soft Touch applicator. This applicator was developed together with Lakota customers to allow the application on arthritic hands with the softest possible touch. This applicator can also be used for gentle massage.

the shower the next morning. That's because water activates the capsaicin.

If the area Lakota was applied to is tightly wrapped or covered up, it may in some cases cause a sensation of extreme heat. This is due to the triggering of the body's heat sensors. If this occurs, avoid getting the skin wet, as water activates the capsaicin. If the product was applied within the last five minutes, it may be possible to limit absorption by washing the area with soap and water. But if it has been more than five minutes since application, apply ice to the area to provide cooling. A bag of frozen vegetables works well.

The Lakota Roll-on and Soft Touch pain relievers are by far the most effective pain rubs available on the market: No other prescription or over-the-counter product works like it. We have received thousands of testimonials from Canadians about how Lakota relieved pain that other products couldn't touch. If you are a Lakota user, why not share your pain relief secret with your friends and family?

Lakota supplements can be used together with the Roll-on or Soft Touch pain relievers. Many customers find the following approach works best: Joint Care Formula for long-term joint health and pain relief and the Roll-on or Soft Touch for day-to-day flare-ups. Joint Care Formula can also be used before arthritis sets in to help keep the joint healthy and to prevent pain.

The supplements are all designed in such a way that they can be used together, as long as no more than nine Lakota pills are taken in any one day. The nine pills can be a combination of different formulas, or a single formula.

If you're taking prescription drugs, your doctor should review the supplements before you take them. Lakota is strong, effective medicine and, as such, it should be used responsibly.

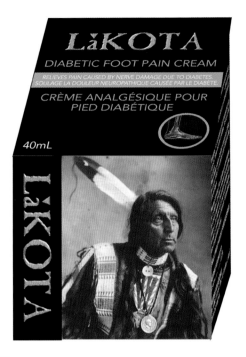

■ DIABETIC FOOT PAIN CREAM

The Lakota Diabetic Foot Pain Cream is different from the rest of the Lakota rubs: It's the only Lakota rub in a silky-smooth cream. Designed for use on pain from nerve damage caused by diabetes, it is a pain reliever and foot cream in one. It contains a potent dose of the natural capsaicin extract to relieve the stinging pain of nerve damage, and also contains shea butter, peppermint oil and green tea extract to help smooth the skin on the feet.

Diabetic Foot Pain Cream can be used on feet and hands for any kind of tingling, stinging or burning pain, especially pain caused by diabetes. As with all Lakota rubs, be sure to wash your hands after use; the natural pepper extract can sting eyes or nose if accidentally touched by hands that have applied the cream.

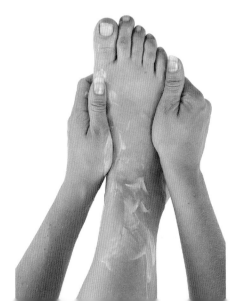

CANINE CARE
Dogs can suffer from arthritis, too. Lakota can help.

It comes as a surprise to some, but Lakota offers incredibly effective pain relief for dogs with sore joints. Pain-free walks for your four-legged friend: Nothing will make your dog happier. And that will make you happier, too.

RELIEVES CANINE ARTHRITIS PAIN
SOULAGE L'ARTHRITE CANINE

FOR DOGS · POUR CHIEN

Canine Joint Care
Arthroformule Canine

75 Chewable Tablets
Comprimés à croquer

■ CANINE JOINT CARE

The Lakota Canine Joint Care is the canine equivalent of the Joint Care Formula. It has many of the same ingredients as the human formula, but is specially tailored for canines. It comes in a beef liver-flavoured chewable tablet, making it easy to administer. In addition to the regular ingredients, it has elk antler velvet. More than just a flavour improvement, elk antler velvet is a key veterinary anti-inflammatory.

We get a number of testimonials about how well the Joint Care Formula for humans work. But for Canine Joint Care, however, the letters are really gushing, telling us that the product completely renewed their dog. Numerous stories have described a dog that was unable to climb into the car or walk up the stairs but that is now able to run and jump like a puppy. Nothing makes true believers faster: You can't fool a dog into feeling better!

OTHER PRODUCTS LAKOTA RECOMMENDS

We know we can't do everything at Lakota; we focus on making the best natural pain relievers in the world. But when it comes to other health areas, there are a few products that we recommend.

If you are considering taking a multivitamin, we suggest the BodyBreak line of multivitamins made by Hal Johnson and Joanne McLeod. These multivitamins are made in Canada using a slow-speed production process that minimizes the chemical additives normally used for large-scale production. The vitamin sources are excellent. Some other multivitamins contain vitamin or mineral sources that are very difficult for your body to absorb. Better vitamin sources make the active ingredient easier for you body to access. The BodyBreak multivitamins are available in some drugstores or online at www.bodybreak.com

For colds and flu, we recommend Cold FX®. Cold FX® is the leading natural cold remedy. It is made using specially selected and tested materials—the process is similar to Lakota's. It is best taken right at the onset of a cold or flu.

For all women over 40, we recommend a calcium supplement. The best kind of calcium is calcium citrate, the kind of calcium most easily absorbed by the body. Calcium is best taken with Vitamin D. If you don't get enough salmon, tuna, beef, liver, eggs or milk, we also recommend supplementing with Vitamin D, especially during the Canadian winter.

As with any supplements, make sure that you purchase a good-quality brand. Natural health products vary greatly from one brand to another. Even products with the same ingredient list can be quite different, as the quality and processing of the ingredients varies. Also check the expiry date: All natural products have a limited shelf life. And don't forget to consult your health care practitioner when combining supplements or taking them with prescription drugs.

Photo credits

LaKOTA

$5 OFF
JOINT CARE FORMULA
(ANY SIZE)

Valid only for September 2015

LaKOTA

$3 OFF
ARTHRITIS ROLL-ON

Valid only for October 2015

LaKOTA

$4 OFF
DIABETIC FOOT PAIN CREAM

Valid only for November 2015

LaKOTA

$5 OFF
TRIPLE ACTION BACK PAIN

Valid only for December 2015

LaKOTA

$4 OFF
JOINT CARE FORMULA 120

Valid only for January 2016

LaKOTA

$7 OFF
ANY LAKOTA PRODUCT

Valid only for February 2016

LaKOTA

$5 OFF
EXTRA STRENGTH SOFT TOUCH

Valid only for March 2016

LaKOTA

$3 OFF
LAKOTA PM

Valid only for April 2016

LaKOTA

$4 OFF
ANY ROLL-ON

Valid only for May 2016

LaKOTA

$4 OFF
JOINT CARE FORMULA
(ANY SIZE)

Valid only for June 2016

189

To the dealer: Upon presentation of this coupon by your customer toward the purchase of the specified product, HPI Health Products will reimburse the face value of coupon plus regular handling fee provided you accept it from your customer on purchase of item specified. Other applications may constitute fraud. Failure to send in, on request, evidence that sufficient stock was purchased in previous 90 days to cover coupons presented, will void coupons. Coupons submitted become our property. Reimbursement will be made only to retail distributor who redeemed coupon. For redemption, mail to HPI Health Products, Box 3000, Saint John, N.B. E2L4L3.

Expires October 31 2015

Also works at lakotaherbs.com

To the dealer: Upon presentation of this coupon by your customer toward the purchase of the specified product, HPI Health Products will reimburse the face value of coupon plus regular handling fee provided you accept it from your customer on purchase of item specified. Other applications may constitute fraud. Failure to send in, on request, evidence that sufficient stock was purchased in previous 90 days to cover coupons presented, will void coupons. Coupons submitted become our property. Reimbursement will be made only to retail distributor who redeemed coupon. For redemption, mail to HPI Health Products, Box 3000, Saint John, N.B. E2L4L3.

Expires September 30 2015

Also works at lakotaherbs.com

To the dealer: Upon presentation of this coupon by your customer toward the purchase of the specified product, HPI Health Products will reimburse the face value of coupon plus regular handling fee provided you accept it from your customer on purchase of item specified. Other applications may constitute fraud. Failure to send in, on request, evidence that sufficient stock was purchased in previous 90 days to cover coupons presented, will void coupons. Coupons submitted become our property. Reimbursement will be made only to retail distributor who redeemed coupon. For redemption, mail to HPI Health Products, Box 3000, Saint John, N.B. E2L4L3.

Expires December 31 2015

Also works at lakotaherbs.com

To the dealer: Upon presentation of this coupon by your customer toward the purchase of the specified product, HPI Health Products will reimburse the face value of coupon plus regular handling fee provided you accept it from your customer on purchase of item specified. Other applications may constitute fraud. Failure to send in, on request, evidence that sufficient stock was purchased in previous 90 days to cover coupons presented, will void coupons. Coupons submitted become our property. Reimbursement will be made only to retail distributor who redeemed coupon. For redemption, mail to HPI Health Products, Box 3000, Saint John, N.B. E2L4L3.

Expires November 30 2015

Also works at lakotaherbs.com

To the dealer: Upon presentation of this coupon by your customer toward the purchase of the specified product, HPI Health Products will reimburse the face value of coupon plus regular handling fee provided you accept it from your customer on purchase of item specified. Other applications may constitute fraud. Failure to send in, on request, evidence that sufficient stock was purchased in previous 90 days to cover coupons presented, will void coupons. Coupons submitted become our property. Reimbursement will be made only to retail distributor who redeemed coupon. For redemption, mail to HPI Health Products, Box 3000, Saint John, N.B. E2L4L3.

Expires February 29 2016

Also works at lakotaherbs.com

To the dealer: Upon presentation of this coupon by your customer toward the purchase of the specified product, HPI Health Products will reimburse the face value of coupon plus regular handling fee provided you accept it from your customer on purchase of item specified. Other applications may constitute fraud. Failure to send in, on request, evidence that sufficient stock was purchased in previous 90 days to cover coupons presented, will void coupons. Coupons submitted become our property. Reimbursement will be made only to retail distributor who redeemed coupon. For redemption, mail to HPI Health Products, Box 3000, Saint John, N.B. E2L4L3.

Expires January 31 2016

Also works at lakotaherbs.com

To the dealer: Upon presentation of this coupon by your customer toward the purchase of the specified product, HPI Health Products will reimburse the face value of coupon plus regular handling fee provided you accept it from your customer on purchase of item specified. Other applications may constitute fraud. Failure to send in, on request, evidence that sufficient stock was purchased in previous 90 days to cover coupons presented, will void coupons. Coupons submitted become our property. Reimbursement will be made only to retail distributor who redeemed coupon. For redemption, mail to HPI Health Products, Box 3000, Saint John, N.B. E2L4L3.

Expires April 30 2016

Also works at lakotaherbs.com

To the dealer: Upon presentation of this coupon by your customer toward the purchase of the specified product, HPI Health Products will reimburse the face value of coupon plus regular handling fee provided you accept it from your customer on purchase of item specified. Other applications may constitute fraud. Failure to send in, on request, evidence that sufficient stock was purchased in previous 90 days to cover coupons presented, will void coupons. Coupons submitted become our property. Reimbursement will be made only to retail distributor who redeemed coupon. For redemption, mail to HPI Health Products, Box 3000, Saint John, N.B. E2L4L3.

Expires March 31 2016

Also works at lakotaherbs.com

To the dealer: Upon presentation of this coupon by your customer toward the purchase of the specified product, HPI Health Products will reimburse the face value of coupon plus regular handling fee provided you accept it from your customer on purchase of item specified. Other applications may constitute fraud. Failure to send in, on request, evidence that sufficient stock was purchased in previous 90 days to cover coupons presented, will void coupons. Coupons submitted become our property. Reimbursement will be made only to retail distributor who redeemed coupon. For redemption, mail to HPI Health Products, Box 3000, Saint John, N.B. E2L4L3.

Expires June 30 2016

Also works at lakotaherbs.com

To the dealer: Upon presentation of this coupon by your customer toward the purchase of the specified product, HPI Health Products will reimburse the face value of coupon plus regular handling fee provided you accept it from your customer on purchase of item specified. Other applications may constitute fraud. Failure to send in, on request, evidence that sufficient stock was purchased in previous 90 days to cover coupons presented, will void coupons. Coupons submitted become our property. Reimbursement will be made only to retail distributor who redeemed coupon. For redemption, mail to HPI Health Products, Box 3000, Saint John, N.B. E2L4L3.

Expires May 31 2016

Also works at lakotaherbs.com

LaKOTA
$3 OFF
**MUSCLE
PAIN
ROLL-ON**

Valid only for July 2016

LaKOTA
$5 OFF
**EXTRA
STRENGTH
ARTHRITIS 75**

Valid only for August 2016

LaKOTA
$3 OFF
**MAXIMUM
STRENGTH
MUSCLE PAIN**

Valid only for September 2016

LaKOTA
$3 OFF
**BACK
PAIN
ROLL-ON**

Valid only for October 2016

LaKOTA
$3 OFF
**JOINT CARE
FORMULA120**

Valid only for November 2016

LaKOTA
$3 OFF
**ARTHRITIS
ROLL-ON**

Valid only for December 2016

LaKOTA
$4 OFF
**RHEUMATOID
FORMULA**

Valid only for January 2017

LaKOTA
$9 OFF
**ANY
LAKOTA
SUPPLEMENT**

Valid only for February 2017

LaKOTA
$4 OFF
**ANY
LAKOTA
ROLL-ON**

Valid only for March 2017

LaKOTA
$4 OFF
**JOINT CARE
FORMULA
120**

Valid only for April 2017

To the dealer: Upon presentation of this coupon by your customer toward the purchase of the specified product, HPI Health Products will reimburse the face value of coupon plus regular handling fee provided you accept it from your customer on purchase of item specified. Other applications may constitute fraud. Failure to send in, on request, evidence that sufficient stock was purchased in previous 90 days to cover coupons presented, will void coupons. Coupons submitted become our property. Reimbursement will be made only to retail distributor who redeemed coupon. For redemption, mail to HPI Health Products, Box 3000, Saint John, N.B. E2L4L3.

Expires August 31 2016

Also works at lakotaherbs.com

To the dealer: Upon presentation of this coupon by your customer toward the purchase of the specified product, HPI Health Products will reimburse the face value of coupon plus regular handling fee provided you accept it from your customer on purchase of item specified. Other applications may constitute fraud. Failure to send in, on request, evidence that sufficient stock was purchased in previous 90 days to cover coupons presented, will void coupons. Coupons submitted become our property. Reimbursement will be made only to retail distributor who redeemed coupon. For redemption, mail to HPI Health Products, Box 3000, Saint John, N.B. E2L4L3.

Expires July 31 2016

Also works at lakotaherbs.com

To the dealer: Upon presentation of this coupon by your customer toward the purchase of the specified product, HPI Health Products will reimburse the face value of coupon plus regular handling fee provided you accept it from your customer on purchase of item specified. Other applications may constitute fraud. Failure to send in, on request, evidence that sufficient stock was purchased in previous 90 days to cover coupons presented, will void coupons. Coupons submitted become our property. Reimbursement will be made only to retail distributor who redeemed coupon. For redemption, mail to HPI Health Products, Box 3000, Saint John, N.B. E2L4L3.

Expires October 31 2016

Also works at lakotaherbs.com

To the dealer: Upon presentation of this coupon by your customer toward the purchase of the specified product, HPI Health Products will reimburse the face value of coupon plus regular handling fee provided you accept it from your customer on purchase of item specified. Other applications may constitute fraud. Failure to send in, on request, evidence that sufficient stock was purchased in previous 90 days to cover coupons presented, will void coupons. Coupons submitted become our property. Reimbursement will be made only to retail distributor who redeemed coupon. For redemption, mail to HPI Health Products, Box 3000, Saint John, N.B. E2L4L3.

Expires September 30 2016

Also works at lakotaherbs.com

To the dealer: Upon presentation of this coupon by your customer toward the purchase of the specified product, HPI Health Products will reimburse the face value of coupon plus regular handling fee provided you accept it from your customer on purchase of item specified. Other applications may constitute fraud. Failure to send in, on request, evidence that sufficient stock was purchased in previous 90 days to cover coupons presented, will void coupons. Coupons submitted become our property. Reimbursement will be made only to retail distributor who redeemed coupon. For redemption, mail to HPI Health Products, Box 3000, Saint John, N.B. E2L4L3.

Expires December 31 2016

Also works at lakotaherbs.com

To the dealer: Upon presentation of this coupon by your customer toward the purchase of the specified product, HPI Health Products will reimburse the face value of coupon plus regular handling fee provided you accept it from your customer on purchase of item specified. Other applications may constitute fraud. Failure to send in, on request, evidence that sufficient stock was purchased in previous 90 days to cover coupons presented, will void coupons. Coupons submitted become our property. Reimbursement will be made only to retail distributor who redeemed coupon. For redemption, mail to HPI Health Products, Box 3000, Saint John, N.B. E2L4L3.

Expires November 30 2016

Also works at lakotaherbs.com

To the dealer: Upon presentation of this coupon by your customer toward the purchase of the specified product, HPI Health Products will reimburse the face value of coupon plus regular handling fee provided you accept it from your customer on purchase of item specified. Other applications may constitute fraud. Failure to send in, on request, evidence that sufficient stock was purchased in previous 90 days to cover coupons presented, will void coupons. Coupons submitted become our property. Reimbursement will be made only to retail distributor who redeemed coupon. For redemption, mail to HPI Health Products, Box 3000, Saint John, N.B. E2L4L3.

Expires February 28 2017

Also works at lakotaherbs.com

To the dealer: Upon presentation of this coupon by your customer toward the purchase of the specified product, HPI Health Products will reimburse the face value of coupon plus regular handling fee provided you accept it from your customer on purchase of item specified. Other applications may constitute fraud. Failure to send in, on request, evidence that sufficient stock was purchased in previous 90 days to cover coupons presented, will void coupons. Coupons submitted become our property. Reimbursement will be made only to retail distributor who redeemed coupon. For redemption, mail to HPI Health Products, Box 3000, Saint John, N.B. E2L4L3.

Expires January 31 2017

Also works at lakotaherbs.com

To the dealer: Upon presentation of this coupon by your customer toward the purchase of the specified product, HPI Health Products will reimburse the face value of coupon plus regular handling fee provided you accept it from your customer on purchase of item specified. Other applications may constitute fraud. Failure to send in, on request, evidence that sufficient stock was purchased in previous 90 days to cover coupons presented, will void coupons. Coupons submitted become our property. Reimbursement will be made only to retail distributor who redeemed coupon. For redemption, mail to HPI Health Products, Box 3000, Saint John, N.B. E2L4L3.

Expires April 30 2017

Also works at lakotaherbs.com

To the dealer: Upon presentation of this coupon by your customer toward the purchase of the specified product, HPI Health Products will reimburse the face value of coupon plus regular handling fee provided you accept it from your customer on purchase of item specified. Other applications may constitute fraud. Failure to send in, on request, evidence that sufficient stock was purchased in previous 90 days to cover coupons presented, will void coupons. Coupons submitted become our property. Reimbursement will be made only to retail distributor who redeemed coupon. For redemption, mail to HPI Health Products, Box 3000, Saint John, N.B. E2L4L3.

Expires March 31 2017

Also works at lakotaherbs.com

LiKOTA

$4 OFF
MAXIMUM STRENGTH MUSCLE PAIN
Valid only for May 2017

LiKOTA

$4 OFF
MUSCLE PAIN ROLL-ON
Valid only for June 2017

LiKOTA

$4 OFF
TRIPLE ACTION BACK PAIN
Valid only for July 2017

LiKOTA

$4 OFF
EXTRA STRENGTH ARTHRITIS 75
Valid only for August 2017

LiKOTA

$4 OFF
DIABETIC FOOT PAIN CREAM
Valid only for September 2017

LiKOTA

$4 OFF
JOINT CARE FORMULA
(ANY SIZE)
Valid only for October 2017

LiKOTA

$4 OFF
EXTRA STRENGTH SOFT TOUCH
Valid only for November 2017

LiKOTA

$10 OFF
ANY ROLL-ON
Valid only for December 2017

LiKOTA

$5 OFF
BACK PAIN ROLL-ON
Valid only for January 2018

LiKOTA

$5 OFF
MUSCLE PAIN ROLL-ON
Valid only for February 2018

To the dealer: Upon presentation of this coupon by your customer toward the purchase of the specified product, HPI Health Products will reimburse the face value of coupon plus regular handling fee provided you accept it from your customer on purchase of item specified. Other applications may constitute fraud. Failure to send in, on request, evidence that sufficient stock was purchased in previous 90 days to cover coupons presented, will void coupons. Coupons submitted become our property. Reimbursement will be made only to retail distributor who redeemed coupon. For redemption, mail to HPI Health Products, Box 3000, Saint John, N.B. E2L4L3.

Expires April 30 2018

Also works at lakotaherbs.com

80816573

To the dealer: Upon presentation of this coupon by your customer toward the purchase of the specified product, HPI Health Products will reimburse the face value of coupon plus regular handling fee provided you accept it from your customer on purchase of item specified. Other applications may constitute fraud. Failure to send in, on request, evidence that sufficient stock was purchased in previous 90 days to cover coupons presented, will void coupons. Coupons submitted become our property. Reimbursement will be made only to retail distributor who redeemed coupon. For redemption, mail to HPI Health Products, Box 3000, Saint John, N.B. E2L4L3.

Expires March 31 2018

Also works at lakotaherbs.com

80816560

To the dealer: Upon presentation of this coupon by your customer toward the purchase of the specified product, HPI Health Products will reimburse the face value of coupon plus regular handling fee provided you accept it from your customer on purchase of item specified. Other applications may constitute fraud. Failure to send in, on request, evidence that sufficient stock was purchased in previous 90 days to cover coupons presented, will void coupons. Coupons submitted become our property. Reimbursement will be made only to retail distributor who redeemed coupon. For redemption, mail to HPI Health Products, Box 3000, Saint John, N.B. E2L4L3.

Expires June 30 2018

Also works at lakotaherbs.com

80816599

To the dealer: Upon presentation of this coupon by your customer toward the purchase of the specified product, HPI Health Products will reimburse the face value of coupon plus regular handling fee provided you accept it from your customer on purchase of item specified. Other applications may constitute fraud. Failure to send in, on request, evidence that sufficient stock was purchased in previous 90 days to cover coupons presented, will void coupons. Coupons submitted become our property. Reimbursement will be made only to retail distributor who redeemed coupon. For redemption, mail to HPI Health Products, Box 3000, Saint John, N.B. E2L4L3.

Expires May 31 2018

Also works at lakotaherbs.com

80816586

To the dealer: Upon presentation of this coupon by your customer toward the purchase of the specified product, HPI Health Products will reimburse the face value of coupon plus regular handling fee provided you accept it from your customer on purchase of item specified. Other applications may constitute fraud. Failure to send in, on request, evidence that sufficient stock was purchased in previous 90 days to cover coupons presented, will void coupons. Coupons submitted become our property. Reimbursement will be made only to retail distributor who redeemed coupon. For redemption, mail to HPI Health Products, Box 3000, Saint John, N.B. E2L4L3.

Expires August 31 2018

Also works at lakotaherbs.com

80816629

To the dealer: Upon presentation of this coupon by your customer toward the purchase of the specified product, HPI Health Products will reimburse the face value of coupon plus regular handling fee provided you accept it from your customer on purchase of item specified. Other applications may constitute fraud. Failure to send in, on request, evidence that sufficient stock was purchased in previous 90 days to cover coupons presented, will void coupons. Coupons submitted become our property. Reimbursement will be made only to retail distributor who redeemed coupon. For redemption, mail to HPI Health Products, Box 3000, Saint John, N.B. E2L4L3.

Expires July 31 2018

Also works at lakotaherbs.com

80816603

To the dealer: Upon presentation of this coupon by your customer toward the purchase of the specified product, HPI Health Products will reimburse the face value of coupon plus regular handling fee provided you accept it from your customer on purchase of item specified. Other applications may constitute fraud. Failure to send in, on request, evidence that sufficient stock was purchased in previous 90 days to cover coupons presented, will void coupons. Coupons submitted become our property. Reimbursement will be made only to retail distributor who redeemed coupon. For redemption, mail to HPI Health Products, Box 3000, Saint John, N.B. E2L4L3.

Expires October 31 2018

Also works at lakotaherbs.com

80816645

To the dealer: Upon presentation of this coupon by your customer toward the purchase of the specified product, HPI Health Products will reimburse the face value of coupon plus regular handling fee provided you accept it from your customer on purchase of item specified. Other applications may constitute fraud. Failure to send in, on request, evidence that sufficient stock was purchased in previous 90 days to cover coupons presented, will void coupons. Coupons submitted become our property. Reimbursement will be made only to retail distributor who redeemed coupon. For redemption, mail to HPI Health Products, Box 3000, Saint John, N.B. E2L4L3.

Expires September 30 2018

Also works at lakotaherbs.com

80816632

To the dealer: Upon presentation of this coupon by your customer toward the purchase of the specified product, HPI Health Products will reimburse the face value of coupon plus regular handling fee provided you accept it from your customer on purchase of item specified. Other applications may constitute fraud. Failure to send in, on request, evidence that sufficient stock was purchased in previous 90 days to cover coupons presented, will void coupons. Coupons submitted become our property. Reimbursement will be made only to retail distributor who redeemed coupon. For redemption, mail to HPI Health Products, Box 3000, Saint John, N.B. E2L4L3.

Expires December 31 2018

Also works at lakotaherbs.com

80816661

To the dealer: Upon presentation of this coupon by your customer toward the purchase of the specified product, HPI Health Products will reimburse the face value of coupon plus regular handling fee provided you accept it from your customer on purchase of item specified. Other applications may constitute fraud. Failure to send in, on request, evidence that sufficient stock was purchased in previous 90 days to cover coupons presented, will void coupons. Coupons submitted become our property. Reimbursement will be made only to retail distributor who redeemed coupon. For redemption, mail to HPI Health Products, Box 3000, Saint John, N.B. E2L4L3.

Expires November 30 2018

Also works at lakotaherbs.com

80816658